THE MANY FACES OF THE CHRIST

THE MANY FACES
OF THE CHRIST

The Christologies
of the New Testament
and Beyond

BEN WITHERINGTON III

A Crossroad Herder Book
The Crossroad Publishing Company
New York

To Dennis Campbell and Leander Keck
and to all those who care deeply
about our christological heritage and the
ἄρχη τοῦ εὐαγγελίου Ἰησοῦ Χριστοῦ

The Crossroad Publishing Company
370 Lexington Avenue, New York, NY 10017

Printed in the United States of America

Library of Congress Cataloging-in-Publication Data

Witherington, Ben, 1951–
    The many faces of the Christ : the Christologies of the New
Testament and beyond / Ben Witherington, III.
        p.   cm. — (Crossroad companions to the New Testament
series)
    Includes bibliographical references.
    ISBN 0-8245-1705-9 (pbk.)
    1. Jesus Christ—History of doctrines—Early church, ca. 30–600.
2. Jesus Christ—Person and offices—Biblical teaching.   3. Bible.
N.T.—Theology.   I. Title.   II. Series.
BT198.W55   1998
232'.09'015—dc21   97-37547
                                                                           CIP

1   2   3   4   5   6   7   8   9   10   02   01   00   99   98

Contents

Preface

THE COMPANIONS TO THE NEW TESTAMENT SERIES aims to unite New Testament study with theological concerns in a clear and concise manner. Each volume:

- engages the New Testament text directly;
- focuses on the religious (theological/ethical) content of the New Testament;
- is written out of respect for the integrity of the religious tradition being studied. This means that the New Testament is studied in terms of its own time and place. It is allowed to speak in its own terms, out of its own assumptions, espousing its own values;
- involves cutting-edge research, bringing the results of scholarly discussions to the general reader;
- provides resources for the reader who wishes to enter more deeply into the scholarly discussion.

The contributors to the series are established scholars who have studied and taught the New Testament for many years and who can now reap a wide-ranging harvest from the fruits of their labors. Multiple theological perspectives and denominational identities are represented. Each author is free to address the issues from his or her own social and religious location, within the parameters set for the series.

It is our hope that these small volumes will make some contribution to the recovery of the vision of the New Testament world for our time.

Charles H. Talbert
Baylor University

Introduction:
Finding a Path through the Maze

T HE SUBJECT OF CHRISTOLOGY has gone through long periods of intense scrutiny, followed by somewhat shorter periods of relative neglect or stagnation in the twentieth century. Since we are in the midst of a period of ferment, furor, and fervor in regard to the historical Jesus, the time seems ripe for a review of the evidence about the Christologies of the New Testament era once again. This particular study is not intended to be a definitive or ground-breaking contribution to the discussion but rather a summing up of the New Testament evidence as we have it, intended to help students, pastors, and lay persons obtain a grasp of the breadth and depth and importance of this subject matter.

There are many ways this subject could be approached, and we will discuss methodological matters shortly, but the obvious premise behind this work is that the study of Christology is important, perhaps especially so now as our culture becomes increasingly Biblically illiterate. And yet our Western culture still has a tremendous fascination with questions about Jesus—who he was, what he did and said, why his life ended as it did, and why he still has such a wide following today. I will not be raising or answering the difficult historical questions here, except in passing (on these subjects see my other works relating to this subject, particularly *The Christology of Jesus*, and *Jesus the Sage*, and *The Jesus Quest*). Rather I will be concentrating on the theological substance of the discussion. This is not because I think

1

these two subjects can be separated from one another or have no bearing on each other.

To the contrary, it is my own conviction that the various Christologies of and in the New Testament are ultimately grounded in who Jesus actually was, what he did and said, and what happened to him during his earthly life and ministry and its aftermath. I do not agree with the conclusion that Christology is a subject foisted on us by the early church because it read too much into the life and person of Jesus of Nazareth. Jesus was not a plebian and mundane person whom the church only later dressed up in royal robes. This, however, does not mean that there was not growth and development in the understanding of Jesus and his significance over the course of the first century C.E. and beyond, a growth and development reflected in the various Christologies of and in the New Testament and in other early church literature.

Something must also be said about the members of early churches who produced the christological material we will be perusing in this study. So far as can be told, with the probable exception of Luke, who seems to have been a Gentile, all the authors of New Testament documents, and the vast majority of those who contributed to the christological reflection we find in the New Testament were Jews, or more specifically Jewish Christians. It follows from this that the study of Christology is certainly not by and large the study of the effect of pagan thinking about Jesus. Jesus himself was a Jew who aroused passionate Jewish discourse, dialogue, and debate about his significance, a debate that spilled over into various Gentile contexts as the church grew and expanded, but by no means began for the first time in those contexts. In my view, M. Hengel is basically correct to insist that "with regard to the development of *all* the early Church's Christology, . . . more happened in the first twenty years [after Jesus' death] than in the entire later centuries-long development of dogma."[1]

Furthermore, I find absolutely no solid historical evidence that there ever were communities of followers of Jesus who did not reflect on him in ways we would today call christological. All of the documents we have in the New Testament, and even the sources we might ferret out from some of them (Q, M, L, the christological hymns, creedal fragments) are christological in character to one degree or another. Even the New Testament book we call James has a submerged Christology, as we shall see. I must conclude from this that the earliest Christians thought or believed there was no non-christological Jesus to be found or discussed, and if there had been, there would never have been all this christological discussion in the first place. Christology, for the earliest Christians, was no marginal or optional subject. It was at the heart of their contemplations, proclamations, and writings. It is my view that it should be at the heart of ours as well, and this indeed is the ultimate rationale for writing this book in the first place.

It does not follow from what I have just said that we can speak simply of the Christology of the New Testament, as is still sometimes done. There was a wide variety of terms and concepts used by the writers of the New Testament to bring out the significance of Jesus, and so we must speak of Christologies of and in the New Testament. Jesus was a tremendously complex historical figure, and like light shining through a prism, reflections on the man who fits no one formula produced a variety of colors and depths of shade that cannot and should not all be blended today into some sort of monochromatic image. For example, Son of Man Christology cannot be simply subsumed under the heading of Son of God Christology. This said, it is still "this same Jesus" whom all these different terms and images were being used to describe and characterize. Thus, this study is entitled *The Many Faces of the Christ*, not because his image cannot be brought into proper focus but because it was felt early and often and is still felt today that no one term, title, or image is adequate to encapsulate the meaning of Jesus.

FIRST PRINCIPLES AND THE QUESTION OF METHOD

The term "Christology" means different things to different people. Properly speaking, the term in its narrowest sense as used in Christian contexts refers to the discussion of Jesus as the Christ or Messiah ("anointed one") of God. Since, however, in early Judaism the term *māšîaḥ* was rarely used—and when it was used, it referred to a special human being, usually a kingly (Davidic?) or priestly figure—it is clear that in Christian discussions the term "Christology" is normally used in ways that go well beyond the attempt to see Jesus as a special *human* being, even if the term "Messiah" or "Christ" is used to refer to a king like but greater than David. Specifically, the term "Christology" is often used to refer to Jesus as more than merely mortal, as divine or deity. This usage, like the usage that limits the term to mean Jesus as God's Anointed One, seems too narrow to encompass all the discussion that follows in this book. Accordingly, I must make clear at the outset that by Christology I mean the study of Jesus as a more than ordinary person. Sometimes that *more* entails viewing Jesus as an extraordinary human being—a prophet, a priest, a king. Sometimes that *more* involves viewing Jesus as a more-than-mortal being—as divine or deity. In other words, I propose to use the term "Christology" to encompass elements both of what is traditionally called Jesus' humanity and his divinity. Put this way, it should be clear that we are not merely interested in the so-called titles applied to Jesus, though those will figure significantly in the discussion that follows.

Often the term "Christology" has been assumed to focus on the person rather than the work of the Christ. While in a broad sense this is true, the assumption is somewhat problematic because there is a sense in which the two are clearly intertwined—Jesus would not have been who he was if he had not done what he did or in some cases had not experienced what he experienced. In particular, from a Christian theological point of view he could not have been the Savior unless he died on the cross and he could not have been the risen Lord, if God had not raised him from the dead. What this shows us is that Christology in the New Testament is grounded in what the early Christians claimed were historical events. To put this in broader terms, there is a narrative character to much of the christological discussion in the New Testament. This is why R. E. Brown's recent study is so helpful. He points out that christological terms and ideas tend to cluster around certain moments in the career of Jesus. Thus, there is Parousia Christology or Resurrection Christology or Ministry Christology or Birth Christology.[2]

The key insight that comes from this sort of discussion is that the New Testament writers were telling us that Jesus assumed various roles at different points in the trajectory of his career. For example, he could not be the risen Lord sending the Spirit to the believers until after he had died. This is a matter of believing that Jesus assumed some new roles at various points in his life and even after his death, not a matter of thinking that Jesus became someone he wasn't before at one or more points in the trajectory of his existence. These insights must be kept steadily in view throughout the discussion that follows in this book.

The previous paragraph says something about how historical and narrative factors affect christological discussion, but something must also be said about how theological factors affect the discussion as well. Christology as it is presented in the New Testament is a subset of theology. In view of the fact that most of New Testament theology, however, has to do with Christology, this clearly makes it the largest portion of New Testament theology, involving more ink than the discussion either of the Father or of the Spirit or both put together. Furthermore, Christology is significantly intertwined with both eschatology and soteriology in the New Testament. The term "Savior" as applied to Jesus makes clear the latter connection, while the association of Jesus with the kingdom, with resurrection, and even the identifying of Jesus as God's Anointed One or Christ makes plain why Christology is properly speaking an eschatological term in the New Testament.

Another initial factor that must be taken into account is that most of the so-called titles applied to Jesus are relational terms, and this applies even to terms such as Lord or Christ. This is more obvious when we are dealing with phrases such as "the Son of Man" or "the Son of God." I would suggest that the relational character of these terms reflects the character of the culture of which Jesus was a part. In this culture a person's identity was established relationally, by who his parents or relatives were or what ethnic group he or she was a part of. Other factors, such as what religious or political group one was a part of, also came into play in establishing one's identity (cf., e.g., Simon the Zealot). Rugged individualism was neither taken for granted nor seen as a goal; nor was it seen as desirable in the culture in which Jesus spent his whole life.

Christological discussion has tended to assume that the subject at issue is the uniqueness of Jesus, and to a real degree this is true, but one must not overlook the relational terms in which the matter was originally couched. One suspects that the reason that Jesus is not depicted in the Synoptic Gospels as spending much time reflecting on or discussing who he was is that it was the common practice of his world to be told rather than to tell who a person was.[3] As we shall see in the second chapter when we discuss the Christology of Jesus himself, there is a good deal to be learned from examining how Jesus related to a variety of other persons and to God. Christology at the end of the day involves an assessment of the person, works, experiences, relationships, roles, and career of Jesus.

Another crucial point that must be kept in view throughout our christological discussions is that it would appear that either Jesus or his earliest followers (or both) changed or modified some of the basic Jewish ideas about what it meant to be Messiah or Son of God or Son of Man. Sometimes this amounted to a stretching of old categories;

sometimes it involved giving new meaning to old labels and concepts; sometimes it meant coming up with new terms and images. Some of these changes were brought about of necessity since a crucified Messiah had to be explained. Early Jews do not seem to have expected such a thing to happen to God's Anointed. Some of these changes were brought about by the larger attempt to reread the Old Testament in light of what was known about the life, words, and deeds of Jesus in general, not just what was known about his death.[4]

If there is any truth to the various hints in the Gospels that Jesus claimed at various points to be a fulfiller of, or one who brought about the fulfillment of, Old Testament prophecies and ideas, then it would have been natural for the earliest followers of Jesus to turn to the Old Testament to help them express their new faith in Jesus. 1 Corinthians 15:3–4 makes evident that already in the 50s or before a tradition had been passed on among the early Christians that Jesus had died, been buried, and been raised *according to the Scriptures.* It was this sort of imaginative rereading of the Old Testament that characterized various of the earliest Jewish Christian interpreters of Jesus and explains some of the remarkable christological developments we find in the New Testament.

In terms of methodology, as an exegete and a New Testament theologian, I take it as axiomatic that exegesis must be the basis of and starting point for discussing New Testament Christology. We cannot start with Calvin's or Luther's or Wesley's or Aquinas's theological formulations or for that matter with the formulations of the councils of Nicaea or Chalcedon or with the creeds. Exegesis must precede theologizing or systematizing, or the formulating of creeds or confessions. Though I will not be able to display most of the details of my exegesis in what follows in this book, all that I will say is based on that sort of close study of the text.

This in turn leads to some comments about other methodological matters. It has often been the way that New Testament Christology has been discussed using a topical approach (e.g., a chapter on Jesus as Son of Man, a chapter on Jesus as Son of God, etc.). This approach is synthetic in character and synchronic in assumption. Both of these factors are problematic, not least because it is often assumed that a phrase like "Son of Man" is univocal, having one basic meaning in all its occurrences, and that it does not usually allow for development over time in the use of the term or phrase. As we have done in *Jesus the Sage* we will basically be attempting a diachronic approach to our subject matter, and, not surprisingly, we will be stressing the variety of Christologies found in the New Testament, though unifying themes and factors will not be overlooked or be omitted from discussion.

Thus, after a discussion of the background and foreground of Jewish messianism, we will discuss Jesus' self-presentation. These two sections will serve as our basic discussion of the origins of New Testament Christologies. The following chapters will be more about the development of these Christologies by various early Christians than about origins, though clearly various New Testament authors had some original thoughts about Jesus which we will highlight. After the discussion of background issues and of Jesus' self-presentation, we will attempt to look at the period between Jesus' ministry and the teachings of Paul, by looking at the material we find in a variety of places (in Paul's letters, in the Gospels, in Acts) that likely goes back to the earliest Jewish Christian believers. Here we will be discussing Aramaic phrases, creedal formulae, hymn fragments, and Q material.

This in turn will be followed by a rather detailed discussion of the christological material to be found in the Pauline corpus. The material in the earlier Paulines will be discussed first, and the material from the Pastorals last. I have chosen this approach because of course many of the later Pauline letters are disputed as to authorship, but also because whether one thinks all these letters are by Paul or not, on two things there is widespread agreement: (1) this is the proper chronological arrangement of these letters; (2) even the later Paulines reflect a development of Pauline thought.

The discussion of the Christologies of the Gospels will begin with a discussion of what we find in Mark and Matthew and this will be followed by a chapter on Luke and Acts, followed finally by a discussion of the Johannine literature including the Fourth Gospel, the epistles, and the book of Revelation. The latter are placed together because I believe they came forth from and addressed the same community in Asia Minor using some of the same ideas and language, not because I think it likely one author wrote all these documents. The discussion of the General Epistles follows, where we will examine the Petrine literature, the so-called minor witnesses of James and Jude, and Hebrews. The study will end with a brief glimpse into the Christologies of the period that led up to Nicaea and Chalcedon.

This order is of course not entirely diachronic, because of the need to take the Johannine literature together, or the Pauline material, or some of the Petrine material. Within these larger groupings, however, the material will be discussed in what I take to be the chronological order in which these works were written. It is only when one takes the diachronic task seriously that one can even begin to talk about the *development* or unfolding of New Testament Christology, much less the evolution of New Testament Christology.

There has been unfortunately a lot of loose talk about the evolution of New Testament Christology, involving a lot of questionable assumptions about the chronological ordering of both New Testament ideas and documents. I agree with J. D. G. Dunn that the term "unfolding" often does more justice than "evolution" to describe the way New Testament Christology developed, but in fact in many ways we must talk about devolution, for some of the highest Christology was some of the earliest (found, for example, in the christological hymns).[5] The term "evolution" is also misleading, for it suggests that one sort of Christology developed into another sort as time went on, when in fact some Christologies (e.g., Jesus as Son of Man) seem to have fallen into relative (and for some authors complete) disuse well before the end of the first century c.e.[6]

In terms of general assumptions, I follow the standard solution to the Synoptic Problem, with Mark being the earliest Gospel, and Matthew and Luke drawing on Mark independently of each other. John I take, with the majority of scholars, as an independent testimony, which may be quite early in its origins but was probably written up in the last decade of the first century. The Johannine letters are seen as written by the person who was the source of the Fourth Gospel but not its final editor, and written before the final form of the Gospel. The book of Revelation is seen as the latest Johannine document, written by a member of the Johannine community but not likely the same person who produced the letters or the Gospel.

It should be clear from what we have said to this point that whenever one talks about the development of New Testament Christologies, one is conceding at the outset that the full significance of Jesus did not just dawn on Christians immediately after the Easter experiences. That awareness gradually came to full fruition. The Fourth Gospel reminds us that it was the Spirit that led the disciples into all truth, which is as much as to admit that they did not by any means fully understand Jesus or his ministry before Easter. Indeed, if Jesus was even close to what the church later claimed he was, it is not surprising that the church was left groping for words, concepts, images, and metaphors large enough to explain the person and work of this man. Naturally enough the earliest disciples would draw on their own immediate contexts and knowledge and experiences, including using the theological vocabulary familiar to them to explain how they viewed Jesus. But it could not be simply a case of applying old terms to a new figure in history. New wine could not just be poured into old wineskins; there had to be new wineskins as well. This means that we must be prepared for both similarities and differences between what we find in the New Testament and what we find in early Jewish literature in general in regard to matters touching on christological issues. We must be prepared to be both surprised and reassured. We must be prepared to see where analogies help us and where analogies break down. Above all we must be prepared for grappling with the amazing variety we will find when we examine the New Testament Christologies. Having said this, we are prepared to start our exploration of the relevant data.

NOTES

1. See M. Hengel, "Christological Titles in Early Christianity," in *The Messiah: Developments in Earliest Judaism and Christianity*, ed. J. H. Charlesworth (Minneapolis: Fortress Press, 1992), pp. 425–48, here p. 443.

2. R. E. Brown, *An Introduction to New Testament Christology* (New York: Paulist Press, 1994), pp. 105ff.

3. One should pay particular attention to the crucial text in Mark 8:27–30, where Jesus asks about how he is viewed, or in Mark 14:61–62, where he responds to questions rather than comes with assertions. Equally telling is the baptismal scene in Mark 1:9–11 (cf. Mark 9:2–8), where God informs Jesus about his identity. On the matter of dyadic personality in the Mediterranean world, see B. Malina, *The New Testament World* (Louisville: Westminster John Knox, 1993), chapter 3.

4. I would suggest that it was the events of Jesus' life, especially the end of his life that led to creative rereadings and reinterpreting of the Hebrew Scriptures. In other words, I would suggest that what we find for instance in the Gospels is not prophecy historicized in narrative form, but rather history creatively related to various sorts of Old Testament texts, *in order to explain the facts about Jesus' life, not in order to explain the Old Testament.*

5. J. D. G. Dunn, "The Making of Christology—Evolution or Unfolding?" in *Jesus of Nazareth: Lord and Christ*, ed. J. B. Green and M. Turner (Grand Rapids: Eerdmans, 1994), pp. 437–52.

6. Paul never uses the phrase "Son of Man" to describe Jesus.

1

Great Expectations?
The Story of Early Jewish Messianism

I T ALMOST ALWAYS COMES as something of a surprise to Christians today when they actually sit down and talk about christological matters with Jews and discover that many Jews, except for the very orthodox, are neither expecting the coming of a Messiah nor are they dismayed that, in their view, one has not shown up. The same may be said about some early Jews as well, but by no means all of them. On the one hand it would be wrong to say that almost every Jew in the first century waited with baited breath for the coming of the Messiah, but it would be equally wrong at the other extreme to minimize the very real evidence of early Jewish messianism. It would also be wrong to assume that there was one particular form of messianism to which most early Jews subscribed. Rather, there were a variety of expectations in the air when Jesus came on the scene in the early first century C.E.[1] This lack of a "normative" view of the Messiah may in fact have made it possible for Jesus to say and do various new things and still stay within the plausibility structure of early Jewish ways of evaluating christological issues.

It is our task in this brief chapter to discuss early Jewish messianism as a backdrop for assessing both Jesus' self-understanding and the Christologies of the early church. While this analysis will help us in various ways, it does not explain all. In particular it does not explain the notable contrast between early Jewish and early Christian literature, the latter being filled with christological terms and ideas, whereas such terms and ideas are for the most part rare in early Jewish literature. I would suggest this contrast is an eloquent, though indirect, testimony to the fact that it was the life and ministry of Jesus which accelerated and in various cases generated christological reflection among a particular group of early Jews who were his followers. If Jesus or his life never suggested such messianic reflections and ideas, it is hard to account for this contrast in interest and emphasis between early Jewish and early Christian literature.[2]

A clear witness to what I am talking about can be seen when we analyze the usage of the term *māšîaḥ* (Hebrew) or *christos* (Greek), both referring to an anointed person. Christians are used to assuming that the Old Testament is littered with prophecies about the future coming Messiah, but in fact if we are talking about the use of these precise terms, *māšîaḥ* is *never* used in the Old Testament of a future coming messianic ruler. The term is used of those who were Davidic kings in the past or present (Pss. 18:50; 89:20; 132:10–17), but it is also used of Cyrus in Isa. 45:1 and in Hab. 3:13 it seems to be used of a presently reigning king. It is clearly not a technical term in the Old Testament for "the Messiah," even though texts like 2 Sam. 7:8–16 expressed the clear hope that God would provide a better Davidic ruler. This stands in dramatic contrast to what we find in the New Testament, where *christos*, when it is not a technical term, becomes almost a second name for Jesus and is used a great number of times.

In part perhaps this lack of use of *māšîaḥ* in the Old Testament can be put down to the fact that the hope for an ideal Anointed One of God did not arise before the demise of the Davidic line and the exile, at the earliest. Indeed, some would say it was only in postexilic times that what we would call messianic hopes really arose, and even then such hopes took a variety of forms. Messianic hope in early Judaism was a response to the experiences of the failure of the Davidic line to sustain itself much less the nation, a failure that in turn led to experiences of exile, and then less than fully satisfactory postexilic experiences, up to and including the Maccabean period.

A further fact deserves our attention at this point: "in all the Jewish history before A.D. 130 . . . we have no evidence that any *living* Jew was ever referred to as the Messiah except Jesus of Nazareth."[3] It is also true that so far as we know, no living Jew, apart from Jesus, was ever identified with the Danielic Son of Man figure during this era.[4] I would submit that these facts are eloquent testimony that it was the life and teachings of Jesus that were the catalyst for the abundant christological discussions that followed his time in Jewish Christian circles. A non-christological Jesus, or a Jesus who neither implied nor suggested anything beyond the norm about himself, fails to explain this sort of data when set against the backdrop of the *lack* of discussion of such matters in early Judaism. It can be no accident that in the lengthy record of Jewish history written by Josephus (the *Antiquities*), the term *christos* occurs only twice and in both cases it refers to Jesus.[5]

When we examine the so-called intertestamental period, there are a few more references to the Anointed One than in the Old Testament, though the terminology is still infrequent (see *Pss. Sol.* 18:5; 4Qpatr 3; CD 12:23–24; 14:19; 19:10–11; *1 Enoch* 48:10; 52:4). As M. De Jonge has said, even here the term "Messiah" does not seem to have been "an *essential* designation for any future redeemer"[6] Furthermore, we find a variety of job descriptions assigned to the "Messiah" in these sources. For example, in *Pss. Sol.* 17–18 we do indeed hear about a future political ruler who is also a spiritual leader. This reminds us that in early Judaism there was not normally any rigid distinction between a political and a spiritual figure when Jews thought about God's coming Anointed One.[7] In the Targums there are a considerable number of messianic passages including some rather militant ones such as the *Targum of Pseudo-Jonathan*, which comments on Gen. 49:11: "How noble is the King, Messiah, who is going to rise from the house of Judah. He has girded his loins and come down, setting in order the order of battle with his enemies and killing kings . . . reddening the mountains with the blood of their slain. With his garments dipped in blood, he is like one who treads grapes in the press." The problem with this material is one of dating, and most scholars would see it not only in its present form but perhaps in its earliest form as postdating New Testament times. What this material shows is that before, during, and after New Testament times a political view of the Messiah was known and discussed. In fact, one may suspect that such a view was the most common one in early Judaism.

Early Jews did not want simply spiritual renewal; they wanted their nation back and self-rule as well. But royal ideas were not always predominant when the Messiah was the subject of discussion. There is, in the Qumran material cited above, evidence for a belief in a coming eschatological priest as God's Anointed One (an idea found also in the *Testaments of the Twelve Patriarchs*), along with evidence in this same literature for a royal messianic figure as well. The latest treatment of the Qumran corpus by John J. Collins shows that there were images of the Messiah as a teacher or prophetic figure as well at Qumran.[8]

It will be worthwhile to pause and consider two of the more important recent Qumran fragments to come to light. The first of these is 4Q521, which speaks of heaven and earth obeying God's Messiah. It goes on to speak of releasing captives, giving sight to the blind, healing the wounded, giving life to the dead, preaching good news to the poor, leading those who have been cast out, and enriching the hungry. There is some debate as to whether these functions are being predicated of God or of God's Anointed One, but in Isaiah 61, which is being drawn upon in this text (along with Ps. 146:1–8), it is clear enough that it is God's messenger who is the herald of good news. Moreover, the mention of obedience to the Messiah in the first line of 4Q521 suggests that God is acting through this anointed agent in the list of activities that follow. This material should be compared to the Q material in Matt. 11:2–5/Luke 7:22, which arguably goes back to Jesus himself. The Qumran material suggests a climate in which, if Jesus made such claims, his audience might well infer that Jesus was making messianic claims. In other words, this recent Qumran material provides additional plausibility to the claim that Jesus could have made some indirect messianic claims using Isaiah 61.[9]

A second fragment from Qumran that deserves comment is 4Q541 (4Q Aaron A). Some scholars have seen reference to a suffering Messiah figure in this fragment, drawing on Isaiah 52–53. This fragment does refer to a figure who atones for all the children of his generation, and then it goes on to say that many words will be spoken against him. Nothing, however, is said explicitly about this figure atoning by means of his *own* death, and Collins concludes that the text may simply mean that this figure is a priest who atones by means of the sacrificial cult. One may also point to the Wisdom of Solomon, which in its first two chapters speaks about the king being opposed and plotted against but not killed.

The second partial fragment in the group 4Q541 is intriguing, even if obscure. It speaks of grieving for some sort of messianic figure and of hanging and perhaps also crucifixion: "Do not afflict the weak by wasting or hanging. . . . [Let] not the nail approach him." In other words, it is not the messianic figure but the weak whose hanging or crucifixion is warned against here, though there may be reference to grieving for this figure. Collins argues that there is no allusion here to the suffering servant of Isaiah 53, but he allows that other servant songs, such as Isa. 42:6 and 49:6 are drawn upon. It is thus possible that the atoning death of a messianic figure is in view in these fragments, but the texts as we have them certainly do not make this clear, and Collins's cautious interpretation, in contrast to some sensationalistic claims that have been made about these texts, is probably correct.[10] There is certainly no clear combination of a discussion about a messianic figure coupled with a quotation of Isaiah 53 here, referring to the atoning death of the servant himself.

Generally speaking, the "Messiah" in the intertestamental literature is not portrayed as a miracle worker, although by the end of the first century C.E. there was Jewish literature that did so (see 4 Ezra 13—in response to Jesus' ministry perhaps?). There is some evidence from this same source that some early Jews believed that the Messiah would come and die (rather than reigning forever), but 4 Ezra 7:29 does not suggest that this death was seen as an atonement of any sort, it simply marks the end of a period of history.[11]

One of the more common themes in these few references to the Messiah in early Jewish literature, whether from before or during the first century C.E., is that he would come and judge and/or destroy the wicked (*Psalms of Solomon* 17–18; 4 Ezra 12; *2 Baruch* 40:72) deliver God's people (*Psalms of Solomon* 17; 4 Ezra 12), and reign in a blessed kingdom (*Psalms of Solomon* 17–18; *2 Baruch* 40). This is not surprising in view of the fact that messianism arose in Israel in the context of disenfranchisement during the exilic and postexilic periods and was apparently further nurtured during the uneasy period of Roman occupation. As I have said, the Messiah was the one looked for who would set the nation back on its feet as an independent entity with Davidic or Solomonic borders.[12]

The term *māšîaḥ* is a relational term, referring to God's Anointed One (whether king, priest, or prophet or some combination of the three), and so it is not surprising that in the literature we are reviewing here there is little use of the absolute form *the Messiah*. Rather it is much more commonly "his Anointed" (*Pss. Sol.* 18:5), or it is used in combinations such as in *1 Enoch* 48:10, where we find "they have denied the Lord of spirits and His Anointed." 4Qpatr speaks of the coming Anointed Righteous One, and we do finally find the absolute phrase "the Messiah" in 1QSam. 2:12—indeed this text speaks of God begetting the Messiah. It is in fact not possible, however, to segregate the messianic texts in early Jewish literature into discrete categories, because clearly enough the phrase Son of God is also used of the messianic figure in some Qumran texts.

4Q246, a pseudo-Danielic fragment in Aramaic that likely antedates the New Testament, says, "the Son of God he shall be said to be, and the Son of the most High they shall call him." This text should not be minimized because it gives us yet further evidence that at Qumran a variety of terms and titles could be applied to the messianic figure, and in view of the context of this fragment it has been plausibly conjectured by Collins that its author saw some connection between the Son of Man figure of Daniel 7 and the Son of God (not merely the saints of God).[13] This conjecture is plausible in view of the evidence of the so-called Parables of Enoch (*1 Enoch* 37–71), which we must now consider briefly.

There has been a considerable amount of debate about the date of this Enochian material, but probably most scholars think that this document is pre-Christian in ideas and probably in origin as well.[14] Collins has recently plausibly suggested, "It is doubtful whether a Jewish author would have made such explicit use of the expression 'Son of Man' for a messianic figure after that phrase had been appropriated by the Christians. . . . Since the *Similitudes* make no allusion to the fall of Jerusalem, a date prior to that event seems most likely."[15] All that we would argue for is that the ideas that this document contains were already extant and probably familiar during Jesus' day.[16] This is of no little significance in view of the similarities between the way the Son of Man issue is discussed in this material and the contexts in which we find the Son of Man phrase in the Synoptic Gospels.

For example, in both the Synoptics and in *1 Enoch* the Son of Man is depicted as a judge. Even more significant is the fact that in both these sources we find the phrase "Son of Man" prefaced by a particularizing term—*the* in the Gospels, *that* in *1 Enoch*. In both cases an attempt is being made to allude to the well-known or aforementioned Son of Man, and in both cases the allusion is likely to be to the Son of Man figure found in Daniel 7. Another important aspect of these parallels is that both in the Synoptics and in *1 Enoch* a particular person is in mind—in the former case Jesus, in the latter case Enoch. Further, in both cases the Danielic overtones of a person who represents God's people (but is not identical with them) is conveyed. In view of the fact that "Son of Man" is the most frequently used messianic phrase in the Synoptic Gospels, and one that is continually found on Jesus' own lips, indeed almost exclusively so, this background information is of considerable importance as we shall see. Also germane is the fact that the Son of Man is equated with the Messiah in *1 Enoch* 48:10 and 52:4.

If we compare the use of "Son of Man" in *1 Enoch* to what we find in 4 Ezra we discover certain similarities—for instance, that in both these sources "Son of Man" refers to an individual, not to a group. In both these sources as well, the Son of Man is identified as the Messiah. Third, in both these sources the Son of Man is seen as preexistent (compare 4 Ezra 13:26 and 7:28 with *1 Enoch* 48:3). "The correspondences between 4 Ezra and the Similitudes point to common assumptions about the interpretation of Daniel 7 in first-century Judaism."[17] These assumptions make it plausible to argue that Jesus could have used "Son of Man" to refer to himself, and that he could have intended messianic overtones when he did so.

Another sort of background material comes to us from a different source—Wisdom literature. Especially important for our purposes is the development of the treatment of the notion of God's Wisdom, a personification of an attribute of God or of his creation. Clearly enough in Proverbs 8–9 we are dealing with a matter of personification, not least because Woman Wisdom is contrasted with Lady Folly in this same context. When we get to the material in the Wisdom of Solomon, a document that is perhaps from just before the turn of the era, we find the role of Wisdom much more fully described, especially in chapters 8–9, where Wisdom is depicted in some of the same terms that are used of Christ in the christological hymns, particularly in Colossians 1.[18] While we will address the implications of this material more fully at various appropriate spots, here it will be useful to give a brief summary of how Wisdom is portrayed in the literature ranging from Proverbs to the Wisdom of Solomon:

1. Wisdom has her origins in God (Prov. 8:22; Sir. 24:3; Wis. Sol. 7:25–26).
2. Wisdom preexisted and appears to have had a role in the work of creation (Prov. 3:19; 8:22–29; 24:3; Sir. 1:4, 9–10; 16:24–17:7; Wis. Sol. 7:22; 8:4–6; 9:2, 9).
3. Wisdom is infused in creation, which accounts for its coherence and endurance (Wis. Sol. 1:7; 7:24, 27; 8:1; 11:25).
4. Wisdom is identified with God's Spirit (Wis. Sol. 1:7; 9:17; 12:1) and seems to be immanent in some sense in the world (Wis. Sol. 7:24; 8:1).
5. Wisdom comes to the world with a mission (Prov. 8:4, 31–36; Sir. 24:7, 12, 19–22; Wis. Sol. 7:27–28; 8:2–3), to address the world personally (Prov. 1:8, 9; Sir. 24:19–22; Wis. Sol. 6:12–16; 8:7–9; 9:10–16), and to her followers she offers life, sometimes prosperity and various other blessings (Prov. 1:8, 9; Sir. 1:14–20; 6:18–31; 15:1–8; 24:19–33; Wis Sol. 7:7–14).

6. Wisdom is especially associated with Israel, dwelling in Israel by divine command (Sir. 24:8–12), sometimes identified with or as Torah (Sir. 24:23; Bar. 4:1), and is at work in Israel's history guiding, guarding, even saving God's people (Wis. Sol. 10:1–21).
7. Wisdom finds no permanent dwelling place on earth and so returns to heaven and resumes her rightful place there (*1 Enoch* 42:1–3).[19]

As we shall see, this Wisdom material proved influential not only on the material we find in the Gospels but also on the material we find elsewhere in the New Testament, particularly the Pauline epistles.

Notable by its absence, though in no way surprising, is any use of terms such as "Lord" or "God" for early Jewish messianic figures. The discussion of Wisdom, especially in Wisdom of Solomon comes much nearer to ascribing some form of divinity to Wisdom, but Wisdom in this literature is seen not as a human figure but rather as a personification of a divine attribute or an attribute of God's creation. The material we have discussed provides the context in which the presentations of Jesus as Son of Man or Son of God or Messiah, or as God's Wisdom in the Gospels and elsewhere in the New Testament begin to make some sense. In short, the christological terminology in the New Testament is for the most part not unprecedented, but both the fact and the way that it is used to describe Jesus are often surprising and innovative. The earliest Christologies in the New Testament did not arise in a total vacuum, but drew on concepts already in the air and being discussed in Jewish contexts before, during, and after the time of Jesus, though with a fresh sense or nuance.

Something must be said about the christological use of the Old Testament at the turn of the era. First, probably a majority of scholars would argue that many of the prophetic Old Testament texts that normally come up for discussion when messianism is the subject were not originally intended as prophecies of the coming Messiah. For example, the Immanuel passage in Isaiah 7 speaks of a young woman (probably assumed to be a virgin) who will bear a child. Verse 16 says that before he comes to the age of moral discernment the land "before whose two kings you are in dread will be deserted." The reference to kings is made clear in v. 18, which explains that God will bring Egypt and Assyria to judge God's people. In other words, this prophecy is tied to a specific historical context that existed before the time of Jesus and, more to the point, did not exist in his own day. Or again, if one reads 2 Sam. 7:4–17 carefully one sees that vv. 12–15 are probably in the first case about the near future, namely, about Solomon, though v. 16 speaks clearly enough of the establishment of David's house forever thereafter. Again the point is that the prophecy had an application on the near horizon. It was not in the first instance a "messianic" prophecy about some distant king or Anointed One.[20] In such cases we may wish to talk about the christological fulfillment of prophecies, but perhaps not about these texts as predictions of an eschatological *māšîaḥ,* unless one wants to argue for a fuller sense to such texts. In the latter case, one would maintain that Solomon and whichever king was Immanuel did not in fact completely fulfill the promises and expectations suggested in these prophecies, and thus the prophecies were viewed as not yet completed before the coming of the Messiah. There are of course also texts like Ps. 110:1, which in their original context seem to have been the comments of a third party about the relationship between Yahweh (the Lord) and the existing Davidic priest-king (my lord), and how God helps him against other kings and foes.

There are, however, other Old Testament prophecies of a more general or apocalyptic character that have less historically particular contours, for example, Isaiah 53 or Daniel 7 or perhaps Isaiah 11 or Zechariah 7–11. These texts seem to envision a more ultimate state of affairs when the final kingly figure will rule, not merely an already existing or soon-to-arise king. In these cases we may perhaps speak of prediction and fulfillment. In all cases, however, we can certainly talk about the christological use of the Old Testament, which did not begin with early Christians.

It is now clear from the careful study of various non-Christian early Jewish documents, not the least of which is the Qumran corpus, that by the time of Jesus what we may call the christological interpretation of the Old Testament was already something of a cottage industry. In some cases this entailed the giving of a particular reference to a general Old Testament prophecy such as we find in Daniel 7 or Zechariah 7–11 in a "this is that" kind of interpretation, where figures such as the Teacher of Righteousness (the founder of the Qumran community) or his eschatological successors are seen as fulfilling various Old Testament prophecies. In other cases it involved the christological interpretation of texts such as 2 Samuel 7, which, in the view of various early Jews, had not been fully or satisfactorily brought to fulfillment in any previous age of the history of God's people (see, e.g., the treatment of 2 Samuel 7 in 4QFlorilegium). In still other instances very creative midrashic procedures were used on even non-prophetic portions of the Old Testament to provide a relevant message to the current situation.

The belief that the world was already in the eschatological age, or that the last age was about to dawn, was not just a belief of many early Christians. It was also the belief of at least many who produced the Qumran literature, and it seems also to have been the belief of those who produced such documents as the Parables of Enoch (see above) and 4 Ezra. This climate of eschatological expectation in various quarters should not be underestimated when we evaluate the New Testament documents. It produced many interesting interpretations of the Old Testament and a general proclivity to see the whole of the Hebrew Scriptures as in some sense foreshadowing if not predicting the final state of affairs. It also produced some results we certainly don't find in the New Testament, for instance, the celebrated references in the *Damascus Document* (CD) and the *Manual of Discipline* (1QS), where there is reference to the Anointed Ones of Aaron and of Israel, who seem to assume priestly and kingly roles (see CD 14:19 and 19:10) respectively.[21] This idea of two messianic figures seems indebted to what we find in Zech. 4:1–14. In most of the relevant material, even when christologically interpreted, the messianic figure (or figures) is seen as a human being especially endowed by God to perform certain necessary final tasks to regather and restore Israel, and sometimes the destruction of enemies is seen as the means of accomplishing this end.[22]

We must now sum up some of the most important conclusions about early Jewish messianism: (1) Only a distinct (though important) minority of early Jewish writings speak about messianic matters or a Messiah or Messiahs. (2) The terms *christos* and *māšîaḥ* are by no means common in this literature and are not used at all in the Old Testament of a future messianic figure. (3) Nevertheless, there is more than sufficient evidence that there was considerable eschatological ferment and hope at the turn of the era, with some groups of Jews, such as those at the Qumran community, interpreting various Old Testament texts messianically and eschatologically. (4) There were a variety of views about the coming Messiah or Messiahs, not one conventional view, though the majority of the relevant writings seem to envision some sort of political and military role for this kingly figure. (5) Early Jewish messianic hope led to varying ways of handling the Old Testament, including prediction-fulfillment, midrashic exegesis, and even the christological use of non-prophetic portions of the Old Testament.

We have seen that some Old Testament prophecies, which were originally focusing on the near horizon, were reapplied, and some more
general and apocalyptic prophecies such as we find in Daniel 7 or
Zechariah 7–11 were seen as specifically applying to the final messianic figure or figures. (6) Though there is considerable similarity in
use of terms and in ways of handling the Old Testament, there are also
significant differences in the treatment of christological issues in the
New Testament, including in the Gospels, to what we find in early
Jewish literature more generally. Specifically, the New Testament
speaks much more often on the subject, says a good deal more about it,
and is sometimes willing to suggest things no other early Jewish literature really suggested, such as the divine status of the Messiah or the
applicability of the Wisdom personification to the Messiah.[23] The differences stand out as much as the similarities between the sorts of
christological reflection we find in the New Testament and the sorts
we find in other early Jewish literature. For example, the claims for the
divinity of Jesus in the New Testament went beyond anything one
finds in the non-Christian Jewish texts, and as far as we know now
"Jesus of Nazareth was the only historical figure who was eventually
identified with Daniel's Son of Man."[24] It is my view that Jesus himself was the catalyst for the frequency and fervency of discussion of
these matters and that he sparked the discussion of the christological
matters in new and fresh ways,[25] and so we must now turn to the evaluation of the Christology of Jesus himself.

NOTES

1. See J. J. Collins, *The Scepter and the Star: The Messiahs of the Dead Sea
Scrolls and other Ancient Literature* (New York: Doubleday, 1995), pp.
195–209; J. Neusner et al., eds., *Judaisms and their Messiahs at the Turn of the
Christian Era* (Cambridge: Cambridge University Press, 1987), passim.

2. This chapter will not involve detailed analyses of various important Old
Testament texts because the focus is on the climate Jesus would have been
part of at the turn of the era and just afterwards and therefore primarily on the
literature of that period, and only to a lesser degree on the Old Testament literature that was very influential during that period. For a very helpful and
detailed study of the life of Jesus in light of the Old Testament prophecies, see
now N. T. Wright, *Jesus and the Victory of God* (Minneapolis: Fortress Press,
1996). Some analysis of the relevant portions of the Old Testament will be
undertaken at various points in the following chapters.

3. R. E. Brown, *An Introduction to New Testament Christology* (New York: Paulist Press, 1994), p. 73 (emphasis added).

4. See rightly Collins, *Scepter and the Star*, pp. 208–9.

5. In fact, one of these references may be a Christian interpolation, in which case the Jewish evidence becomes even slimmer.

6. M. De Jonge, "The Use of the Word 'Anointed' in the Time of Jesus," *Novum Testamentum* 8 (1966): 132–48. See also his "The Earliest Christian use of *Christos:* Some Suggestions," *New Testament Studies* 32.3 (1986): 321–43.

7. See the discussion of this material by G. L. Davenport, "The 'Anointed of the Lord' in Psalms of Solomon 17," in *Ideal Figures in Ancient Judaism: Profiles and Paradigms*, ed. G. W. E. Nickelsburg and J. J. Collins (Chico, Calif.: Scholars Press, 1980), pp. 67–92.

8. See Collins, *Scepter and the Star*, pp. 102–26.

9. See the helpful discussion in Collins, *Scepter and the Star*, pp. 117–22.

10. See ibid., pp. 123–26.

11. See J. H. Charlesworth, "From Messianology to Christology: Problems and Prospects," in *The Messiah: Developments in Earliest Judaism and Christianity*, ed. J. H. Charlesworth (Minneapolis: Fortress Press, 1992), pp. 3–35, here p. 8.

12. See now Collins's conclusion in *The Scepter and the Star*, that there "was a dominant notion of a Davidic messiah, as the king who would restore the kingdom of Israel, which was part of the common Judaism around the turn of the era" (p. 209).

13. See J. J. Collins, "The Son of God Text from Qumran," in *From Jesus to John*, ed. M. De Boer (Sheffield: JSOT Press, 1993), pp. 65–82.

14. But see G. W. E. Nickelsburg, "Salvation without and with a Messiah: Developing Beliefs in Writings Ascribed to Enoch," in *Judaisms and their Messiahs*, ed. Neusner et al., pp. 49–68, here 56–64.

15. Collins, *Scepter and the Star*, p. 177.

16. See my more extended discussion in the *The Christology of Jesus* (Philadelphia: Fortress Press, 1990), pp. 234–35.

17. Collins, *Scepter and the Star*, p. 188. See his entire discussion of this matter on pp.187–89.

18. On this matter, see pp. 81ff. below.

19. See my discussion of this material in *Jesus the Sage: The Pilgrimage of Wisdom* (Minneapolis: Fortress Press, 1994), pp. 114ff. In this composite list I am following the suggestions of R. Murphy, in his *The Tree of Life* (New York: Doubleday, 1990), pp. 145–46.

20. The establishment of an eternal dynasty is not the same as the idea of God intervening late in time and restoring Israel's fortunes with an unexpected royal figure. The one speaks of historical continuum, the other of restoration by eschatological action after long interruption.

21. Charlesworth is uncertain whether the Qumran texts refer to one or

two messianic figures, but at least several of these texts suggest that two were in view ("From Messianology to Christology," pp. 27–28).

22. See the discussion by S. Talmon, "The Concept of *Masiah* and Messianism in Early Judaism," in *Messiah,* ed. Charlesworth, pp.79–115, and by L. H. Schiffman, "Messianic Figures and Ideas in the Qumran Scrolls," in ibid., pp. 116–29.

23. It is important to note that some Jewish ideal figures, such as Enoch in the Parables of Enoch, do take on certain quasi-divine attributes or traits, but the point is that such attributes were not being predicated of an existing historical figure in this literature. Not even the Teacher of Righteousness is described as divine or quasi-divine in the way Jesus was.

24. Collins, *Scepter and the Star,* p. 209.

25. Here I must disagree with Charlesworth when he says, "I find it difficult to comprehend how the Jewish man Jesus could have thought he was Messiah and yet one 'very different' from the Messiah expected by the Jews" ("From Messianology to Christology," 7). On the one hand there is a frequent theme in Jewish literature of a political messianic figure who will right wrongs, banish enemies, and restore Israel, even if one cannot speak of this being the normative view of the Messiah in early Judaism. Precisely because there was no "normative view" but only some dominant ideas and expectations, Jesus was free to use the ideas and terminology in fresh ways without breaking out of the plausibility structure of early Jewish thought. It is also worth bearing in mind that the Gospels, especially Mark, suggest that Jesus' meaning was difficult to understand, that he was to some extent an enigmatic, though not a completely incomprehensible, figure.

2

The Christology of Jesus

ENTION THE CHRISTOLOGY OF JESUS and in some scholarly
circles you are likely to get a snicker or a wry smile. For
many scholars it is axiomatic that Jesus had no exalted self-
understanding, if by that one means that he understood himself to be
more than a Jewish sage or perhaps a prophet. M. Borg speaks for a variety of scholars when he says "the self-understanding and message of
the pre-Easter Jesus were in all likelihood *nonmessianic*. . . . According to the earliest layers of the developing Gospel tradition, he said
nothing about having such thoughts."[1] It is precisely this conclusion
that I wish to dispute in this chapter. I believe it is based on faulty
assumptions about the character of the material in the Synoptic
Gospels. Much nearer the mark is J. D. G. Dunn, who says:

> I have become increasingly persuaded that the best *starting* point for
> studying the main body of the Synoptic tradition is to view it as the ear-
> liest churches' memories of Jesus as retold and reused by these churches.
> . . . I see the earliest tradents within the Christian churches as preservers
> more than innovators, as seeking to transmit, retell, explain, interpret,
> elaborate, but not create *de nova*. . . . Through the main body of the Syn-
> optic tradition, I believe, we have in most cases direct access to the
> teaching and ministry of Jesus as it was remembered from the beginning
> of the transmission process (which often predates Easter), and so fairly
> direct access to the ministry and teaching of Jesus through the eyes and
> ears of those who went about with him.[2]

If this is even close to being an accurate assessment of the Synoptic
Gospels, then we can speak of the Gospel writers (or those who passed

traditions to them) not as the creators of the christological images of Jesus but rather as the expounders, refiners, and re-presenters of these images. We shall see that even taking a very critical approach to the data and limiting ourselves to the arguably authentic words, deeds, relationships, and experiences of Jesus recorded in the Synoptic Gospels (I am, for the sake of argument, leaving the Gospel of John for the most part out of account at this juncture), we still come up with a Jesus who speaks and acts and relates in ways that deserve to be called messianic.

THE INDIRECT EVIDENCE

Jesus and His Relationships

Though it has been traditional to begin with the direct evidence of the titles, in some ways the indirect evidence of Jesus' christological self-estimation is more compelling than the direct evidence, as it was probably less likely to be tampered with in a christologically tendentious way by the Gospel writers and/or those who provided them with their source material. We will begin by reviewing briefly the major ongoing relationships of Jesus as portrayed in the Gospels: (1) John the Baptist; (2) the Pharisees; (3) the revolutionaries; and (4) his disciples. The data relevant to discussing any one of these relationships are in themselves revealing, but even if one discounts this or that text, the combined effect of looking at all these relationships is very close to compelling. We shall see that even if Jesus made no overt christological claims whatsoever, the way he related to others would suggest that he viewed himself in such a light.[3]

Jesus and John the Baptist

No little ink has been spilt in the discussion of Jesus' relationship to John the Baptist. John Meier, for instance, in the second volume of his magisterial three-volume work entitled *A Marginal Jew*, devotes well over two hundred pages to the discussion of this subject alone. A good deal of the debate about the evangelists' portrayals of John has been about whether they are polemicizing against John (and an ongoing Baptist sect?) or whether they are trying to claim John as a witness to and for Jesus and the Gospel. On the whole, the latter seems to be the case, though the Gospel writers are keen to make clear that John was overshadowed by Jesus, not merely followed by him. W. Wink's detailed analysis has yielded the following conclusions: (1) Mark portrays John as Elijah incognito, paralleling the messianic secret motif in that Gospel; (2) Matthew uses John as an ally of Jesus against the hostile front of opposition they both encountered in Judaism; (3) Luke basically accepts Mark's portrait but adapts it to suit his historical purposes in presenting an orderly chronicle of salvation history; (4) the Fourth Evangelist portrays John as the ideal and first real witness to Jesus as God's Christ and Lamb.[4] If we take account of these redactional tendencies, all of which tend to view and use John in a positive way to bolster the presentation of Jesus, we should be able to envision how the sources the Gospel writers used presented Jesus' relationship with John.

The figure of John is striking. On first examination he appears to be an isolated ascetical prophet of doom, like Jeremiah or Joel. Yet he seems to have performed no miracles or signs, like Elijah or Elisha, and his practice of baptizing has no real precedent in the Old Testament prophetic literature. On this latter front, he seems rather more like those who practiced baptism of initiates at Qumran. Yet he is unlike at least some of the Qumranites in that he has not withdrawn from Israelite society, and indeed he sees it as his task to address Israel as a whole, calling all of God's people to repentance in view of the coming judgment of God. In other words, John is not simply a reformer like the Pharisees, for he exhorts even the ritually pure and "righteous" to be baptized, and, from what we can tell, John's baptism is not to be seen as a repeatable ritual ablution. There is nothing in the Gospel evidence, nor in Josephus's portrayal of John (see, e.g., *Antiquities* 18.5.2), to suggest that John presented himself as more than a prophet, for instance, as the leader of a messianic movement. Nor is he just another reformer or revolutionary, for he urges no levitical regimen or revolutionary program on Israel. What is in a sense revolutionary about John, however, is that he seems to see the whole nation of Israel as so corrupt and in danger of judgment that it needs to start over from scratch with God, on the basis of repentance and baptism, not relying on heredity or a renewed keeping of the levitical laws. He seems to have appeared on the stage of Jewish history at an uneasy time. Luke 3:1 informs us that he appeared during the fifteenth year of Tiberias, sometime between autumn of 27 C.E. and the summer of 29 C.E., and to judge from Josephus he was apparently executed by Herod Antipas around 32 C.E. (*Antiquities* 18.109–19).

If we begin with Mark 1:1–11 and take account of the author's redactional tendencies, we still are left with the following likely historical data: (1) John baptized people in the Judean wilderness; and (2) his baptism was for the forgiveness of sins.[5] If we supplement these conclusions with the doubly attested tradition that John baptized anyone who was willing to come, repent, and submit to this baptism, even harlots and tax collectors (compare Luke 3:12–14 with Matt. 21:31–32), we gain a picture of John as something of a radical, who believed that the old solutions of offering sacrifices in the Temple for forgiveness of sin were no longer necessary or sufficient in view of the coming judgment of God. Forgiveness could be had by anyone directly through repentance and baptism by anyone. The idea of forgiveness offered apart from the following of the levitical rituals also appears in the ministry of Jesus, and it is possible that Jesus got this idea from John.

There is one further element in the Markan text that seems likely to be authentic, namely, that John did not see himself as the final revealer of God's will; rather he spoke in terms of some sort of successor who would come and judge God's people by means of a baptism of Spirit and fire. Mark 1:7–8 should be compared to the independent Q version of this tradition in Matt. 3:11/Luke 3:16. The Gospel writers saw John as playing an essential but preparatory role, and in fact John's ministry could be said to be the beginning of the Good News, which means he was not its consummation.

If we look closely at Matthew 3/ Luke 3:1–22 we learn a few more pertinent pieces of information about John. First, he seems to have believed that the spiritual leadership of Israel was desperately corrupt, and this would seem to include the Pharisees, for the idea is attested not only in this text but also independently in Luke 7:29–30. Second, it appears that he did not expect all to respond positively to his message. Indeed, he did not expect the "brood of vipers" to respond that way at all, which means that he had the idea of some sort of righteous remnant. Third, John's association of the Coming One with judgment seems clear from this text, which will help to explain the perplexity of John as we find it in the next arguably authentic piece of material.

Matthew 11:2–19/Luke 7:18–35 has various marks of authenticity, not the least of which is that the early church was not likely to make up the idea that John had doubts about Jesus' true identity, since all four Gospel writers show interest in making John a positive witness to the ministry of Jesus. The quandary of John seems to have been caused by the fact that instead of coming and bringing judgment on Israel, Jesus came and brought Good News and healing. The inbreaking dominion of God in the first instance meant liberation and healing, though if it was rejected judgment would follow. Jesus' response here is revealing. He came to live up to not John's expectations but God's call on his life. This presupposes that Jesus sensed a call and that he saw this Isaianic prophecy being fulfilled through his ministry (cf. Isa. 29:18–19; 35:5–6; 61:1). Most interesting about Jesus' response is that he seems to have left out the references to judgment in the Isaianic material he is using (cf. Isa. 29:20; 35:5; 61:2). With this material about how Jesus interacted with John we are beginning to get a picture of how Jesus viewed himself.

Jesus' estimation of John was clearly positive. The Q tradition in Matt. 11:7–11/Luke 7:24–28 in fact tells us that John was viewed as more than just a prophet—indeed, the greatest person ever "born of woman." What are we to make of this? One suggestion, perhaps the most plausible, is that Jesus saw John as the last great eschatological prophet and so more than an ordinary prophet. It is hardly plausible that the early church would invent the idea that Jesus would call John more than a prophet, for such an idea could have been taken to mean that Jesus saw John in a messianic light. But this saying also suggests that Jesus saw John as the last in the line of prophets, bringing closure to an age, or perhaps as a transitional figure with one foot in each of two ages (something Matt. 11:12–13/Luke 16:16 probably also independently suggests). Probably the saying contrasts two ways of evaluating people—by their physical descent and human characteristics or by their place in the inbreaking dominion of God. Jesus' point, then, would not be to necessarily or forever place John outside the kingdom but to stress that the old ways of evaluating things should be given up. Perhaps Jesus had picked up John's contrast between physical descent and repentance and faith and expanded it to discuss the significance of participating in God's dominion.

The next text that can help us in our inquiry is Matt. 11:16–19/Luke 7:31–35. Even the most rigorous sifters of the Gospel traditions are in agreement that this tradition likely goes back to a situation in the life of Jesus, if one subtracts the Matthean and Lukan redactional features. The saying suggests a social environment of criticism and rejection of the ministries both of John and of Jesus, even though they had contrasting styles of ministering. The analogy is drawn between the rejecters of "this generation" and petulant and spoiled children who were pleased neither with John's ascetical approach nor with Jesus' celebratory style. John they saw as a fanatical madman, Jesus as immoral and an aesthete. Though these views are caricatures, there is enough justice in the assessment to tell us that John and Jesus did not approach Israel or minister in exactly the same way. Furthermore the ministries of these two figures invited comparison (and contrast).

A final tradition that is arguably authentic, even though it comes from the Gospel of John is John 3:22–4:3. Here we learn several things that the church would probably not have invented: (1) that Jesus was perhaps indebted to John for several aspects of his own ministry; (2) that Jesus either participated in or was a supporter of John's ministry beyond the Jordan in Perea for a considerable time and established a parallel practice in that region; (3) that Jesus drew some of his earliest disciples from John's flock; and (4) that Jesus' followers, if not Jesus himself, followed the example of John in practicing baptism—only he did it presumably in his native region of Galilee (or perhaps in Judea as well). That Jesus believed John's baptism had divine approval can be established independently from the tradition in Mark 11:27–33. It is possible and believable that Jesus may have wanted not to detract from John's ministry and so called a halt to a similar practice among his own followers when they began to draw bigger crowds than John. It is also possible that it was not until John was imprisoned, and so out of the picture, that Jesus came to the conclusion that he was called to a rather different sort of ministry that involved preaching, healing, practicing fellowship, and going forth and calling disciples, rather than waiting for them to come to him.

There is a delicate balance to be maintained in evaluating these traditions, so that one neither minimizes the similarities nor the differences between Jesus' ministry and John's, and how they viewed themselves (and each other). Let us emphasize the similarities first. Jesus, like John, had ministries that called Israel to change its ways, even and perhaps especially Israel's leadership. The ministry of both of these men involved hostile responses and rejection by various people, which suggests that neither was offering a familiar nonthreatening message. Both believed that forgiveness could be had apart from the sacrificial system in Jerusalem. Both believed that God's eschatological action was about to or was breaking into human history and that Israel must be prepared to respond properly or be judged. In other words, both seem to have believed that judgment begins with the household of God and that salvation hinges on how one responds to their respective ministries. Both believed that baptism was an appropriate symbol of response to their preaching, a symbol of preparation for what was to come. Both men believed that the eschatological hour of decision was dawning for Israel and that it was critical that Israel respond appropriately.

Unlike John, Jesus does not seem to have expected a successor.[6] Also unlike John, Jesus seems to have believed that his task was not merely to announce but to bring in the eschatological blessings announced in Isaiah. Unlike John, Jesus participated fully in the society of which he was a part, even to the extent of banqueting with the bad and the unclean. Unlike John, Jesus eventually went out and called disciples, and one particular symbolic action (baptizing) did not characterize his whole ministry. Unlike John, Jesus was known as a healer.

It is important that of all the figures in his society with whom Jesus could have compared and contrasted himself in terms of words and deeds (for example, Herod Antipas, Caesar, the Pharisees, the Sadducees, the priests and Levites, the revolutionaries) John was the one he chose to mention as his reference point and human touchstone. It appears that Jesus had a normal progressive historical consciousness such that it was only after he had been baptized by John, and perhaps not until after John was out of the picture, that Jesus concluded that God's call on his life involved an independent ministry in Galilee, after a period of being involved either with John's ministry or in a parallel ministry in the same region. If it is true that Jesus saw John as the last great prophet, or as a transitional figure, the eschatological prophet (like Elijah?), by implication this says something about how he viewed himself. Jesus did not see himself as just another in a long line of Israel's prophets.

Jesus and the Pharisees

If there was a particular sect or party in Israel in Jesus' day that could be said to be the most popular with ordinary Jews, it was the Pharisees. It was their goal to reform the nation by spreading the message of "scriptural holiness" throughout their land, which chiefly meant that they wished for the nation writ large to embrace the stringent levitical standards of ritual purity that previously only priests had been expected to follow. Like John and Jesus, the Pharisees saw their nation in a state of spiritual, ritual, and moral corruption, and their solution to the problem was to extend the way the ritual (and moral) law was implemented so that it encompassed all the aspects of everyday life, even of ordinary people. J. Neusner sums up the matter thus: "In a very specific way the Pharisees claimed to live as if they were priests, as if they had to obey at home the laws that applied to the Temple."[7] Since there was not a law for every occasion in the Torah, the Pharisees elevated various oral traditions, giving legal guidelines to all sorts of other issues and matters. In their view, the oral Torah was also given to Moses at Sinai and had been carefully passed down through the generations to the first century C.E. The claim of the Pharisees was that their scribes, or experts in the law, knew the correct way to interpret, explain, and expand the law to meet every need. In this manner they asserted a "biblical" authority over against other interpretations and interpreters, and so a spiritual authority over Jews in general. It is no surprise that, since their authority was so grounded in assumptions about a certain sort of interpretation of the Old Testament and the value of various oral traditions that they did not pass over lightly any challenge to these fundamental assumptions. The Mishnah later encapsulated this attitude well: "It is more culpable to teach against the ordinances of the [Pharisaic] scribes than against the Torah itself" (*Mishnah Sanhedrin* 11:3).

Though it has become fashionable in some circles to follow E. P. Sanders and his views that in fact Jesus had no serious conflicts with the Pharisees, I remain unpersuaded in view of the considerable evidence to the contrary in the New Testament, not the least of which is the Pauline evidence that Saul the Pharisee persecuted Christians (see, e.g., Gal. 1:13; 1 Cor. 15:9).[8] This latter was surely only a continuation of the animus that had already existed between the Pharisees and Jesus and his followers, not some new development first concocted by Paul. While it is possible and plausible to argue that some of the Gospel polemics against the Pharisees may be put down to the ongoing disagreements between the church and the synagogue after the time of Jesus, it is simply not possible to place all of this material under such a heading, as it is found in too many strands of the tradition. It stretches credulity to the breaking point to suggest that Christian communities throughout the Diaspora were having major controversies with Pharisaic Jews of the sort that the Synoptic Gospels reflect. Not only do we have no clear evidence of extensive Pharisaic influence all over the Diaspora, but one must reckon with the fact that many of the issues raised in the Gospels as bones of contention between Jesus and the Pharisees were surely dead or moot issues for the majority of Christians by the time the Gospels were written, especially after 70 C.E., and before Pharisaic Judaism had managed to truly reorganize

Judaism in the Holy Land. One would have to argue that the Synoptics were all written to audiences in close touch with Judaism in the Holy Land to explain such a widespread polemic as mere ecclesiastical broadsides.[9] Especially in the case of Luke's Gospel, probably written in the 70s or 80s to an audience in the West, perhaps in Rome, is it implausible to argue that the controversies reflected in this Gospel mirror later church difficulties with Pharisees and specific Pharisaic concerns.[10] Mark's Gospel as well seems clearly written for those who are not even in contact with Aramaic-speaking Christians, never mind with Pharisaic controversies in the Holy Land (e.g., notice the inserted explanatory remarks in Mark 7:3 and 19). I thus conclude that we must take seriously the suggestion of a variety of traditions that Jesus had some controversies with the Pharisees and that this can teach us something about Jesus' self-understanding. These controversies are all the more likely if any of the leading Pharisees were scribal retainers of the Temple hierarchy and leadership in Jerusalem, a group that was indeed concerned to regulate the behavior of Jews both in Judea and Galilee.

In an important study, M. Borg has documented how one of the essential characteristics of Jesus' ministry was controversy, particularly over holiness issues.[11] In fact, the controversies between Jesus and the Pharisees were caused largely by the fact that they had two rather different visions of how to reform the nation, and of what real holiness was. That Jesus healed people on the Sabbath is a multiply-attested notion in the Gospels, as is the idea that he ate with ritually unclean and even with immoral people. If the latter is true, it is also highly probable that he ate unclean food as well. Furthermore, a variety of Gospel traditions portray Jesus as touching and being touched by unclean persons or even as touching corpses, but there are no traditions which suggest that Jesus performed rituals of purification after such occasions. The implications of these deliberate practices of Jesus is that either he was a careless or bad Jew or else he assumed an authority over both the oral traditions and the law that the Pharisees would not have recognized or respected.

Let us consider one controversial piece of evidence that supports this latter suggestion. Mark 7:15 is an aphoristic contrast saying, and as such is characteristic of the kind of contrast sayings that seem to have typified Jesus' teaching (cf., e.g., any of the antitheses in Matthew 5).

That the saying is allusive or elliptical and subject to various interpretations is clear enough from the fact that the Gospel writer feels he must explain it (Mark 7:19). This elliptical quality may explain in part why the early church did not immediately understand the saying's implications and had various arguments about clean and unclean food at least until the Apostolic Council recorded in Acts 15 seems to have largely settled the matter for the church. The saying at its most basic level denies that what really defiles a person is something that he or she touches or eats. This may be seen as Jesus' justification for why he banqueted with even the unclean and the immoral. Jesus was not one who saw ritual cleanliness as next to godliness. The important point to be made at this juncture is that Jesus assumed an authority over the Torah (not just over oral traditions) that led him to set aside certain of its provisions, perhaps because he saw them as no longer applicable now that the dominion of God was breaking in.

There are of course various other texts in which we see Jesus intensifying the law's requirements (e.g., Jesus' teaching on divorce in Mark 10 and par.), adding new authoritative teaching to what the law said (see Matthew 5), or simply affirming the validity of some portions of the law (Mark 12:28–31 and par.; Mark 10:19 and par.). The point is, however, that he felt free to do all of these things, including abrogating some of the law. Furthermore, he never cites previous Jewish teachers as authorities for his teaching, but simply speaks on his own authority. The multiply-attested motif of Jesus prefacing his own teaching with the word "Amen," found in both the Synoptic and Johannine traditions, is very striking and reveals Jesus testifying to the truth of his own words in advance of giving them! In most of these respects Jesus stood apart from the Pharisees and would have been seen as a challenge to both their values and their approach to the Torah.

In at least three different sources we have confirmation that Jesus dined with the unclean and the immoral, indeed perhaps even with the intentionally wicked. We find stories to this effect in Mark 2:15–17, in the L tradition in Luke 7:36–50 and 19:1–10, and in the Q material found in Matt. 11:19/Luke 7:34. The use of the term "sinner" in Mark 2:15–17 in all likelihood includes the intentionally wicked, and dining with them would have been seen as scandalous behavior by the Pharisees not only on ritual but also on moral grounds. Nothing suggests that Jesus limited his fellowship to those who had already reformed and were back on the right track toward practicing a moral life-style.

Now it must be said that the Pharisees had plenty of scriptural ammunition to use to object to Jesus' behavior. The Psalms and also Proverbs are very clear that God scorns the wicked and favors the upright (see Prov. 14:9; 2:22; 10:30; Pss. 10:15; 141:5). The question is whether God was now doing things differently in view of the coming of the eschatological dominion of God breaking into history. Jesus' answer was that this was the case. Now Jesus, acting for God, must come as a physician to try to heal the sick and sinful, not merely to shun or condemn them (see Mark 2:17; Luke 4:23). It seems clear from a variety of traditions that Jesus saw it as part of his ministry to come and help and heal the least, the last, and the lost, even if it meant setting aside certain Old Testament traditions to accomplish this end. The question that all of these traditions raise is, What sort of person thinks he is free to change the rules of the road, long after they have been set up and been recognized to have sacred status? At the very least, Jesus' banqueting with the bad and the underlying new vision of what defiled a person suggest a person with a very exalted sense of his own authority and importance.

We may sum up this brief review of some of the relevant data by drawing a few conclusions. To be fair to the Pharisees, it must be understood not only that they were very devout Jews but also that they believed that their approach to the law was the means, if followed, by which Israel would be able to survive their current situation without the nation dissolving and would be prepared to face whatever judgment God might bring upon the land because of the laxness or unfaithfulness of many Jews. When Jesus came and suggested things that undermined their approach to the law and perhaps also their authority, it is not surprising that there were heated exchanges and some animosity. The Pharisees would have seen Jesus as a bad Jew or perhaps even as a threat to the nation's survival. Jesus' freedom in handling and applying the law suggests that he saw himself as considerably more than a prophet, who was chiefly and sometimes only a mouthpiece for God. Jesus by contrast spoke on his own authority, as if he had some personal divine authorization to change the situation and the way the law was interpreted. In view of this, U. Luz's conclusion is apt:

> Jesus was certainly also rejected by many Pharisees. His liberal interpretation of the Sabbath laws and especially his freedom regarding the regulations governing ritual cleanliness must have appeared problematic to the Pharisees, one of whose chief concerns was the ritual purity of the *whole* people of God. . . . I for one do not consider the numerous scenes in the Gospels which speak of conflict between Jesus and the Pharisees have all been fabricated.[12]

Jesus and the Revolutionaries

The question about Jesus' relationship with the revolutionaries of his day has gone through a series of permutations and alterations over the years. Few scholars today would see Jesus as a Zealot, if by that one means an advocate of armed revolt against Rome in the name of God, the only ruler (a theocratic view). There are, however, numerous scholars who think that in a nonviolent way Jesus was setting about to deconstruct the oppressive society of which he was a part. For example, R. Horsley has argued that Jesus set out to reorganize local village life in Galilee, with his radical ethical teaching as a basis of a new community. This was a response to the urban elite's attempts to squeeze the small landholders by extracting money, and eventually land itself, from Galilean peasants who are thought to have made up close to 90 percent of Jewish society in this era.[13] Jesus identified with the least and the last and had a program to help alleviate their plight.

Another scholar who sees Jesus as in some respects revolutionary though not an advocate of violence would be John Dominic Crossan.[14] In Crossan's view Jesus was an advocate of radical egalitarianism, being opposed to any sort of hierarchical authority structure. In order to prevent such a structure being set up by his followers in any one place, Jesus practiced an itinerant life-style and had his followers do the same. He also practiced what Crossan calls open commensality, being willing to eat and fellowship with anyone, and he was something of a therapist, healing people's psychosomatic illnesses, apparently brought on by living in a culture where many things including illnesses made one unclean and a potential outcast from society.

There are some significant problems with both of these views, not the least of which is that there is not a shred of hard historical evidence for Jesus' having confronted the urban elites in Galilee who lived in places like Tiberias and Sepphoris, nor that he set up egalitarian communities in various places in Galilee, nor that Jesus was opposed to all sorts of hierarchical authority structures. The idea that Jesus chose twelve followers as the inner circle of his disciples is well attested in both the Gospels and Paul's letters (see 1 Corinthians 15), as is Jesus' teaching about parents being honored and not deprived of financial support (the *Corban* controversy in Mark 7:10–13). There also is little doubt that he spoke about God's dominion, which is certainly a hierarchical notion. Furthermore, Jesus' dining with the likes of a tax collector such as Zacchaeus or a wealthy Pharisee such as Simon suggests that he attempted to fellowship with the oppressors as well as the oppressed, the up and in as well as the down and out, calling them all to repent and believe the Gospel. Jesus' followers were not, so far as we can tell, drawn primarily from the peasant class; rather they seem to have been mostly fishermen, merchants, and a few people who were somewhat more well-to-do.

This is not to deny that there is plenty of evidence that Jesus was a liberator of sorts, healing various people and setting them free from the shackles of being unclean or outcasts from society, and allowing various women to be his disciples. Nor is there any doubt that Jesus had little regard for Herod Antipas, whom he once called "that fox." The point is that Jesus' reforms were not those that modern advocates of radical egalitarianism would find totally satisfactory, even though clearly there was a social component to Jesus' Gospel that involved the reforming of a strongly patriarchal society so that women and men had more equal standing and status in the community of Jesus' followers (and in God's dominion).[15]

The usual evidence trotted out to make even more radical claims about Jesus as a revolutionary involves the following. First, Luke 6:15 is cited, which refers to Simon the Zealot. But even if this term is used in the technical sense of one who was so zealous for God and the law that he advocated armed resistance to the foreign oppressors,[16] a moment's reflection will show that in the context of Jesus' inner circle it must mean Simon the former Zealot, for he is now part of a group that includes one of his sworn enemies—a tax collector, named either Levi or Matthew (or both), whose job it was to help the foreign powers oppress (by collecting burdensome taxes) one's own people.

Mark 12:13–17 and par. are often cited as well. In this narrative Jesus is questioned about the legality of paying tribute money to Caesar. Jesus does not in this story refuse to pay the tribute, but it is also clear that he does not carry such money on his person. There are of course various traditions that Jesus had little positive regard for money and in fact stressed its potential to corrupt the human spirit or impede one's entering the dominion of God (Matt. 6:24; Luke 16:9; Mark 10:25 and par.). It may be, then, that Jesus' response to the query is meant to show the insignificance of the issue, though to any revolutionaries in the audience it probably would have been seen as an immoral compromise. He would not have pleased the revolutionaries, but also he would have given his other opponents (Herodians, Pharisees) no reason to report him to the Roman authorities. The key saying is not about doing one's civic duty or the separation of church and state but rather about the fact that one owes one's whole self to God, for humans are created in God's image, while only little pieces of metal are created with Caesar's image. In fact, this saying may suggest that Jesus' vision of things was even more theocratic than that of the Zealots. In Jesus' view what needed to be done to bring in the kingdom was not to take up arms but rather to teach and preach and heal and have fellowship with various people and let God work his transformation of the situation directly through these means.

Two further traditions often thought to show Jesus' revolutionary potential are Jesus' grand entrance into Jerusalem, the last time he went into that city, and Jesus' sayings about the destruction of the Temple, coupled with his "cleansing" of the Temple. The former evidence is clearly weak, for if his riding into town on a donkey suggests anything, it suggests that Jesus came in peace, perhaps attempting to fulfill Zech. 9:9. It would also suggest that Jesus saw himself as some sort of shepherd king in the Zecharian mold.

The cleansing of the Temple, perhaps coupled with Jesus' prediction of the Temple's demise, provides more plausible evidence that Jesus had some sort of social agenda that affected the heart of Judaism. Two things, however, need to be said about these traditions. The prophecy does not advocate the destruction of the Temple, but suggests that the Temple will be destroyed by someone (compare Mark 14:58 with John 2:19). The former tradition of the Temple cleansing, found in all four Gospels (cf. John 2 and par.) suggests why: the Temple is seen as corrupt and in need of a total house-cleaning. On this latter point, Jesus would be holding views little different from what we find in some of the Qumran literature, and there is no evidence that the Qumranites were Zealots. In fact, it is possible that the sign act was simply a visible way of signifying the coming destruction of the Temple, if things did not radically change there.[17]

Perhaps here is the place to say something about the only miracle attested in all four Gospels—the feeding of the five thousand. There must have been something special about whatever happened on this occasion for all four evangelists to give it significant attention when each writer was presenting only a representative account of Jesus' life. The Synoptic presentations give little clue to what might have been especially notable about the event, but we do find a clue in John 6:14–15, about which Raymond Brown remarks: "If John was written toward the end of the first century when Roman persecution of Christians under Domitian was all too real, then the invention of the information in vss. 14-15 seems out of the question . . . . we believe that in these verses John has given us an item of correct historical information."[18] What do we learn from these verses? That the crowds sought to make Jesus king after this miraculous feeding, but that Jesus was having none of it. When it was clear to him what was happening, he withdrew. This suggests that we must evaluate this event in light of other sign acts performed during that era. For instance, we can set up the following chart about various prophetic or messianic figures during the period 27–57 C.E.:

Ruler	Messianic Figure	Messianic Activity	Location	Audience
Pilate	The Baptist	baptizing	wilderness	great crowd
Pilate	Jesus	feeding 5,000	wilderness	5,000 men
Pilate	Samaritan	revealing Temple vessels	Mt. Gerizim	great crowd
Fadus	Theudas	dividing Jordan	Jordan	great crowd
Felix	Egyptian	Jerusalem walls to fall	wilderness	4,000 men[19]

What we learn from a close scrutiny of these parallels is that there were certain settings and certain activities that were bound to prompt speculation about who a particular person was. In particular, activities in the wilderness, which brought back memories of the exodus-Sinai events; and activities in and around the Holy City, especially the Temple area, were bound to trigger certain conjectures. In Samaritan territory the same would be true for activities undertaken around or on Mount Gerizim. We could easily add Jesus' cleansing of the Temple to the list as well. Of course it is true that not all the figures listed above saw themselves in messianic terms. In particular, the Baptist did not, but it may be that his followers did, for otherwise it is hard to explain what we find in Acts 18–19, where there is evidence of the Baptist having an ongoing following and effect long after his death.

If we turn back to the story of the feeding of the five thousand, what do we learn? That Jesus' feeding event in the wilderness prompted speculation that Jesus was making some sort of royal claims, perhaps that he was the latter-day prophet like Moses spoken of in Deut. 18:15 and

Num. 27:17. Jesus' intentions, however, were different from the crowd's deductions. Possibly Jesus saw this event as an eschatological sign that the dominion of God had broken in and that the messianic banquet was being foreshadowed. Be this as it may, the parallels between Mark 6/John 6 and the material in Josephus's *Antiquities* 20.169 and *Jewish War* 2.261, which record the story of the Egyptian, are impressive and strongly suggest that Jesus was implying something about the significance of his person and ministry by this sign act in the wilderness. Nevertheless, what he intended and what the crowd took him to mean were two different things. If we compare this sign act to the riding into Jerusalem on a donkey, the suggestion is ready to hand that the crowd took Jesus to be one sort of king, perhaps a benevolent ruler who would provide great benefactions of food to his people. Jesus, by contrast, modeled his activities on a different royal model, perhaps the one found in Zechariah. At the very least one must say that Jesus himself would have had to have been exceedingly obtuse not to realize that if he performed the sorts of acts we find in Mark 6 and par. and Mark 11 and par. that they would be understood in a messianic light. The feeding of the five thousand, according to both the Markan and Johannine outlines, was the event that climaxed and in effect ended Jesus' Galilean ministry. It is hard to believe that this is accidental, any more than one can believe that it was accidental that it was on his last trip up to Jerusalem that Jesus rode into town on a donkey and cleansed the Temple. It is precisely evidence such as this that shows that even if one were to discount all, or almost all the sayings tradition, and even if Jesus never openly made any messianic claims in so many words, his actions would speak loudly and point us in this direction.

What do we learn from this discussion about Jesus' relationship with the revolutionaries? First, one cannot really speak of Jesus having such a relationship, unless one counts Simon the Zealot as still among their number. This *lack* of relationship probably says something about Jesus and his intentions. Second, there is no evidence that Jesus proposed armed revolt against Rome. Third, it seems clear that Jesus was more theocratic and theocentric in his approach than even the Zealots. He believed that God was intervening directly through his ministry (and afterwards) and that therefore armed struggle was unnecessary. One must worry about rendering unto God his due and remember that all things ultimately belong to God, all other debts or duties paling into insignificance compared to what one owes God. Furthermore, while there is no evidence that Jesus was interested in leading a peasant revolt or participating in class struggle or confronting oppressing urban elites in Galilee or advocating modern notions of radical egalitarianism, there is certainly some evidence that his ministry intentionally had a social dimension and that Jesus did indeed set about to make clear that among his followers and in the kingdom things would be more just and equitable for the disenfranchised and oppressed. Finally, we see already in John 6:14–15 a hint that Jesus' intentions could be and were misread along more political lines. It is not for nothing that he was crucified for claiming to be "the King of the Jews." This latter fact itself sheds considerable light on Jesus' life and ministry. This leads us to discuss Jesus' relationship with a group he clearly had a lot of contact with—his own disciples.

Jesus and His Disciples

That Jesus had a relationship with his followers no one would dispute. There has occasionally been a scholar (for instance recently J. D. Crossan), who disputed that Jesus had an inner circle of twelve, but this is a decidedly minority opinion, not least because we have independent evidence quite apart from the Gospels that there was such a group—1 Cor. 15:5. It is, furthermore, not believable that early Christians would make up the idea that there was a Judas, who is regularly identified as one of the Twelve (Mark 3:14–19; Luke 6:13–16; Matt. 10:2–4; John 6:67). There are references to the Twelve found in the double tradition (see Matt. 19:28; Luke 22:30), and also in John 6:67, which shows that the idea of the Twelve can be found in various non-Markan layers of tradition.

Furthermore, texts like Mark 4:10 and Luke 8:1–3 make evident that the Twelve were not Jesus' only disciples, indeed not even Jesus' only itinerant disciples. It has on various occasions been disputed that Jesus meant to set up a community of followers, but this is unlikely in the extreme if one agrees that Jesus proclaimed the inbreaking of God's dominion. As R. Schnackenburg has said, to deny that Jesus intended to gather some sort of community "misunderstands the messianic-eschatological thought of Israel, in which eschatological salvation cannot be separated from the people of God and in which the community of God necessarily belongs to his reign."[20] Salvation was viewed in a corporate sense—one was saved as part of or at least into a body or community of people.

That Jesus had other disciples beyond the Twelve (e.g., Mary and Martha, attested in two sources—Luke 10 and John 11–12) surely seems to mean that Jesus did not see the Twelve as a sort of righteous remnant of Israel, gathered to the exclusion of others participating in his ministry. Perhaps the most one can get out of the fact that Jesus chose Twelve is that he saw himself as the eschatological gatherer of Israel, and the Twelve symbolized this fact. More important for our purposes, Jesus chose twelve, and *did not include himself among the Twelve.* This suggests that Jesus saw himself in a special relationship to Israel, as some sort of shepherd or leader or representative figure, rather than that Jesus identified himself as or with Israel. Neither Jesus himself nor the Twelve were to be Israel, but both, as we shall see, came to free (or if rejected judge) Israel.

One of the more secure facts about Jesus' Galilean ministry is that Jesus called people to be his disciples, an act that made him stand out from other early Jewish teachers, who simply received disciples but didn't go looking for them. Mark 1:17 is an important, arguably authentic saying of Jesus. It is arguably authentic because we have no evidence either that early Jewish teachers or that the early church spoke of missionary work in terms of fishing for followers. The Old Testament background to this saying (Jer. 16:16; Ezek. 29:4ff.; 38:4; Amos 4:2; and Hab. 1:14–17) suggests that there may have been an ominous undercurrent to this saying. The prophetic texts especially suggest the catching of people for judgment with either God or God's agent doing the catching. The saying should probably be seen in the light of Jewish notions about bodies of water as a symbol of chaos and evil, being the dwelling place of demons, spirits, and dangerous creatures (see Ps. 74:13), in which case the image is one of a rescue mission for Israel "lost at sea." Since Jesus' ministry was confined to Israel, it is probable that we should see this saying as not about missionary work among non-Jews but about the rescuing of lost Jews, even the least and the last. I suggest that this saying makes good sense if we take account of the factors mentioned by G. B. Caird:

> Jesus was working against time to prevent the end of Israel's world, that the haste of the mission was directly connected with the many sayings which predict the fall of Jerusalem and the destruction of the temple. He believed that Israel was at the crossroads, that she must choose between two conceptions of her national destiny. . . .[21]

There is implicit in the Markan saying we have just discussed the idea that at some appropriate point Jesus' disciples would themselves go out among Jews on missionary ventures. There are at least two versions of the charge to the disciples, one in Mark (6:8) and one in Q

(Matt. 10:10/Luke 9:3). Without going into detail about how one gets back to the earliest form of this saying, we should stress the fact that the disciples will be called upon, even if for a limited period of time, to perform the same functions Jesus was performing, such as exorcism, healing, and preaching. The question then becomes whether or not Jesus saw the Twelve as his agents, his *šālîḥîm*. The Jewish concept of agency largely had to do with one who was authorized to carry on certain important transactions for the one who sent them to do so. For a limited period of time they had the power and authority of the one who sent them, and it was expected that they would be treated by the ones they were dealing with as if they were that person, for "a man's agent is as himself," according to Jewish thinking on these matters. The evidence from the Mishnah shows that even in the time of Gamaliel the First (*Mishnah Rosh Hashanah* 4:9) there was already a rather well-defined concept of a congregational agent who fulfills some obligation for the larger group, having been commissioned and empowered to do so (see *Mishnah Rosh Hashanah* 1:3; *Mishnah Yoma* 1:5). Let us consider the relevant evidence in the light of these facts.

First of all, the relevant Gospel commissioning saying refers to the disciples being sent out two by two (thus six different groups of two). The reason for this may be that in Judaism the veracity of any statement needed to be corroborated by the testimony of two witnesses, not just one. Notice also that the commission is for them to go to the lost sheep of Israel, in contrast to going to either Gentiles or Samaritans. This probably tells us something about how Jesus viewed his own ministry, but of course the real debate is over the referent in the phrase "the lost sheep of Israel." Does this refer to all Israel as lost, or to a particular group within Israel? In view of the contrast with other whole groups of people (Gentiles, Samaritans), it probably refers to Israel as a whole.

It is also important to note the content of their message. Mark's form of the saying suggests that it involved a call to repentance, which is historically plausible for Jesus, it would appear, continued the message of John as part of his own message to Israel. The Q form of the saying, however, also speaks of a message about the nearness of God's dominion (cf. Luke 10:11 and Matt. 10:7). Probably both of these subjects were raised, as they both seem to have characterized Jesus' own preaching—especially if it was really believed that all Israel needed to be rescued in view of the inbreaking dominion of God (which could mean either rescue or judgment depending on how one responded).

In the light of the *šālîḥîm* concept, texts such as Matt. 10:40 also become readily intelligible. Just as the Twelve were Jesus' agents, so Jesus was God's special agent on earth. If someone rejected Jesus' agents, it was as though they had rejected Jesus himself, and likewise Jesus believed the same about himself and God—to reject the one was to reject the other. Jesus is seen in a saying like Matt. 10:40 as God's agent on earth, one commissioned by God to perform certain tasks, to speak for the one who sent him with divine authority, one who is to be treated as if he were the one who sent him. Even if some of the titles applied to Jesus do not go back to him, if this concept of Jesus as God's agent is authentic it suggests strongly a exalted self-understanding, indeed a messianic self-understanding, especially in the light of Mark 1:17.

From time to time one comes across a saying of Jesus that seems so radical that it is hardly plausible that the church invented it, nor can it be explained by reference to prevalent Jewish customs or ideas. Such a saying is the Q saying found in Matt. 8:21–22/Luke 9:59–60. In early Judaism one of the most sacred family duties was the burying of the dead, particularly members of one's own family. Some early Jews even saw the commandment "honor thy father and mother" as necessarily entailing a decent burial for them. *Mishnah Berakot* 3:1 says that attending to the duty of burying the dead supersedes even the most binding of other religious obligations. Only Nazirites and the high priest were said to be exempt from such a duty (see Lev. 21:11; Num. 6:6–7). Taken at face value, at the very least this saying is suggesting that Jesus thought that the duty to follow him superseded even the requirements of Jewish piety and of the Torah. This is not the attitude of an ordinary sage or teacher of Israel. The saying reflects a belief not only that a time of crisis confronted Israel but also that following Jesus, being his disciple, was the most important obligation of all, something Luke 10:38–42 also suggests in a story that is quite independent of the Q text we are now examining. Upon critical reflection, it is not clear whether the person Jesus was addressing was already a disciple or not. The word "first" ("first let me go bury . . .") suggests that the issue is one of priorities in the mind of the inquisitor, and the word may also suggest that the inquirer saw himself as already a follower of Jesus. What he obviously didn't understand is that in Jesus' view the obligations of the family of faith supersede the obligations of the physical family. This attitude on Jesus' part is attested elsewhere in Mark 3:31–35 and par., which because of its offensiveness is also likely an authentic saying of Jesus.

The saying helps confirm two impressions we have already gotten in studying Jesus' relationships: (1) Since this saying likely means "Let the spiritually dead bury the physically dead, you come and follow me," the implication is that those who are not Jesus' followers are spiritually dead or lost. (2) This saying reflects the sovereign way in which Jesus handled the Mosaic law, even setting aside some of its hallmark demands in the light of the new thing that was happening through his ministry. M. Hengel, who has devoted a monograph to this saying, is right that in all probability it ought to be judged "in light of the messianic authority of Jesus."[22]

A final saying that tells us something about Jesus' relationship to his followers is Matt. 19:28/Luke 22:30. The saying has strong claims to authenticity in view of the fact that it seems to envision an earthly eschatological kingdom for Israel in which the Twelve would have special roles (this would originally have included Judas), something that did not transpire in the first century and something that the early church, especially as it became increasingly Gentile in character, was not likely to dream up as a vision of the eschaton. As for the meaning of the saying, Israel here is distinguished from both Jesus and the Twelve. One of the hopes in Judaism was for the regathering of the Twelve tribes of Israel as the center of God's rule or dominion on earth. Are we to envision the Twelve acting as judges for Israel in the reconstituted nation, or more likely as judges of the Twelve tribes at the final judgment? Probably the latter. This means that Jesus foresaw a leadership role for the Twelve both in the present and in the future in relationship to Israel. What this saying then implies about Jesus is not only that he believed he had vast authority, even in relationship to what would happen to Israel at the eschaton, but also that he saw himself, with the aid of his agents, as the one to gather for salvation or judgment the twelve tribes of Israel. This saying probably alludes to Dan. 7:22 and it should probably be compared to the sayings where the Son of Man's role in the final judgment is discussed.[23] In any case, this saying, if authentic, suggests that Jesus had some sort of messianic self-consciousness.

In this section of our discussion we have found plentiful evidence that Jesus did not view himself as an ordinary Jew, or even as yet another Jewish sage or prophet. Especially revealing was the material that dealt with Jesus' relationship with John the Baptist and with his own disciples, the two most ongoing positive relationships in the Gospels. Our conclusion that Jesus had an exalted and christological view of his message and mission, and so of himself, is based not on any one of these pieces of evidence but comes as a result of the cumulative effect of a variety of different traditions. It does not stand or fall on the authenticity of any one of these traditions. As we shall now see, a closer study of Jesus' experiences and his deeds provides further confirmation of such a conclusion.

Jesus' Experiences and Deeds

When we discuss Jesus' experiences, we are referring to things that happened to Jesus, things that he did not initiate but that nonetheless tell us something about how Jesus understood himself. In this category would fall something that few scholars would dispute, namely, his death on the cross. But also in this category would fall a number of revelatory or visionary events which many feel have no basis in historical reality. In the latter category would be included what happened to Jesus at his baptism, what happened to him thereafter in the wilderness, what happened to him on the Mount of Transfiguration, and finally certain sayings of Jesus that allude to other visionary experiences. We will deal with these more controversial experiences first before discussing Jesus' death on the cross, and this in turn will lead to a discussion of a few of Jesus' special "mighty works."

According to Marcus Borg, Jesus should be seen as an example of a common type of religious person, a "person of the Spirit." This type of person has vivid and in some cases frequent experiences of another dimension or level of reality, the realm of God or the Spirit. We might call this person a mystic. Equally important, this type of person relates these experiences to others, and in some cases becomes a conduit through whom the power of God or the Spirit is conveyed to others. It is characteristic of this type of person that he or she has a deep relationship with God and often this person becomes a healer. Borg rightly points out that in every age of human history there have been persons of this sort and that it is a mistake to reduce all reports of dreams, visions, or miracles to psychological phenomena that tell us something about the person's mind-set but nothing about objective reality. He argues:

> But the reality of the other world deserves to be taken seriously. Intellectually and experientially, there is much to commend it. The primary intellectual objection to it flows from too rigid an application of the modern worldview's definition of reality. Yet the modern view is but one of a

large number of humanly constructed maps of reality. . . . To try and understand the Jewish tradition and Jesus while simultaneously dismissing the notion of another world or immediately reducing it to a mere psychological realm is to fail to see the phenomena, to fail to take seriously what the charismatic mediators experienced and reported.[24]

This means that we ought not to peremptorily dismiss the accounts of Jesus' religious experiences as later church theologizing about Jesus, myths, or the like. They may in fact be like the accounts we find in the book of Revelation or like what Paul relates in 2 Cor. 12:1–7, and at the very least they may indeed tell us a great deal about how Jesus viewed reality and his place in the world.

Let us consider first a saying from Luke's Gospel, 10:18. Here Jesus reports that he *watched* Satan fall from heaven like lightning. Commentators are rather evenly divided about whether this is a description of an actual visionary experience of Jesus or a metaphorical way of speaking about his disciples' (and his own) triumphs over the powers of darkness. This may relate to what Jesus refers to in Mark 3:23–37. If we evaluate Luke 10:18 in light of the language we find in apocalyptic literature—for example, in the book of Revelation, it is plausible that this is a brief allusion to a visionary experience. Since it would be a private and interior experience it would be difficult to prove that such an experience actually happened. I suggest, however, that there may be an independent version of this same tradition in John 12:31, where Jesus is reported to have said: "Now is the judgment of this world; now the ruler of this world will be driven out."

Moving on to Mark 1:9–11 and par. we have a more promising source of evidence. Few scholars would dispute that Jesus was baptized by John, and probably the majority of scholars think that this event had something to do with Jesus' taking up his ministerial tasks, for it is apparently only after this event that Jesus goes forth preaching, teaching, and healing. Unlike the case with Luke 10:18, here it is plausible that Jesus might have spoken about this experience on more than one occasion to one or more persons when he sought to explain why he began his Galilean ministry. There is a clue in Mark 11:27–33 and par. that Jesus' baptism, if one will pardon the pun, was a watershed event in his life. It is not plausible that the church originated this latter Markan tradition because it could be interpreted to mean either that John had authority equal to that of Jesus, or that Jesus derived his authority from John when he was baptized.

Whatever else we make of the text in Mark 11, it strongly suggests that Jesus believed that it was at his baptism that he was authorized to do what he was doing. This supports the contention that Jesus had occasion to speak of the experience of his baptism and its significance. If Jesus even to a small degree saw himself in a prophetic light, it would hardly be surprising that he had some sort of prophetic call experience.

On close analysis, the text of Mark 1:9–11 has a variety of apocalyptic features—the rending of the heavens, the voice from heaven, and the reference to the Spirit coming down. It is telling that Matthew takes Mark's account of a personal visionary experience and turns it into a public report. Instead of the voice saying to Jesus alone, "You are my beloved Son . . . ," in Matthew we have, "This is my beloved Son." Notice that Mark 1:10 indicates that only Jesus saw the Spirit coming down.

Jesus probably had some sort of spiritual experience when he was baptized, for we must account for why Jesus began his ministry after being baptized by John, whereas others baptized by John apparently did not take up such ministries. Let us suppose, then, that we do have in Mark a summary of what Jesus believed happened to him on this important occasion and later reported. What do we learn from the report of what the voice said? In all probability this is an allusion to Ps. 2:7, which refers to the "begetting of the king," by which is meant the divine empowering and authorizing of the king on the occasion when he takes the throne and takes up his tasks. On that occasion the word of God to the king was: "You are my son, today I have begotten you." If Jesus did report such an experience, he would be indicating his authorization to be a royal or messianic figure, empowered by God's Spirit to take up his tasks of bringing in the dominion of God on earth by preaching, teaching, and healing. Furthermore, the temptation narrative fits in nicely as a sequel to the baptism story and as a further visionary experience during the time when Jesus was wrestling with his call and ministry. The Q version of the temptation story found in Matthew 4/Luke 4 attempts to prove in various ways that Jesus is the Son of God. In other words, Jesus' identity is being questioned, or what sort of Son of God Jesus will be is being tested. At another turning point in his life, Jesus seems to have had another spiritual experience— on the Mount of Transfiguration, as Jesus faced the prospect of going to Jerusalem to die. Once again the question of identity comes up. Only this time it is the disciples who are being informed on this matter. If Luke's version of this story is any clue, this experience for Jesus was meant to prepare him for his "exodus"—in other words, for his shocking death in Jerusalem.

What do we learn from these stories? All three of these narratives— the baptism story, the temptation story, and the transfiguration story—have something to do with Jesus' identity as God's Son, and all three seem to have come at a time of transition or crisis in Jesus' life. Jesus may in fact have had such visionary experiences during these times. After all, there are clear precedents for this in the Old Testament prophetic literature, whether we think of Daniel or Ezekiel or Zechariah. Are there any other hints in the Gospel tradition that might confirm these conclusions?

There are various texts that imply that Jesus believed he had unique revelatory experiences and encounters with God. For example, in Matt. 11:25–28 and par. Jesus speaks directly to God, presumably in an audible prayer, but what he is thanking God for is that God has given him uniquely intimate knowledge of God, and that God knows him uniquely, and furthermore that it is Jesus who has been called on to reveal the Father to others. The language of things hidden and then revealed in v. 25 is apocalyptic language, and this text as a whole suggests not only that Jesus is the unique bearer of revelation about God to others but that he was first the unique recipient of such revelation.

Of a similar character is the material in John 12:27–32. Once again we have an audible prayer, which is followed in this case by a voice from heaven, a unique phenomenon in the Fourth Gospel and so not something that reflects Johannine redaction. In other words, the sequence again is Jesus' prayer, followed by revelation described in apocalyptic fashion.

Finally, there is Matt. 10:32–33/Luke 12:9. This tradition speaks of Jesus acknowledging people before the Father. It suggests that he had unique and open access to the Father in heaven. While the saying could refer to Jesus doing this acknowledging once he enters heaven, it is equally plausible that it refers to what Jesus will do when he is "taken up in the Spirit" into the heavenly council during a visionary experience, just as the author of the book of Revelation and other Jews of that period and earlier believed they were.

The one experience of Jesus that is almost never disputed is of course his crucifixion. The most primitive narrative of this event in Mark 15 recounts that Jesus was crucified as King of the Jews. Now, the account we have suggests that the *titulus* would have read *basileus, rex, melek,* not *christos, christus,* and *māšîaḥ*. In other words, the title on the cross does not reflect the way the church later addressed Jesus, and thus this report is not likely to derive from ecclesiastical redaction. Nils Dahl, reiterating his earlier conclusions, puts the matter this way: "It is highly unlikely that Christians introduced this title into the narrative since it was otherwise used in clearly political contexts (see Josephus *Ant.* 14.36; 15.373; 16.311; *War* 1.282)."[25] More critically, Dahl aptly points out that the resurrection experiences, including the empty tomb, would not have led the disciples to proclaim Jesus the Messiah; for post-mortem appearances, assumption into heaven, and the like were not part of early Jewish thought about the Messiah, *unless* Jesus had first been crucified as an alleged messianic figure. In other words, Christology must have begun before Easter, even for the disciples.[26]

Dahl goes on to stress that it was precisely the crucifixion and its sequel that led the church to call Jesus the Christ so frequently, for the earlier traditions taken from the ministry itself spoke of Jesus as Son of Man or God's Son. *Christos* is notably absent from the earliest sayings collections that go back to Jesus. It is also Dahl's thesis that the crucifixion and the Easter experiences led to a radical reevaluation of what it meant to say that Jesus was king, which apparently in turn led to the use among the earliest Jewish Christians of slightly less political but nonetheless royal terminology to refer to Jesus. The important points to note about this in terms of historical development are these: (1) Something about the life, ministry, or perhaps especially the actions of the last week of Jesus' life suggested to outsiders that Jesus was a messianic figure who was politically dangerous. This in turn led to his death as "King of the Jews." The title was meant to be ironic, coming from Pilate, but had there not been some political charges against Jesus, it is doubtful he would have suffered the "extreme penalty," as the Romans called it. (2) The disciples were not looking for a crucified and risen Messiah any more than other early Jews were; thus, these experiences led to a reevaluation of Christology—or, if one prefers the term "messianism"—on the part of Jesus' followers. (3) Events in the life of Jesus, including what happened to him at his death, suggested a christological evaluation of him by his followers. The disciples' christological reflections were reformulated and refined in the fires of the crucifixion and Easter experiences, but they did not begin at that point.

The discussion of Jesus' mighty deeds or miracles has often been thought to be a fertile ground for finding christological evidence. The problem is that already in the Old Testament there are stories of healings and even raisings of the dead by prophets of God. In other words, such deeds would show no more than that Jesus was one of Israel's great prophets, like Elijah or Elisha. There are, however, three traditions that suggest to us something more about Jesus' mighty works: (1) indications of how Jesus interpreted his own deeds; (2) the performance of acts that were associated with royal traditions in early Judaism, in particular with Solomon; and (3) the performance of types of miracles nowhere recorded in the Old Testament—in particular, giving sight to the blind. We will examine each of these traditions in turn.

Matthew 12:28/Luke 11:20 is a crucial Q saying for understanding Jesus' view of his mighty works, in particular his exorcisms. This saying has good claims to authenticity for two reasons: (1) Later Gospel traditions—for instance, what we find in John—show no interest in Jesus as an exorcist; in fact they avoid the subject, perhaps because it led to the charge that Jesus was in league with the powers of darkness (see Mark 3). (2) The tendency in Christian redaction was to attribute Jesus' power directly to his person, but here it is God's or the Spirit's power by which Jesus casts out demons.

What is important for our purposes is that this saying connects Jesus' exorcisms with the dominion of God, which distinguishes Jesus' exorcisms from those of others.[27] In other words, these exorcisms are not just random acts of kindness or healing. Rather they announce the inbreaking of God's eschatological rule upon the earth and the casting out of evil from the earth. G. Theissen has rightly stated that one thing that made Jesus unique was his combination of apocalyptic expectation of complete salvation in the future with the episodic bringing of salvation in the present through miracles. "The eschatological view of miracles is generally and rightly held to be a peculiarity of Jesus' preaching. Because the negative web of evil has already been broken it is possible for salvation to come in individual instances. Because individual instances of salvation occur, the presence of the end can be proclaimed here and now."[28] This whole tradition must be compared to Matt. 11:4–6/Luke 7:22–23, where Jesus interprets his miraculous actions as a fulfillment of Old Testament promises and prophecies about the coming age of restoration and final blessing (cf. Isa. 35:4–6; 61:1).

As has often been noticed, exorcisms are not predicated of the Old Testament prophets, nor are there any promises that God's Anointed

One will come and perform such actions. Jesus would seem in this regard to stand neither in the prophetic nor in the messianic tradition. This conclusion, however, overlooks some very important early Jewish evidence. From Qumran Cave 11 a recension and comment on Psalm 91 provides rather clear evidence that Solomon the son of David was associated with exorcisms and cures. This evidence should be compared to the *Testament of Solomon,* the Aramaic incantation bowl evidence, the later rabbinic evidence that saw Psalm 91 as a song for exorcising demons (see Palestinian Talmud, *Šabbat* 6.8b; Babylonian Talmud, *Šebiʿit* 15b; especially Palestinian Talmud, *ʿErubin* 10.26c). But see especially what Josephus says about Solomon in *Antiquities* 8.45:

> And God granted him knowledge of the art used against demons for the benefit and healing of human beings. He also composed incantations by which illnesses are relieved, and left behind forms of exorcisms with which those possessed by demons drive them out, never to return. And this kind of cure is of very great power among us today. . . .

In short, knowledge of exorcism is associated with Solomon's wisdom. These data make it quite plausible that Jesus' exorcisms would have been interpreted as implying that Jesus had royal status. This evidence also sheds new light on other traditions where Jesus is called "Son of David," which may well mean a Solomonic figure, like *the* most famous son of David.

There are no Old Testament stories about prophets giving sight to the blind, but the idea that Jesus did so is well attested in various layers of the Gospel tradition: (1) in the uniquely Markan story in Mark 8:22–26; (2) in the familiar Bartimaeus story, Mark 10:46–52 and par.; (3) in the summary in Matt. 15:30; (4) in John 9; and (5) in Jesus' response to John in the Q material in Luke 7:22/Matt. 11:5. By the criterion of multiple attestation at least some of this is likely to go back to the time of Jesus. We must consider here briefly the Bartimaeus story.

This story seems primitive in several respects, not the least of which is the cry of the blind beggar, calling Jesus Son of David. This is not a title for Jesus that occurs with any frequency elsewhere in our earliest Gospel (but see Mark 12:35, though only by implication is it being applied to Jesus).[29] It is clear enough from texts like Mark 1:1 that Mark's own tendency was to call Jesus either Christ or Son of God; he shows no special interest in the Son of David title, and no one other than Bartimaeus addresses Jesus in this fashion in Mark's Gospel. The suggestion is probable that the cry in our story then is an authentic memory of how Jesus was addressed on this occasion. The question then is, What would have been meant by "Son of David." Why should someone wanting healing call Jesus this? I submit the answer is that Solomon was the person associated with cures in early Judaism and Jesus was being addressed as a latter-day Solomonic healer, based on Jesus' well-known reputation for working a variety of cures. If this is correct, then we have another piece of evidence that Jesus' ministry suggested to those who witnessed it that Jesus was some sort of messianic figure.

In retrospect, in view of the traditions we find in the Isaianic material (e.g., Isa. 35:5), it is not surprising that there were at least some early Jews who expected that the eschatological age of blessing would include miracles such as even the prophets had never performed. It is no accident that perhaps two of the most frequently attested *types* of miracles recorded in the Synoptic tradition are exorcisms and the giving of sight to the blind. Both of these types of mighty deeds could have and probably would have been interpreted in a messianic light, a fact of which it is very unlikely Jesus was ignorant. Here again we see further evidence of the messianic contours of Jesus' ministry even without our entering into a debate about the direct evidence, the so-called titles of Christ. It is now time, however, to turn to this evidence, but before we do so, it is well to bear the following in mind. Even if one discounts all of the many Gospel passages where the issue of Jesus' identity is directly raised or discussed, the evidence we have examined in this chapter, even with a very critical or minimalist approach to the data, strongly suggests that there was a messianic character to Jesus' life and in particular his ministry. Furthermore, Jesus was conscious of this fact and acted in particular ways because of it—attempting to avoid a misunderstanding of who he was and what he was doing, especially avoiding being cast as a Zealot leader or political claimant to the throne formerly held by Herod the Great, without denying the eschatological character and significance of his life and work.

THE DIRECT EVIDENCE—THE "TITLES" OF JESUS

Son of Man

If there is one title or descriptive phrase that most scholars believe Jesus did use of himself repeatedly, it is not Son of David, or Son of

God, or Messiah, but rather Son of Man. There has long been a debate about when a Jewish conception of a Son of Man as a messianic figure arose. Much of the debate centers on the dating and meaning of the early Jewish material we find in *1 Enoch* 37–71 and 4 Ezra 13. The latter text is widely believed to have originated near the end of the first century C.E., but it may well reflect earlier ideas. In regard to the Enochian material, however, most scholars think that at least the ideas it contains are of earlier provenance. These texts show that in the first century C.E. in early Judaism there was considerable speculation about the Son of Man figure. In such an environment, Jesus' frequent use of the phrase would at least have raised some messianic questions, even if the use did not in itself provide any clear messianic answers.[30] This is especially so because we know that the book of Daniel was extremely popular among Jews in the first century, as Josephus (*Antiquities* 10.267–68) and the various fragments of the book at Qumran show.

We must begin our discussion with the originating point of this whole tradition, which is not the *ben ʾādām* material in Ezekiel or in Psalm 8, but rather the Aramaic material in Daniel 7. It must first be noted that in Daniel the phrase is used not as a title but as part of an analogy—the author saw one like a human being, or "son of man." There is no little debate over who this figure is. Some scholars think the figure refers to one or more angels, though this is a minority view. Others see him as simply a symbol for Israel or in particular the faithful Israelites, called in Daniel the saints of the Most High. The third view, held by probably a majority of scholars, is that the Son of Man is seen as a representative figure, a representative of Israel who comes into the presence of the Almighty.

All of these views have a certain plausibility. For example, elsewhere in the Old Testament "holy ones" is a phrase applied to angels, and, more to the point, in Daniel itself the angel Gabriel is described as having a human voice and appearance (8:5–16; 10:16), and as being a "man" (9:21, cf. 10:5; 12:6, 7). Against this identification is the fact that elsewhere in the Old Testament "holy ones" can also refer to human beings (Ps. 34:20, cf. Wis. Sol. 18:9; 1 Macc. 1:46), and Dan. 7:27 tells us that the kingdom will be given not to angels but to the people of God.[31] Furthermore, if the Son of Man is an angel who has not suffered with Israel, how is giving such a creature a kingdom comforting to the author's audience? The second view, which identifies the Son of Man as a symbol for corporate Israel has more plausibility, for clearly

enough the larger context of Daniel 7 refers to the saints, and they will
benefit from this bestowal of the kingdom by God. Yet it is a mistake
to identify this human figure with Israel writ large because then the
contrast with the beastly empires breaks down. It will be recalled that
in Dan. 7:27 and 8:21 we have clear evidence that kings and not just a
people are being referred to as the source of Israel's problems. There is
of course a close connection—a king was seen as the representative of
his kingdom, and was to some extent seen as the embodiment or
essence of his people. On this second view, we have the further problem that the Son of Man is seen in essence as a symbol, not a real being.
But a king was not merely a symbol, though he was certainly that as
well, and in the ancient Near East the idea of royal rule of the people
was a foreign idea. A kingdom without a king was not what ancients
hoped for or expected. Surely the vast majority of ancients, including
ancient Jews, would have read Dan. 7:13–14 to be referring to a royal
individual who in turn represented and embodied God's people and
their experiences. Furthermore, both in *1 Enoch* 37ff. and in 4 Ezra, as
well as in Revelation in the New Testament "son of man" seems
clearly enough to be an individual, and so this is surely the most probable interpretation of the figure in Daniel 7, whatever we make of him.
Further confirmation for the third view comes from the fact that when
we read of this human figure being given a kingdom it is probable that
what is meant is not just a piece of real estate, but both a land and a
people. In other words, the Son of Man is not the kingdom or the people; he is their ruler and representative. The conclusion of the careful
study of B. Lindars about the Enochian Son of Man is also to be com-
mended for the Danielic material:

> ... "that Son of Man," is a leader of the righteous ... i.e. the faithful
> Jews. Consequently he must be seen as a representative figure, embody-
> ing the expectations of the Jews that their righteousness before God will
> be vindicated, their enemies will be liquidated, and they will reign with
> God. ... It would be a mistake to suggest that he is in some way a cor-
> porate figure, i.e., identical with the faithful Jews.[32]

That the human figure in Daniel 7 is seen as a royal figure is clear
enough from the fact that he is given a kingdom, especially after the discussion which precedes Dan. 7:13–14 about other rival kings and king-
doms. Furthermore, Daniel 7 seems to be presenting an investiture
scene. Finally, in the Enoch material it is probable that the Son of Man
is seen as a messianic figure. That Jesus drew on and alluded to this
material in his teaching seems secure from the fact that here alone in

the Old Testament do we find the two concepts juxtaposed that are more often found on Jesus' lips in the Synoptic Gospels—Son of Man and dominion of God. We must now examine several of the Synoptic traditions that include this phrase and try to discover how Jesus used it.

The phrase "the son of the man," to translate it literally, is found some eighty-one times in the Gospels: sixty-nine of these are in the Synoptics, and all but three of these (Mark 2:10; Luke 24:7; John 12:34) are found on Jesus' own lips.[33] The phrase is found in all levels of the Gospel material—Mark, Q, M, L, and John, and only three times outside the Gospels (Acts 7:56; Rev. 1:13; 14:14).[34]

The latter two of these reflect the Danielic material directly because the analogy "one like a son of man" is used, and so there is likely no connection between the material in Revelation and the sayings tradition per se. What this tells us is that the early church did not use this phrase to confess their faith in Jesus (notice its total absence from the Pauline corpus). Its enigmatic and apocalyptic quality made it especially impenetrable for Gentile converts not familiar with the Old Testament or Jewish apocalyptic literature in general. We may be almost completely certain, then, that this phrase did characterize how Jesus referred to himself, and not how others, whether disciples or inquirers or enemies, referred to him.[35]

The Son of Man sayings have often been categorized into three groups: (1) ministry sayings; (2) suffering and death sayings; (3) future coming sayings. This categorization has led to one or another group of sayings being declared a church creation (especially group 2), but each saying's authenticity should be evaluated on its own merits. There is overlap in the case of some of these sayings, and some fall into more than one category.

The first saying we must consider, widely regarded as authentic, is the Q saying found in Luke 9:58/Matt. 8:20. This saying seems to be a comment on Jesus' itinerant life-style, but it may also have a more ominous tone, reflecting his rejection in various places, or his inability to find any congenial place he could call home and from which he could base his operations. What is interesting about this saying is that it seems to be echoing what we find in some of the Enochian literature about Wisdom being unable to find a home on earth.[36] There are perhaps intended implicit warnings in this saying for Jesus' would-be followers about the cost of following him (they too become homeless vagabonds), but it is doubtful that this is the primary thrust of the saying in view of the Enochian background (*1 Enoch* 42:1–3). In other words, it is unlikely that the original Aramaic phrase Jesus would have used here, *bar ʾănāšāʾ*, means in a generic sense "a person in my position." Jesus means this as a comment on himself and only by implication on his disciples. The overtone of rejection and the humanness and frailty of Jesus must not be missed here, which means that this saying has affinities with the Son of Man sayings in the passion narrative. This leads us to our next arguably authentic saying—Luke 9:44b.

Luke 9:44b is a saying that quite readily can be translated from Greek back into Aramaic, and more to the point even in the Greek seems to betray Aramaic ways of phrasing things, showing its earlier origins. There is no evidence that the author of the Third Gospel knew any Aramaic, so these features cannot be attributed to him. A roughly literal translation of this saying would be the following: "The Son of Man will be delivered up into the hands of the sons of humanity...," with a wordplay on *bar ʾănāšāʾ* and *bene ʾănāšāʾ*. This saying implies a violent end to Jesus' life, but it does not specify what sort. The "divine passive" here ("will be delivered up") implies that it is ultimately God doing the delivering. Here we may compare texts like Rom. 4:25 or 8:31–32. There is no reference to the resurrection in this saying, nor is the crucifixion itself mentioned, which speaks for the authenticity of this saying. The saying is reminiscent of the parable of the workers in the vineyard (Mark 12:1–9 and par.). Probably the majority of scholars think that this parable is authentic precisely because it ends by simply referring to the killing of the son and heir, with no word about his vindication afterwards.[37]

If it is true that Jesus' ministry received a significant amount of resistance and rejection, it is quite believable that Jesus would have anticipated his premature death, even if Jesus had only seen himself as some sort of prophet (cf., e.g., Matt. 23:37). What is of special importance is that this saying probably implies that God's hand will be in this coming death. It will be part of the plan, not just a senseless tragedy. If it is true that Jesus had some sense of messianic identity, it is hard to doubt that he would have believed that God would have something to do with his death as he had with his life.

This in turn may mean that the question of the authenticity of Mark 10:45 should be reopened by the many scholars who simply dismiss it as a later church creation, especially in view of the fact that there is evidence from the Maccabean literature that it was believed that a martyr's death could have an atoning benefit for other Jews (see 4 Macc. 6:27–29; 2 Macc. 7:37–38; 1 Macc. 2:50; 6:44). There is also evidence elsewhere in early Jewish literature for such an idea (1QS 5:6; 8:3–10; 9:4; Palestinian Talmud, *Yoma* 38b). Whether we accept Mark 10:45 as a saying of Jesus or not, we have from three different sources and traditions the notion that Jesus saw his destiny as "Son of Man" involving a coming violent death—(1) Luke 9:44b; (2) Mark 8:31; 9:31; 10:32–34; (3) the parable in Mark 12, to which Mark 10:45 can be added as further corroboration.

This is why as critical a scholar as R. Pesch has concluded that the violent death of the Son of Man was announced by Jesus himself.[38] This is especially believable if Jesus had reflected on and drawn on the nuances of the Danielic portrait of the Son of Man, who comes before God during the time of the suffering of God's own people at the hands of the beastly empires. Why should the Son of Man be any different, especially as the representative of God's people? This leads us to the discussion of one further saying thought by many scholars to be authentic in some form—Mark 14:62.

Recall that the one category of Son of Man sayings that R. Bultmann thought might include some authentic material is the future coming sayings. This is plausible not least because it is these sayings that best match up with what is said about the Son of Man in Daniel 7. Mark 14:62 has some interesting features. It does not mention the exaltation of the Son of Man, but rather that he is already seated at the right hand of God and will be seen coming on the clouds. The saying has a certain self-authenticating quality, for of course those present at the Sanhedrin did not live to see the Son of Man coming on the clouds, and so it is unlikely that the church made the saying up. Furthermore, the correcting—or, better said, qualifying—of the remarks of the questioner who speaks of Jesus as Messiah/son of the blessed but is answered in terms of Son of Man is unlikely to reflect later church theology, since the church (and Mark) much preferred the titles Christ or Son of God. This qualifying of an identity statement by referring to himself as the Son of Man is also of course attested elsewhere in Mark 8:29–31 and par. and seems to have been characteristic of Jesus. He was more comfortable referring to himself as Son of Man, though he did not reject other suggested titles (see below).

In Mark 14:62 it would appear that Jesus is deliberately combining insights from Daniel 7 and Ps. 110:1. It is an idea about the Son of Man that also crops up in *1 Enoch* 45:3; 55:4; 62:5. The saying, if it did come from the hearing of Jesus before the high priest, is laced with irony. The high priest and others thought they sat in judgment of Jesus, but Jesus

was indicating that quite the reverse would ultimately be the case!
The saying suggests that Jesus saw himself in the future assuming a
position of power and authority as God's right-hand man. Jesus would
also be implying that how one reacts to the Son of Man now will affect
one's own future destiny, an idea found in other places in the Gospel
traditions (see Luke 12:8–9 and par.).

This evidence suggests that Jesus' use of the phrase "Son of Man"
implied a messianic self-understanding that entailed frailty, rejection,
and death, but also authority, empowerment, and the hand of God on
one's life and ministry. Jesus probably chose this phrase to refer to himself (in the third person) in order to distinguish himself from some of
the more conventional ways of looking at God's Anointed One.

This image admirably conveyed the idea of both suffering and ultimate glory and vindication, of both human rejection and divine
approval that Jesus saw as defining his mission and ministry. It was an
image he found in texts like Daniel 7 and perhaps a text like Isaiah 53,
but it was also an image alive among early Jews in the first century C.E.
in the form of other Son of Man traditions found in *1 Enoch* and 4 Ezra.
These other traditions provide a plausible Jewish and historical matrix
out of which Jesus' chosen self-designation made good sense in its original context, even though when the Gospel spread beyond Israel and
Jewish contexts the phrase was less well understood and so went
almost unused by the early church when it wished to discuss who
Jesus was.

The Messiah or Christ

Earlier in this study we discussed the etymology of the term "Messiah" and its use in early Judaism. We concluded that it was used but
not in abundance and that there was no normative concept of what the
Messiah would be like.[39] The variety of uses of the term may have
opened the door for Jesus to give the term a new significance. Yet when
Jesus was addressed as Messiah or Son of God or both, he chose to reply
as Son of Man, clearly his preferred form of self-identification. We need
to look now more closely at several texts to see whether Jesus may
have spoken or alluded to himself as God's *māšîaḥ*. It is, however,
important to point out, since the New Testament is written in Greek,
that in secular Greek *christos* was by no means a technical term for a
religious figure. In fact it was basically an adjective found on bottles of

anointing oil or perfumes and meant "for external application," apparently always used of the ointment and not of the one anointed. When Biblical Greek uses *christos* for an anointed *person* this is a new usage, or at least a departure from normal secular usage. Furthermore, as C. F. D. Moule has noted, though prophets and priests were anointed in Jewish contexts, when the discussion is about "an anointed one" or even "the anointed one" without further specification, it "would almost certainly mean nothing except the divinely appointed King."[40] Texts such as *Pss. Sol.* 17:32 or 18:37 (cf. 1 QSa 2:12, 14, 20; CD 12:23f.; 14:19; 19:10; 20:1) confirm this conclusion and make clear that if there was a dominant notion of Messiah in early Judaism it was of a royal or kingly figure.

We have already noted that Jesus was crucified as "king of the Jews," but it is unlikely that Christians would simply perpetuate in a title the notion that Jesus was crucified, apparently as a revolutionary.[41] In other words, it is not likely that the words on the *titulus* generated New Testament christological application of the term *christos* to Jesus, but they do likely reflect a term like *basileus/melek/rex* that was already being used of Jesus—and this term may well have been *māšîaḥ*. To my mind, J. J. Collins has recently put the matter rightly:

> Herein lies the anomaly of the messianic claims of Jesus of Nazareth. That he was crucified "King of the Jews" cannot be doubted. The claim to Davidic kingship also figures prominently in early Christian sources. The title *Christos*, messiah, is treated as a virtual name by Paul. It is unlikely that Jesus' followers would have given him such a politically inflammatory title after his death if it had no basis in life. . . . The messianic identity of Jesus must be grounded in some way before his crucifixion.[42]

Let us now consider several relevant Synoptic texts. If the cross did anything, it demonstrated that Jesus was not the political Messiah that some had hoped for, the one who would come and free Israel from foreign powers and internal strife (cf. Luke 24:21—"we had hoped that he would be the one to redeem Israel").

We may say immediately that the evidence is more sparse than we might have expected, considering the plethora of references to *christos* elsewhere in the New Testament and even within the narrative framework of the Gospels. This suggests that the Synoptic writers did not regularly insert titles into the dialogue or sayings portions of their source material, though occasionally it is clear that this has been done by a later Christian scribe (cf. the textual variants in Mark 9:41 and note that Matt. 10:42 seems to reflect an earlier form of this tradition that spoke of disciples instead of Christ). Some texts are of no real help to our inquiry—for instance, Mark 13:21, in which Jesus speaks of those who falsely claim to be the Messiah, but Jesus does not identify himself as the true one. Matthew 23:10 is nearer the mark, but even here Jesus does not say explicitly that he is the Messiah that is being discussed, though it seems to be implied.

The famous occasion at Caesarea Philippi recorded in Mark 8:27–30 and par. involves the acclamation of a disciple about Jesus, and according to Mark Jesus told his disciples not to tell anyone that Peter had said "You are the Messiah." Furthermore, when Jesus began to teach them after this acclamation he seems to have deliberately spoken again of himself as Son of Man, in particular, a Son of Man who must suffer. The point of mentioning this is that here Jesus does not reject the acclamation that he is the Messiah, but he strongly qualifies its meaning by referring to the future destiny of the Son of Man; and if it is not simply a Markan addition, we also learn that the disciples were very sternly warned to tell no one about Peter's words. Historically this is plausible if Jesus did not want to be mistaken for a particular sort of messianic figure. Perhaps with the deeds of the Maccabees fresh in people's minds Jesus was being cautious so that he could make clear his own identity in his own way.[43]

This brings us to Mark 12:35–37 and par. Again, Jesus does not say clearly that he is speaking about himself; he simply raises a conundrum of how David as the psalmist could call the Messiah Lord, if in fact he was David's son. Some scholars have taken this as a critique of the traditions that existed about the Davidic Messiah, and this may be correct. At most one can argue that Jesus implied something about his own messianic identity here in this riddle.

Finally we must take one more look at Mark 14:61–62 and par. Otto Betz has made an impressive case for reading all of Mark 14:53–65 in light of the eschatological interpretation of 2 Samuel 7 at Qumran (4QFlor 1–13). Notice that the prophecy in 2 Samuel 7 speaks of David's offspring, whose reign will be established and who will build God's house, and finally we have the saying "I will be his Father and he will be my Son." In Mark we find the discussion about the possibility of Jesus claiming he would destroy (and rebuild?) the Temple (Mark 14:58/2 Sam. 7:13), the Messiah, Son of the Blessed (Mark 14:61/ 2 Sam. 7:14), and finally the mention of enthronement (Mark 14:62, cf. Luke 22:69/2 Sam. 7:13). Betz concludes that the sequence of the discussion before the high priest and Jesus' response makes good sense historically in light of current Jewish discussion about 2 Samuel 7.[44] I agree, and scholars on other grounds have argued that the high priest's question and Jesus' response are plausible.[45] There is unfortunately a textual problem in regard to Jesus' response: some manuscripts read "I am," and others read something close to what we find in the Matthean parallel, "You say that I am." The weight of the evidence strongly favors the simple "I am," especially in light of the fact that in the church already by the second century Matthew's Gospel had become the most popular, and the readings in Mark were then subject to alteration to conform to the more popular Gospel. What we learn from this text, if it does reflect a historical incident, and from the others we have examined as well, is that while Jesus did not ever directly proclaim himself to be the Messiah, he may have alluded to himself occasionally using this sort of terminology; and when others suggested he was the Messiah, he affirmed their remarks but then proceeded to qualify them with a remark about the destiny of the Son of Man. Another reason Jesus was reluctant to use this term may have been because in early Judaism it was sometimes thought that no one could claim to be the Messiah until he had completed the tasks of the Messiah. If this was on Jesus' mind, then the climactic moment before the high priest would have been the right moment to say "I am" directly.

In sum, the prevalent use of the term "Christ" of Jesus in the New Testament must have some foundation in the actual ministry of Jesus, though the evidence is not plentiful at this point. I agree with Moule that the tenacity and prevalence of the usage are best explained if Jesus accepted the royal title during his ministry but radically qualified and reinterpreted it using the Son of Man material.[46]

The Son of God

Very few scholars would dispute that Jesus used the Aramaic word *ʾabbāʾ* to address God. There is disagreement, however, about the significance of this fact. Much of the recent scholarly debate has centered on the issue of whether Jesus was unique in addressing God this way. We cannot rehearse that debate here,[47] but suffice it to say that the evidence trotted out, while it certainly indicates that God was increasingly being addressed as Father in early Judaism, does not provide us with evidence that outside the Jesus tradition God was being addressed or prayed to as *'abbā'*. The Qumran documents 4Q371 and 372 provide evidence that God was addressed as *'ābî*, but even this does not involve the use of the Aramaic term *'abbā'*, much less the use of *'abbā'* in prayer language, as we find in such disparate New Testament texts as Mark 14:36; Rom. 8:15; and Gal. 4:6. The further work of James Barr on this term, has shown that *'abbā'* does not mean "Daddy," but Barr was unable to deny that the term connotes intimacy even when used of God.[48] Nor does he deny that there is clear evidence that *'abbā'* was used as a term of endearment by children ("father dearest") even of a beloved Jewish teacher such as Hanin ha Nehba.

It is surely not an accident that in the three New Testament examples of the use of the term *'abbā'* the context suggests that the intimacy of the speaker's relationship with God is being expressed in a moment of real passion. Moreover, we still have no evidence besides these three texts of anyone apart from Jesus or his followers invoking God as *'abbā'*. It still appears, therefore, that the use of this term seems to have been a unique, or at least characteristic, mark of Jesus' own and his disciples' devotional relationship with God.

Since Mark 14:36 appears to be an example of a private prayer that the sleeping disciples did not overhear, the question to be raised is, Why would Mark have thought that this form of speech characterized Jesus' prayer life? Here we may point to the beginning of the Lukan form of the Lord's Prayer in Luke 11:2 (which really should be called the disciple's prayer) in which God is simply addressed as "Father" in the Greek, not as "our Father" as the Matthean form has it. This prayer seems to be a modification of the traditional Jewish Kaddish prayer ("Exalted and hallowed be his great name in the world which he created according to his will. May he let his kingdom rule in your lifetime . . .") and, in its most primitive form as Jesus gave it, probably involved the simply invocation "Father." Translated back into Aramaic, this is surely *'abbā'*. In other words, Jesus not only prayed this way to God; he taught his disciples to do so as well.

The question for us is: What does this tell us about Jesus' relationship to God? In all likelihood it implies a filial consciousness on the part of Jesus that seems to have involved a degree of intimacy unprecedented, so far as we can tell, in early Judaism. Further, it was only by being Jesus' disciple that one also could dare to take up this form of intimate address and use it of God. It may also be germane to point out that Jesus seems to have insisted that no ordinary mortal or human teacher should be called *'abbā'* (Matt. 23:9), though there was certainly

Jewish precedent for this. Since both Jesus and the disciples can address God as ʾabbāʾ there is no exclusive christological weight to the term, but it does strongly suggest that Jesus saw himself as God's son, involved in an intimate relationship with God and, more telling, able to mediate such a relationship with God for his disciples, so they could relate to God in this fashion as well.

As we noted in a previous chapter, there is evidence from Qumran (4Q246) of an Aramaic fragment that speaks of a messianic figure as the Son of God, even though the formal title "the Son of God" never appears in the Hebrew Bible. There is, then, a possibility that Jesus could have used such a phrase during this era.

Our first saying of significance is Mark 13:32/Matt. 24:36, a saying so surprising that Luke, who used Mark, simply left it out. It is interesting that this saying and the next one we will scrutinize, the Q saying Matt. 11:27/ Luke 10:22, both have to do with the state of the Son's knowledge, one denying that he has a certain kind of knowledge, the other affirming it. Not many scholars simply dismiss Mark 13:32 precisely because it is unlikely that the early church would make up the idea that Jesus was ignorant about something, especially something that had to do with his own future role in the divine economy.

Some scholars have attempted to argue that the phrase "not even the Son" or at least the use of the term "Son" is a later addition to this saying, but the textual evidence favors the inclusion of the saying, especially because of its offensiveness. Moreover, those who would omit the word "Son" have failed to notice that the saying is meant to convey the idea of a crescendo of knowledge moving from ordinary humans to angels to the Son, and finally to the Father. As has been pointed out there would be little reason to mention the angels if the phrase "not even the Son" was not also originally part of the saying. Furthermore, the ignorance of the Son becomes problematic only if one thinks of sonship in some special sense. In short, this saying offers offense only if it is someone more than an ordinary mortal claiming ignorance of things divine. It is not plausible to argue that the church would add the reference to the Son in this saying, thereby compounding their own difficulties in defending Jesus.

As to the meaning of this saying, Jesus is telling his disciples that it has not been revealed to him when the parousia will transpire. The phrase "day or hour" does not refer to the precise time of something (as if Jesus knew the general timing but without precision); it simply refers to the time of the event. The saying is apocalyptic in character and is like those in Daniel and elsewhere in apocalyptic literature where the timing of certain events has been hidden or is a divine secret. The fact that the phrase "not even the Son" is last in the ascending chain of knowledge tells us that Jesus saw himself as more intimate in his knowledge than even the angels, presumably because he believed he was the Son in some special sense.

Matthew 11:27/Luke 10:22 has been called the thunderbolt that fell from the Johannine sky, not only because it sounds like various characteristic utterances in the Fourth Gospel but also because it is perceived to be so unlike what we find elsewhere in the Synoptics. Here Jesus is portrayed as being like the truly wise man such as we find in Dan. 2:20–23, who thanks God for his unique revelation to him. One must compare also Wis. Sol. 2:13–16: "He claims to have a knowledge of God, and calls himself a son of the Lord . . . and boasts of having God as his Father." In short, this saying is a wisdom utterance or, better said, reflects the intermingling of wisdom and apocalyptic ideas. The phrase "no one knows the Son but the Father" probably points to the authenticity of this saying, for what early Christian would concoct the idea that no human being knew the Son? This saying is probably conveying, in a different way, the same idea that is expressed by Jesus' praying and teaching his disciples to pray to God as ʾabbāʾ, namely, that Jesus is the revealer of the Father's true identity to others. As for the phrase "no one knows the Son but the Father," we must compare a variety of evidence from the Wisdom corpus that indicates that only Wisdom truly knows God or God's mind and will (see Job 28:1–27; Sir. 1:6, 8; Bar. 3:15–32; Prov. 8:12; Wis. Sol. 7:25ff.; 8:3–8; 9:4, 9, 11). In other words, Jesus would be suggesting that he is assuming Wisdom's function of revealing God's character and mysteries, and that he has access to this information because of the special filial relationship he has with the Father.

It is possible that the verb tense of *paredothē* suggests that at some specific point in time in the past Jesus received this revelation or information, perhaps at his baptism. In short, while the saying suggests a rather high self-estimate on the part of Jesus, at the same time it suggests that the Son is dependent on the Father for this knowledge and so is subordinate to the Father. This subordinationist note is probably original, and it is interesting that it is found in the Fourth Gospel in especially clear fashion. Notice, however, the contrast between "no one" and "all" in this saying, which suggests that Jesus is the exclusive mediator of the true knowledge of God.

In sum, this saying draws out the implications of Jesus' use of *'abbā'* in terms of making clear how he viewed his relationship with God. He saw himself as the unique revealer of God's true nature and plan. The saying also suggests that Jesus relied on the Father to reveal this information to him, but that this information was critical to bringing God's people back to a true knowledge of God. Jesus was not dispensing merely higher knowledge or esoteric extras. Without the knowledge he conveyed, no one would truly know the Father. Clearly, it takes an exceptional person to imply this sort of thing about himself, but all the evidence we have suggests that Jesus was an exceptional person. If the parable of the vineyard is authentic in some form, then it confirms that Jesus saw himself as the Son and heir who was the last chance for God's people to respond properly to what God required of them. This comports with the idea we have just discussed that Jesus saw himself as the true, final, and only revealer of the eschatological secrets of God and God's mind and plan in regard to his people.

These are large claims, but then if Jesus made them, he was not the first or last to make such claims, and they are not historically improbable just because of their magnitude. Nor is the theological issue resolved if one comes to closure with the historical questions. By this I mean that Jesus could have implied or actually openly made various christological claims, but whether those claims were true or not cannot be answered on a purely historical level, except perhaps in a negative way (i.e., if it could be shown that he didn't make any such claims, even implicitly by his actions or by how he related to people, then this would call into question the validity of later theological deductions about his significance). What one is, what one believes oneself to be, and what one claims to be may in fact be three different things. This is often forgotten in the heated debates about the historical Jesus. As we bring this discussion to a close, we must consider evidence of an even larger claim. Did Jesus see himself as God's Wisdom come in the flesh?

Jesus—The Wisdom of God

Usually the fourth title that is discussed is *kyrios*, or Lord, but the evidence that Jesus referred to himself in this way is slim, and further there is the problem that the term, even if we consider the Aramaic equivalent *mārē'*, was often used in a mundane fashion as a form of respectful address to a notable person, including revered teachers. For example, in Mark 7:28 *kyrios* likely means no more than "respected sir," or again in Luke 6:46 and par. the term is used as a means of respectful address, not as an acclamation of Jesus' divinity or the like. It is often and rightly noted that in the narrative framework of the Gospels, Mark and Matthew do not call Jesus *ho kyrios*, but interestingly Luke does, using the later Christian phrasing (Luke 7:13; 10:5),[49] without placing the definite form of the term on either the lips of Jesus as a clear self-reference or on the lips of others as meaning more than "respected sir." Not even Mark 11:3 would seem to be an exception to the rule that Jesus did not refer to himself as "the Lord" in some exalted sense, for here the term may have its more normal mundane sense when referring to a revered teacher, or it may even mean that Jesus was the owner of the colt, though I think that is less likely. The only text that may really suggest that Jesus used the term *mārēʾ* of himself in some exalted sense is Mark 12:35–37, which we have already discussed; but here again the usage is elliptical and it may simply be an example of how one would address a royal figure as "my lord."

In short, there is no incontrovertible evidence that Jesus used *mārēʾ* of himself in an exalted sense. But is there any other evidence that Jesus spoke of himself in exalted terms? I suggest there is, and it has to do with the popular conception of God's Wisdom.

Here again the evidence is more significant than abundant. First, if we revisit the Q saying found in Matt. 8:20/Luke 9:58 we may note that it has strong echoes of what we find in *1 Enoch* 42:2, which refers to Wisdom looking for a dwelling place among God's people, "but she found no dwelling place." In other words, Jesus saw himself as in the position and condition of Wisdom when Wisdom came to earth. One must also take account of the further wisdom tradition found in Sir. 36:31: "So who will trust a man [presumably a sage] that has no nest, but lodges wherever night overtakes him?" In other words, there is a twofold piece of evidence that Jesus was discussing his own situation using Wisdom language. One may also point to how this Q saying comports with Matt. 23:37–39/Luke 13:34–35, where Jesus portrays himself as a mother bird being rejected by her chicks, an image that admirably suits what we have just noted about the rejection of Wisdom, a female personification.

There are at last two different traditions where Jesus seems to identify himself as God's Wisdom. Matthew 11:19 is the first of these: "Yet Wisdom is vindicated by her deeds." As I have argued at some length elsewhere, this is probably the more primitive form of this saying rather than what we find in Luke 7:35, which reflects Lukan redaction to convey a particular vision of the relationship of Jesus and John the Baptist.[50] Clearly, "deeds" is the more difficult reading here in view of the contextual discussion of children (cf. Luke 7:31–35). The context here suits what we have already seen in the previous tradition— namely, that Wisdom faces rejection on earth, but here it is added that she will be vindicated by her deeds.

Our next saying of importance is found only in Luke 11:49 and reads: "The Wisdom of God says, 'I will send them prophets and apostles, some of whom they will kill and persecute. . . .'" Here it is possible that God is spoken of as Wisdom, but more probably the reference is not to some past sending of prophets by God, in view of the reference to apostles, especially in view of the fact that the verb is in the future tense, "I will send." In other words, it is more likely that this refers to Jesus' sending forth of emissaries, who will sometimes be rejected by this generation. This comports with the famous commissioning traditions found in Matt. 10:11ff. and par.,[51] where the possible rejection of Jesus' agents was spoken of. We find a further tradition to this effect in Mark 13:9–13 and par. The term "apostles" may of course be Luke's use of later Christian jargon, but there is no reason to reject the saying as a whole on the basis of this one word. Here then we may have further evidence that Jesus during his ministry identified himself as God's Wisdom on earth.

If this is one way that Jesus viewed himself, we should recall that the Johannine thunderbolt saying Luke 10:21–22/Matt. 11:25–27 speaks of the exclusive knowledge of God's mind by Jesus. In the Wisdom tradition it was Wisdom who was entrusted with the secrets or revelations of God and the task of unveiling them to others (Prov. 8:14–36; Wis. 2:13, 16; 4:10–15). I am suggesting that Jesus creatively combined various Old Testament traditions in order to convey to others a sense of how he viewed himself. Thus, in this saying sonship language is combined with Wisdom material.

If it is true that the ultimate test of a thesis is its ability to explain a wide range of otherwise disparate data, then the theory that Jesus presented himself as God's Wisdom on earth has much to commend it. The following is a list of things that begin to make better sense in light of this proposal: (1) Jesus' use of ʾabbāʾ for God is not at all characteristic of what we find in the Old Testament, but we do find such language frequently in the Wisdom corpus (cf. Sir. 23:1, 4; 51:10; Wis. Sol.

14:3 cf. 3 Macc. 6:3, 8). (2) The use of kingdom-of-God language in conjunction with wisdom language is found almost exclusively in texts like Wis. Sol. 10:10 and various texts in the Synoptic Gospels. (3) Jesus' exorcisms could easily have led people to see him as the "one greater than (but like) Solomon" who came and worked cures no one else could (cf. 11QPs 91 and Josephus, *Antiquities* 8.45). (4) Jesus' clear and frequent use of Son of Man language echoes material that reflects the cross-fertilization of apocalyptic and wisdom traditions—Daniel and the parables in *1 Enoch*. (5) There are many echoes of Sirach in the teaching of Jesus, which receive an explanation if Jesus saw himself as sage and Wisdom (compare, e.g., Sir. 11:18–19 with Luke 12:13–21; Sir. 24:9 and 6:19–31 with Matt. 11:29–30; Sir. 23:9 with Matt. 5:34; Sir. 32:1 with Luke 22:26–27; Sir. 36:31 with Luke 9:58; etc.). (6) Jesus' willingness to portray himself in female imagery makes sense if he saw himself as God's Wisdom on earth (Matt. 23:37–39 and par.).

In other words, the Jesus-as-Wisdom proposal is the sole one I am aware of that makes sense of the fact that Jesus never spoke as a prophet in the oracular mode ("Thus says the Lord") but spoke rather using sapiential forms of speech (parables, aphorisms, riddles); that Jesus performed miracles as Son of David (i.e., one like Solomon, Mark 10:46–52), that Jesus' offering of a yoke to his disciples has a clear parallel in the yoke of Wisdom in Sirach (cf. Matt. 11:29–30 and par. with Sir. 24:9 and 6:19–31); that Jesus referred to the coming of God's Wisdom and the coming of the kingdom; and that he saw himself as bringing in the kingdom or dominion of God. This thesis also explains how it is that at a very early date the early church in its christological hymns (Philippians 2; Colossians 1; John 1) used a wide variety of Wisdom ideas to sing the praises of Jesus.[52] More could be said along these lines but this must suffice, and we must now draw to a conclusion.

A long time ago Professor C. F. D. Moule aptly remarked that at some point in the investigation of New Testament Christology one must make up one's mind whether the term "development" or "evolution" better encapsulates what we find in the New Testament. In other words, one must decide whether the various Christologies of the New Testament are only attempts to describe, draw out, or articulate something that was already at least implicitly there in the person and work of Jesus or whether they are successive additions of something new. One must decide whether the big-bang theory applies to Christology, so to speak. Moule suggests that the truth of the matter was that Jesus was such an impressive and powerful figure that the Christologies we find in the New Testament were not in danger of saying too much about him, but rather were gropings toward adequacy.[53] I agree with this assessment and this is why, though there are many new elements to be found in the various Christologies in the New Testament, I think we must primarily talk in terms of continuity between the Christology of Jesus and the Christologies of the earliest Christians.

There is evidence in the Synoptics, even when critically sifted, that Jesus spoke of himself as Son of Man, probably as Son of God, alluded to himself as Christ and even possibly as Lord, and directly called himself God's Wisdom. The indirect evidence suggests a messianic self-understanding—even if we discount all the direct evidence. In other words, the case for continuity between Jesus and his post-Easter followers in terms of how Jesus was to be evaluated is a strong one. Of course we did not find evidence that Jesus ever called himself God, and for good reason. The term in Jewish circles would surely have been taken to mean Yahweh, not the later Christian notion of the first person of the Trinity. The application of *theos* language to Jesus is a post-Easter development, but this does not mean it had no foundation in how Jesus evaluated himself. The use of the language of Wisdom as a form of self-reference already suggested moving in that direction.[54] We must turn now to the Christologies of the earliest Jewish Christians and see how they handled these diverse data.

NOTES

1. M. Borg, *Meeting Jesus Again for the First Time* (San Francisco: Harper-SanFrancisco, 1994), p. 29.

2. J. D. G. Dunn, "Messianic Ideas and Their Influence on the Jesus of History," in *The Messiah: Developments in Earliest Judaism and Christianity*, ed. J. H. Charlesworth (Minneapolis: Fortress Press, 1992), pp. 365–81, here pp. 371–72.

3. For a fuller and more detailed discussion of these same matters, see my *Christology of Jesus* (Philadelphia: Fortress Press, 1990), pp. 33–143.

4. W. Wink, *John the Baptist in the Gospel Tradition* (Cambridge: Cambridge University Press, 1968), pp. 109–11.

5. The latter is especially likely historically for two reasons: (1) it is unlikely that Christians who believed that forgiveness came as a result of Jesus' death would invent the idea that it was available through John's baptism; and (2) it is virtually certain that Jesus underwent John's baptism.

6. We will say more about this in due course when we examine the Son of Man material on pp. 53ff.

7. J. Neusner, *Judaism in the Beginning of Christianity* (Philadelphia: Fortress Press, 1984), p. 42.

8. See especially Sanders's influential study *Jesus and Judaism* (Philadelphia: Fortress Press, 1985).

9. Only in the case of Matthew's Gospel is such a close connection with Judaism in the Holy Land really very plausible.

10. It is too often forgotten that even in the Holy Land, Pharisees were a minority group. Though they had wide influence among the ordinary folk, it was out of all proportion to their numbers. Is it really plausible to argue that the Gospel writers would have assumed that their audiences would see the term "Pharisee" in their Gospels as a cipher for Jews in general and the controversies in the Gospel as representative of whatever sort of controversies the church might have with the synagogue in the Diaspora? I find this assumption quite unbelievable, not least because Paul's letters do not really suggest that his communities' difficulties were being caused by Pharisees from the synagogue. Judaizers were a problem of a different sort, being strict Jewish Christians—indeed, as Luke suggests in Acts 15:5, Pharisaic Christians. Notice that even they are not said to reside in the Diaspora, but to come from Jerusalem and go to the Diaspora to trouble Paul's churches there (see Galatians). The judaizing issue of circumcision does not arise at all in Jesus' controversies with the Pharisees in the Gospels, nor really does the issue of the basis on which Gentiles might be accepted among God's people come to the fore in the Synoptics, two of the major issues bedeviling the early church.

11. M. Borg, *Conflict, Holiness and Politics in the Teaching of Jesus* (New York: Edwin Mellen Press, 1984).

12. P. Lapide and U. Luz, *Jesus in Two Perspectives: A Jewish Christian Dialog* (Minneapolis: Augsburg, 1985), p. 141.

13. For an introduction to Horsley's views, perhaps *Jesus and the Spiral of Violence* (San Francisco: HarperSanFrancisco, 1987) is his most important and accessible work.

14. See especially Crossan, *The Historical Jesus: The Life of a Mediterranean Jewish Peasant* (San Francisco: HarperSanFrancisco, 1991).

15. See my more detailed critique of Horsley's and Crossan's proposals in *The Jesus Quest: The Third Search for the Jew of Nazareth* (Downers Grove, Ill.: Inter-Varsity, 1995), pp. 58ff. and pp. 145ff.

16. And of course it is possible that it simply means a very zealous believing Jew, without any implications of politically radical views.

17. See the discussion in my *Christology of Jesus*, pp. 111–13.

18. R. E. Brown, *The Gospel of John 1-12*, Anchor Bible (Garden City, N.Y.: Doubleday, 1966), pp. 249–50.

19. See the discussion of these events by P. W. Barnett, "The Jewish Eschatological Prophets" (Ph.D. diss., University of London, 1977).

20. R. Schnackenburg, *Gottes Herrschaft und Reich* (Freiburg: Herder, 1959), p. 150.

21. G. B. Caird, *Jesus and the Jewish Nation* (London: Athlone Press, 1965), p. 8.

22. M. Hengel, *The Charismatic Leader and His Followers* (New York: Crossroad, 1981), p. 15.

23. See pp. 56ff. below.

24. M. Borg, *Jesus: A New Vision* (San Francisco: HarperSanFrancisco, 1987), pp. 33–34.

25. N. A. Dahl, "Messianic Ideas and the Crucifixion of Jesus," in *The Messiah*, ed. Charlesworth, pp. 382–403, here p. 390.

26. In his recent book M. Hengel makes much the same point. He stresses that the first Christians claimed after Easter not merely that Jesus was alive but that he was the Christ (see Acts 2:36). This suggests that the Messiah question must have been alive before Easter, because Christ's exaltation to the presence of God would not in itself suggest messiahship. After all, there were stories in the Old Testament about Elijah and others being taken up into the presence of God with no messianic implications drawn. See Hengel, *Studies in Early Christology* (Edinburgh: T & T Clark, 1995), p. 13.

27. See my *Christology of Jesus*, pp. 164ff.

28. G. Theissen, *The Miracle Stories of the Early Christian Tradition* (Philadelphia: Fortress Press, 1983), pp. 279–80.

29. Notice that in Mark 11:10 the reference is not to the coming king like David, but the coming Davidic kingdom.

30. The careful discussion of J. J. Collins should be consulted: "The Son of Man in First Century Judaism," *New Testament Studies* 38 (1992): 448–66.

31. Recently, M. De Jonge has argued that since the kingdom Jesus proclaimed was God's kingdom promised for the end-times, this should in all likelihood be correlated with Jesus' use of the Son of Man terminology, which in Daniel 7 is connected to the establishing of divine dominion on earth ("The Christological Significance of Jesus' Preaching of the Kingdom of God," in *The Future of Christology: Essays in Honor of Leander E. Keck* [Minneapolis: Fortress Press, 1993], pp. 3–17).

32. B. Lindars, "Enoch and Christology," *Expository Times* 92 (1980–81): 295–99, here p. 297.

33. The first of these references, however, may be a part of a parenthetical remark by Mark.

34. I am not counting the quotation of Psalm 8 in Heb. 2:7, since originally this text has to do with human beings in general, and it may be doubted that the title has a christological reference even in Hebrews.

35. Notice that in the material in John 9, the blind man uses the term only at the prompting of and after the self-disclosure of Jesus himself.

36. See pp. 17–18 above.

37. On this parable see pp. 68ff. below.

38. R. Pesch, "Die Passion des Menschensohnes," in *Jesus und der Menschensohn* (Freiburg: Herder, 1975), pp. 166–95.

39. See pp. 11ff. above.

40. C. F. D. Moule, *The Origin of Christology* (Cambridge: Cambridge University Press, 1977), p. 32.

41. Ibid., p. 33.

42. J. J. Collins, *The Scepter and the Star: The Messiahs of the Dead Sea Scrolls and Other Ancient Literature* (New York: Doubleday, 1995), p. 204.

43. On W. Wrede's theory about the so-called messianic secret motif in Mark, see my *Christology of Jesus*, pp. 263–67.

44. O. Betz, "Die Frage nach dem Messianischen Bewusstsein Jesu," *Novum Testamentum* 6 (1963): 20–48.

45. See the discussion in my *Christology of Jesus*, pp. 256–58, and also in R. E. Brown, *An Introduction to New Testament Christology* (New York: Paulist Press, *1994)*, pp. 75–77.

46. See Moule, *Origin of Christology*, p. 34.

47. For which see my *Christology of Jesus*, pp. 216–18.

48. J. Barr, "Abba Father and the Familiarity of Jesus' Speech," *Theology* 91 (1988): 173–79; idem, "Abba Isn't Daddy," *Journal of Theological Studies* 39 (1988): 28–47.

49. See pp. 160ff. below on Lukan Christology.

50. See my *Jesus Quest*, pp. 184–85, and *Christology of Jesus*, pp. 84–85.

51. See the discussion on pp. 40ff. above.

52. On which see pp. 78ff. below.

53. Moule, *Origin of Christology*, pp. 2–4.

54. See pp. 107ff. below on *theos* language applied to Jesus.

3

The Worship of the Lord:
Pre-Pauline Christology

E ARLY JEWISH CHRISTIANITY in the first decade or two of the existence of the church in Israel was apparently not a monolithic entity. I say "apparently" because what we know of early Jewish Christianity comes to us largely from later sources. The evidence is also mainly indirect and comes to us in the form of elements from early Christian worship—fragments of prayers, hymns, and creeds that were reused by Paul, Luke, and other New Testament authors. Without question, Paul's letters are the earliest access we have to Jewish Christian Christology, but material from other sources such as Q may be equally early. In all cases the evidence must be evaluated critically because it has likely been somewhat modified by the writers in whose works we find this material.[1]

PRAYERS AND CONFESSIONS OF THE CHRIST

The logical place to start our discussion is by examining Aramaic material found in our sources, as this material must surely go back to Palestinian Christianity, and perhaps back to the earliest Jewish Christian community in Jerusalem. Thus, we begin by looking again at the term ʾabbāʾ,[2] only this time we look at its use in two places in Paul's letters—Rom. 8:15 and Gal. 4:6. In both of these texts we are told that it is the Holy Spirit in the life of the Christian believer that prompts one to invoke or cry to God as ʾabbāʾ. It would appear, then, that Paul is linking the use of ʾabbāʾ to a form of ecstatic utterance, or at least that he sees it as an example of the Spirit speaking through the believer. Yet Paul is addressing non-Palestinian Christians who are doing this praying, certainly including some Gentiles (see, e.g., Rom. 10:13; Gal. 2:8), and it is probable that these non-Palestinian non-Jewish Christians did not know Aramaic. Notice too that Rom. 8:15 indicates that *ʾabbā* is the common cry or prayer of both Paul and his audience, which suggests its widespread use, even in Rome, where most Christians may well have been Gentiles. The use of *ʾabbā* is seen as the sign that the speaker is an heir of God, a joint heir with Christ, a child of God. I suggest that the reference to being joint heirs with Christ has to do with the fact that Paul knows that Jesus prayed using *ʾabbā* and was therefore suggesting that just as this was the cry of the Son who is the heir, so also it is the cry of the sons and daughters who are joint heirs.

It is also possible that these texts, especially the Romans text, suggest that the Holy Spirit prompts glossolalia in the form of non-Aramaic speakers addressing God in Aramaic. In fact Gal. 4:6 indicates that it is the Spirit who is crying " *ʾAbbā*, Father,"[3] and this is what Rom. 8:16 suggests as well. Rom. 8:26 may also be about this same phenomenon ("the Spirit intercedes with sighs too deep for words"). In any case, these texts speak of a communication with God that is characterized by a deeply felt intimacy between God and the one who prays. The earliest Christian worship was not only heartfelt; it was Spirit-inspired and probably involved charismatic utterances "in other tongues." In terms of Christology, these texts, especially the Romans text, suggest that it was Jesus by his example and through his mediatorship (joint heirs) who initiated the believer into this filial relationship with God and this prayer language, though now it is the Spirit who enables the believer to pray in this fashion.

Our next Aramaic phrase is found in 1 Cor. 16:22. Here again we seem to have prayer language in Aramaic. There is debate over whether the original phrase involved simply the *maranatha* phrase or whether it was originally *anathema maranatha*, in view of v. 22a. However, if Rev. 22:20 is a translation and further example of the *maranatha* phrase, as many think, then it would seem that *maranatha* stood alone in the prayer (cf. Jude 14). How the key phrase is to be translated is in part determined by whether we divide the phrase *marana tha* or *maran atha*. Does the phrase mean "Our Lord (has or is) come" or "Come, Lord"? In view of the parallels in Revelation 22 and Jude 14, it is probably the latter.

The term *mārēʾ* of course means "lord," but as Moule pointed out, it is hardly plausible that the term merely means "master" or "respected sir" here. One does not pray to a deceased rabbi or revered master teacher to come.[4] The term here must mean more than "lord," perhaps "Lord," with the implication of divinity. This prayer has both christological and eschatological significance, reflecting a belief in Jesus not only as Lord but also as a Lord who would return. At a very early date Jewish Christians prayed to Jesus as Lord, but this was not only the language of prayer; it was also the language of the earliest confession.[5]

If we ask how it was that early Jewish Christians came to address Jesus not merely as lord but as Lord, we must consider the confessional fragments found in 1 Cor. 12:3; Rom. 10:9, and especially Phil. 2:11. The confession "Jesus is Lord" was probably one of the earliest Christian confessions, if not the very earliest, and especially Phil. 2:11 helps us to see what it meant. It meant Jesus is the risen Lord. In other words, it was a title that was appropriate only after Jesus had completed his earthly work, including being obedient even unto death on the cross. The hymn in Philippians 2 tells us that the name was bestowed on Jesus by God as result of the successful completion of his mission. We will say more about this hymn shortly, but here it is important to note that the name being bestowed on Jesus was God's Old Testament (Septuagint) name—*kyrios*, Lord, the divine name that is above all others. In other words, the earliest confession of Christians was a high christological one indeed, going beyond what we have examined in the Jesus tradition itself in the last chapter and reflecting the church's response to the Easter experiences.

1 Corinthians 12:3 provides us with a contrast between saying "anathema Jesus" and "Jesus is Lord." Paul, writing this letter only a little over two decades after Jesus' death, speaks of the confession as something that would be familiar to his Corinthian converts, something that they themselves had probably confessed at conversion. It is the Holy Spirit which prompts and guides the believer to make a true confession. Only one with the Holy Spirit in his or her life can do so. Again we have clear evidence that it was only a very high christological assertion by which one would be recognized as a Christian, at least in the Pauline communities.

There were of course gods many and lords many in the Greco-Roman world, as Paul admits in 1 Cor. 8:5, but the confession of Jesus as Lord was something different. The Greek and Roman gods or heroes being called *kyrioi* were all either mythological figures or legendary figures from hoary antiquity, whereas Jesus was a historical figure whom many still remembered. It is also true that during the first century C.E., beginning really with Augustus, many emperors were being divinized, not only after their deaths but during their lives as well. By the end of the century Domitian felt comfortable insisting that he be called *Deus et dominus noster* (God and our Lord). It is then possible that the Christian confession was in part an attempt to distinguish the worship of Jesus from emperor worship and other forms of pagan worship. This may also in part explain formulations like "the Lord Jesus Christ," which bears a certain resemblance to *Imperator Caesar Augustus.* Notice how in 1 Cor. 12:3 the confession of Jesus is connected with its opposite—cursing Jesus. I suspect that the scholars are right who have suggested that it was not in the first place the study of the Old Testament by early Christians or even the study of Jesus' teachings that prompted this confession but rather the experiences of the risen, and later of the ascended, Lord. Certainly the *maran atha* confession implies the heavenly position of Christ and his divine ability in due course to come.[6]

Our third text is Rom. 10:9, which is clearly in a confessional context. This text is important in several regards. First, we notice the parallel between confessing Jesus as Lord and believing that God raised him from the dead. This strongly suggests that the confessional formula entailed the proposition "Jesus is the risen Lord."[7] Second, in Paul's view, it is not only heartfelt belief but confessing with one's lips that is instrumental to being saved. We notice here again how the earliest post-Easter christological discussions seem to have focused on Jesus as Lord. Rom. 10:9 leads us to examine briefly another text widely regarded as reflecting a primitive confessional formula—Rom. 1:3–4.[8] Here two parallel phrases are applied to Jesus: (1) that he was born of the family of David according to the flesh and (2) that he was appointed or installed Son of God in power according to the Spirit of holiness[9] by resurrection from the dead. The result is that he is (3) Jesus Christ our Lord.

Several exegetical notes are necessary at this point. The phrase "in power" likely modifies Son of God, not "appointed." Second, the key word *horisthentos* most probably means "appointed" or "installed," not "declared." Third, it is possible to interpret the preposition *ek* to mean either "by" or "from" (the time of = since). Finally, it is possible to see three clauses here rather than two: (1) "his Son born of the seed of David according to the flesh; (2) appointed Son of God in power according to the Spirit of holiness; (3) since the resurrection of the dead, Jesus Christ our Lord." The confession then would have three parts, the first having to do with what Jesus was in himself by physical birth and then as a result of the work of God's Spirit in his life after death, and finally what he was to and for believers ever since the resurrection, namely, our Lord.

It is clear enough that Paul is saying not that Jesus became the Son of God at the resurrection, but that he became Son of God in power at that point, having previously been Son of God in weakness. The way the beginning of v. 3 is phrased also suggests that Paul saw Jesus as God's Son already at the point of his physical birth—it was the Son who was born of David's seed.

Whether one accepts the threefold division of the confession or not, it seems clear enough that the text is indicating that Jesus assumed the role of Lord over his followers since (and probably because of) his resurrection from the dead. We have already seen this clear connection between Jesus' resurrection and his Lordship from other texts.[10]

There is a good deal more that could be said about the early prayers and confessions of the first Jewish Christians, but we must summarize here the christological import of this material: (1) It was believed that it was appropriate to pray to or confess Jesus in the same way God was prayed to or confessed. (2) It was believed that it was appropriate to call Jesus, at least after his resurrection, by the title that was used in the Old Testament of God—*kyrios*. This title denoted a relationship between the believer and Jesus that formerly Jewish believers had only recognized as appropriate to describe the relationship of God and the believer. (3) It was believed that Jesus assumed after his resurrection a lordship role that he had not previously undertaken. (4) Closely parallel to (3) is the assumption that Jesus was installed (in heaven) as Son of God in power by means of the Spirit and after the resurrection.[11] (4) It was believed that Jesus as Lord would return at some point and this was prayed for. (5) It was believed that the Christian was enabled to be in a relationship to God the Father of the same level of intimacy that Jesus as a human being had while on earth, such that the Spirit prompted the Christian to call God ʾ*abbā*ʾ as Jesus had, and to recognize their filial relationship to God, which also made them heirs, jointheirs with Christ. (6) It was the Holy Spirit that was said to enable the believer to offer prayers from the heart to God and true confessions from the heart about Jesus to the world. But the early Christian not only prayed and confessed; they also sang, and we must now consider the hymn fragments found a variety of places in the New Testament.

SINGING CHRIST'S PRAISES

Well before the time of Jesus, early Jews were already singing the praises of God's Wisdom and Word as encapsulated in Torah, as can be seen even in the canonical Psalms (see Psalms 1 and 119). This praise developed considerably during the intertestamental time to include the praise of the Personification of Wisdom, as in texts such as Wisdom of Solomon 7–8.[12] Thus, when we come to the New Testament hymn fragments we are dealing not with creations out of nothing but with songs that drew on several sources for their material: (1) the Old Testament song book, Psalms; (2) Wisdom literature and in particular Wisdom hymns; and (3) early Christian material about the life, death, and exaltation of Jesus. It has been said that New Testament Christology was born in song, and to a certain extent this was true, but it is also fair to say that what was not necessarily born in song was certainly amplified and proclaimed in song.

Scholars have often been amazed at the high christological remarks found in these christological hymns, but if more attention had also been paid to the early prayers and confessional fragments the hymns would seem more of a natural development and less of a surprise. What this evidence shows is that to a large extent Christology grew out of early Christian experiences of the risen Lord both individually and in corporate worship, as well as out of early Christian reflection on the Gospel stories and Jesus' traditions. Lest we make too sharp a distinction between before Easter and after Easter, it is important to remember that the earliest christological prayers, confessions, and hymns were in all likelihood first formulated by some of those who had been a part of Jesus' ministry before Easter and could compare and relate the before and after factors that affected christological reflection. In general, the material in the hymns about Jesus' death and resurrection seems to draw on the early Gospel source material, while the material about the Son's preexistence and incarnation draws on the wisdom literature, and finally the material about Jesus' exaltation and roles at the right hand of God tends to draw on the Psalms.

It will be seen from close scrutiny of what follows that the early christological hymns had a characteristic V pattern chronicling the preexistence, earthly existence, and post-existence of the Son. In short, they were exercises in narrative Christology tracing the full career of the Son, not just his earthly ministry. This fuller presentation of Christ involved discussing his role in creation as well as redemption. That we find these hymn fragments in a variety of sources (Pauline letters, in Hebrews, in the Fourth Gospel) shows, as M. Hengel has stressed, that there was a much more unified structure to early christological thinking in a variety of Christian communities than some New Testament scholars are willing to recognize.[13]

The first hymn is found in Phil. 2:6–11. This is in some respects the fullest manifestation of the hymnic structure, with all three portions of the V—or perhaps better, U—pattern manifested. It is characteristic of these hymns that they tend to skip directly from the birth to the death of Christ, focusing on the moments of especial soteriological and christological importance during Jesus' earthly sojourn. We will start with a fresh translation.

Part I   Who, being in the form of God
Did not consider the having of equality with God something to
Take advantage of
But stripped/emptied himself
Taking the form of a servant
Being born in the likeness of human beings
And being found in appearance like a human being
Humbled himself, being obedient to the point of death,
Even death on the cross.

Part II That is why God has highly exalted him
And gave him the name, the one above all names,
In order that at the name of Jesus
All knees will bend—those in heaven, on earth,
   and under the earth
And all tongues confess publicly that Jesus Christ is LORD
Unto the glory of God the Father.

First, this hymn is not likely an attempt to contrast Christ with Adam, the latter the disobedient one who grasped at divinity, the former the obedient one who did not. This interpretation is largely based on a dubious rendering of the key term *harpagmos*. Nothing is said here about Jesus making a choice on earth parallel to Adam's choice in the garden. Rather, the choice to be a servant was made in heaven before the human nature was assumed. The characteristic language about the last Adam, or about Christ beginning a new race, or about Christ being the firstfruits of a new creation by mean of resurrection is entirely absent. Furthermore, an early Jewish Christian person, being thoroughly monotheistic, would not likely have thought it appropriate to call a human being such as Adam, even the last Adam, *kyrios*. The contrast between being in the form of God and becoming in the form of human beings would make little sense if what was being contrasted was two stages in the life of a mere mortal.

Our focus here is on the christological significance of the saying, not on its various sources, and so the following remarks will have to suffice. The term *morphē* always signifies an outward form that truly and fully expresses the real being that underlies it. As applied to Christ, this means that he not merely appeared to have the form of God but that he had a form that truly manifested the very nature and being of God. This is the reason the further phrase says what it does—Christ had equality with God: he had by right and nature what God had. In this matter it is useful to compare the parallel text in 2 Cor. 8:9, where the preexistent Christ is also said to humble himself and become poor for our sake.

The word *harpagmos* has been the subject of endless debate. Does it refer to something the person has and clutches to him, or does it refer to something he desires and tries to seize or grab? The clutching interpretation is nearer the mark, but the most probable way to read the word is that it means not taking advantage of something one rightfully already has. The contrast then between v. 6b and v. 7a becomes clear. Christ did not see being equal with God as something he had to take advantage of; rather, he stripped himself, which likely means he set aside his rightful divine prerogatives or perhaps his glory in order to be fully and truly human. This need not mean that he set his divine nature aside, only that he did not draw on his rightful divine prerogatives while on earth. He took on limitations of time, space, knowledge, and perhaps power while on earth. But in fact Christ went even further, identifying with the lowest sort of human—a slave, a person without any rights. When it says he humbled himself, the term has almost its literal secular sense that he became like a slave, one who must serve all others, one who is obedient even unto death.

The exaltation part of the hymn alludes to Isa. 45:21ff., which says that only God is God and Savior and that one should only bow to God.

Christ now is given God's very name and deserves this sort of homage. What we have here is what N. T. Wright calls "Christological monotheism," a form of monotheism that asserts the divinity of Christ but without taking away from the glory of the Father and without denying that there is only one true God.[14]

The hymn then is divided into two major parts that speak of what Christ chooses to do (vv. 6–8) and what God has done for him as result of what he did (vv. 9–11). In this hymn Christ is portrayed not simply as a wise man who makes good choices and is rewarded by God in the end but as God's very Wisdom, who comes to earth, is rejected, and yet is exalted by God in the end. Read in light of Wisdom of Solomon 1–11, or the more general profile of Wisdom already discussed previously,[15] or some of the material in Sirach 3 and 11, the text makes good sense. Already here we see a rather explicit christological affirmation of the divinity of Christ both before and after his earthly career—and presumably during as well, since the text does not say he gave up his divinity to become human. We shall see that some of these other hymns are no less explicit in their christological affirmations.

The next hymn is found in Col. 1:15–20 and focuses more on Christ's role in the work of creation and very little on his role since the resurrection. Paul and others have adopted and adapted these hymns to serve the specific purposes of the document in which a particular hymn is found.

Part I   Who is the image of the invisible God
Firstborn of all creation,
Because in Him were created all things
In the heavens and upon the earth,
The seen and the unseen,
Whether thrones or dominions
Or sovereignties or powers.
Everything [created] through Him was also created for Him.
And he is before everything and everything coheres in Him.
And he is the head of the body, the Church.

Part II   Who is the beginning (source), The firstborn from the dead,
In order that he might take precedence in all things.
Because in Him is pleased to dwell all the 'pleroma'
And through Him is reconciled everything for Him,
Making peace through the blood of his cross
Whether things on earth or in the heavens.

This hymn has a rather clear parallel structure in the two stanzas, especially at the beginning of each stanza. The first stanza is deeply indebted to Wis. Sol. 6:22–8:1 such that it is rather clear that the author of this hymn has simply taken various ideas and phrases that were applied to Wisdom in the Wisdom of Solomon and has applied them to the story of Christ's preexistence, though with certain subtle modifications. Philippians 2 and Colossians 1 contain the most similar of the hymn fragments, though there is no servant discussion in Colossians 1, and there is more distinctively non-Pauline vocabulary in the Colossians hymn. It is interesting that the nadir of the V pattern in this hymn is not Christ's incarnation or death, but rather the body or church, though Paul goes on to refer to making peace through the blood of the cross. Here as in the Philippians hymn Christ's being the image of God means that he is the exact likeness or representation of God, so much so that it is said that the fullness of God dwells in Christ.

The firstborn terminology is found in each stanza but in neither case should the reference to birth be taken literally. In the first stanza the Christ is said to be the author of all creation, so the term *prōto-tokos* probably doesn't refer to his being created but to his existence prior to all of creation and his precedence and supremacy over it, just as he also precedes all others in the resurrection of the dead. Verse 16 in fact stresses that Christ created even the supernatural powers and principalities, which began as good creatures, as did the human race. Then these powers fell and, like humans, are said to need reconciliation to God through Christ.

It seems that the idea of incarnation is already implied in this hymn as it was in the Philippians hymn, for the author is saying that the person who hung the stars and created the powers is the same person who died on the cross, was the first to experience resurrection, and became the reconciler of all things. This is not unthinkable, for already in Sirach 24 we find the idea of the incarnation of Wisdom on earth in the Torah. The new development here is simply the notion of an incarnation of and in a person. It is then not true to say that in John 1 for the first time we find the notion of incarnation. It is already at least implicit in Philippians 2 and Colossians 1.

Colossians 2:9 provides us with the proper commentary on the idea of *plērōma* in this hymn, which says that the whole "fullness" dwells in Christ bodily. This comment is perhaps polemical, meant to counter the idea that there might be a variety of intermediaries between God and humankind, each with a bit of the divine in them. Both here and in Philippians 2 there is a note of universalism at the end of the hymn. Philippians 2 says that all will bend the knee to Christ, but this may mean that some will do so willingly and some will be forced to recognize the Christ's position. Here too the meaning may be that in the end some will experience the *šālôm*, or peace, of being reconciled to God. Others will simply be pacified, but in either case all hostilities against God and God's people will cease when the work of salvation is complete. One should compare Wis. Sol. 5.1ff. on all of this. This hymn emphasizes the cosmic role of Christ in creation and thus implies his divine status even before he became the savior of all higher beings.

Our next hymn fragment, 1 Tim. 3:16, is also found in the Pauline corpus in one of its latest texts. This fragment says nothing explicitly about preexistence but rather speaks about the Christ's role on earth and beyond. It reads as follows:

> Who was revealed in flesh,
> Vindicated by the Spirit,
> Seen by angels,
> Proclaimed among the nations,
> Believed in throughout the world,
> Taken up in glory.

The first two lines of the hymn remind us of the statements about Christ in Rom. 1:3–4, but most of the ideas in this hymn fragment can also be found in 1 Pet. 3:18–22.[16] It is not surprising that all the verbs in this particular hymn fragment are passives. The second stanza of the hymn in Philippians 2 relates what God does to and for Christ, and this fragment is decidedly a second stanza, though the verb "revealed" in all likelihood presumes the preexistence of the one revealed.

It is not clear whether this hymn manifests a clear chronological order, but it probably does as follows: (1) The first clause alludes to preexistence and speaks of incarnation. (2) The second refers to Jesus' resurrection by the Holy Spirit (cf. Rom. 1:3–4). (3) The third phrase refers to Christ's ascent to heaven, during which he, according to the early tradition found in 1 Peter 3, preached to the spirits (i.e., angels) in prison (cf. also 2 Pet. 2:4 and Jude 6, where the reference is to the sinning angels referred to in Genesis 6). (4) Once exalted to God's side, Christ was first preached to the nations and then (5) believed in the world, (6) which resulted in glory for the Son (cf. how the hymn in Philippians 2 finished on the note of glory). This hymn once again stresses the universal scope of Christ's work, but it also for the first time stresses the role believers play in finishing the task of spreading salvation to the world. The allusions to Christ's preexistence and his glory are the primary portions of the hymn that hint at the divinity of Christ. As we shall see, glory is at the heart of the next hymn fragment.

The hymnic material in Heb. 1:2b–4 includes the entire V pattern, speaking of the preexistence, earthly existence, and post-existence of the Son. In the preexistence portion of the hymn, God is the actor, but thereafter Christ is the initiator of the action:

> Whom he appointed heir of all things,
> Through whom also he made the aeons (= universe);
> Who being the radiance of glory
> And the exact representation of his being,
> Upholding all things by his powerful word;
> Having made purification for sins,
> He sat down on the right hand of the Majesty on high,
> Having become as much better than the angels as he has,
> (He) has inherited a more excellent name in comparison to them.

The hymn fragment is found as part of the prologue of Hebrews meant to make clear that God's revelation in his Son was full, final, and definitive in a way that previous revelations were not, and that no other beings, including angels can compare to God's Son. The Son has more glory, a more excellent name and nature (being the exact representation of God), and he alone has made purification for sins a major issue in this homily. In Greek this fragment is part of one long sentence that stretches from v. 1 to v. 4 and involves alliteration and rhythm not evident in English translations. While the author of Hebrews in the main calls Jesus the Son, in fact in the hymn fragment Jesus is called by no title. Moreover, in none of the hymn fragments we are examining is Jesus called the Son. Sonship Christology seems to have arisen from another source or quarter. There are a variety of Old Testament texts being drawn on in this hymn (see, e.g., Deut. 32:43; Pss. 104:4; 45:6–7; 110:1; Psalm 2), but it is also clear enough that the author is steeped in later Wisdom material such as Wisdom of Solomon 7–8. The hymn says of the Son and his glory what had been previously said of God's Wisdom.

The hymn begins with the affirmation that God had a plan for the redeemer to be the inheritor of all things, and furthermore to be the agent through whom God created the universe. The theme of the Son as both aid in creation and inheritor of all things is by now familiar. It is the similarity of motifs and concepts in all of these hymns that shows that there was a core set of beliefs about Christ that was widely shared in early Jewish Christianity and was propagated through the use of this hymnic material in various parts of the Diaspora by Paul and others. Not only is the Christ involved in the beginning and end of all things, but he is the one upholding the universe by the word of his power. This is not dissimilar to the notion that in Christ all things cohere or hold together. In other words, the author does not see the universe as a watch that God wound up and left to run on its own.

In terms of Christology, v. 3a is very important. Here we find two key terms, *apaugasma* and *charaktēr.* The former word can be taken as active or passive in sense but in view of the background in Wis. Sol. 7:25f. it is likely to be active and to mean "effulgence" rather than simply "reflection." The difference is that a reflection is like a shadow, but not directly connected to the light source, whereas effulgence suggests a beam coming forth from that light source. The normal referent of the second term is to a stamp or impression that a signet ring leaves on wax or that a stamping device would make on a coin. The meaning would seem to be that the redeemer bears the exact likeness of God's nature. This material is remarkably close to what we have already seen in Col. 1:15–17, though with rearranged clauses.

While the author does not want to lead his audience to call the redeemer the Father, he does want to make clear that the redeemer is divine, is God's final self-expression and exact representation, and is thus higher in nature than any angel. The Son is not merely an act or power of God but a person who is the image of the Father, and so is to be worshiped as no mere angel should be. It may be right, as many have concluded, that this hymn is a rejoinder to those who wished to see Christ as some sort of special angelic being, but it is also possible that our author is stressing that the new covenant is superior to the one that was mediated by angels, namely, the Mosaic covenant (cf. Gal. 3:19; Acts 7:53; *Jub.* 1:29). This covenant is mediated by a divine being, not merely a supernatural one. It is striking that the author withholds the human name of the redeemer until 2:9, perhaps because he understood that the redeemer was, properly speaking, not Jesus until he took on a human nature.

It has been noted by various scholars that there is a closeness between this hymn and the one in Philippians 2 on the matter of Christ's obedience. In Philippians obedience is an aspect of Christ's relationship to the Father; obedience is presented in relation to the

way it benefits the Christian community. The discussion of purification followed by the Son's sitting at God's right hand requires a knowledge of sacrificial practices in antiquity. The author's point is that the
purification the Son made was once for all time, and so did not require
repetition. While other priests had to stand and offer sacrifices repeatedly, this priest did the job in such a definitive and final way that he
could sit down thereafter (cf. Heb. 10:11ff.). Here our author may be
drawing on Sir. 24:10, where it is said of Wisdom that she ministered
before God in the earthly Temple. The author's own distinctive christological thrusts can be seen and are served here as well, for he wishes
to say that Christ is the believers' heavenly high priest even now, and
that he is a priest forever, since he is an eternal being. The author is
combining various christological insights at the end of this hymn, in
particular combining the preexistent Wisdom Christology with the
enthronement of the Son at or after the resurrection Christology.[17]

The end of the hymn stresses God's endorsement of what the Son
has done. Not only is he given the favored right-hand seat, the side of
honor and power next to a ruler, but he is given a divine name or
throne name as well. This theme of receiving a name is found also in
Philippians 2, though here in Hebrews 1 we are not told explicitly
what the name is, only that it is a higher name than angels could have.
Notice, however, that here it is a matter of *inheriting* a better name.
The concept of a messianic figure not being called such until he has
completed his work is found elsewhere in *Testament of Levi* 4:2, 3 and
3 Enoch 12:15. The influence of *1 Enoch* 42 is also possible at the end
of this hymn, for in the Enoch text Wisdom takes her seat among, but
as one superior to, the angels when she returns from earth to heaven.

This christological hymn shows how a variety of rich traditions can
be drawn on and blended together to present a striking and divine
image of God's Son as an eternal being who bears God's exact likeness.
It is another example of christological monotheism, which perhaps
receives its ultimate expression in our final hymn text—the prologue
in John 1.

There are at least four stanzas to the hymn material in John 1, and
most scholars see this material as the apex of the expression of incarnational thinking about Christ in the canon. We have seen that the
idea of incarnation was likely present in Philippians 2, Colossians 1,
and Hebrews 1, if not also in 1 Timothy, and so what we find in this
hymn is not a radical departure from what we have seen in the christological hymns, but a further development thereof. There are several

major themes in this hymn including: (1) the preexistent Word (*logos*); (2) the Word and creation; (3) the response of those created (rejection); (4) incarnation and revelation; (5) the response of the faithful community ("we have seen his glory"). The first two stages of the V pattern is what this hymn concentrates on (preexistence and earthly existence). Like the hymn in Hebrews 1, the material in John 1 is used to establish at the outset the character and career of the main person of the book. The author of the Fourth Gospel is, however, concerned about where the Word is going as well as where it came from. Especially in this Gospel it is evident that one cannot truly understand the Christ and his character unless one knows about his divine origins and destiny. In all probability vv. 6–9 on John the Baptist are not an original part of the hymn, which in its most primitive form would likely be as follows:

> In the beginning was the Word
> And the Word was with God,
> And the Word was God.
> He was with God in the beginning.
>
> Through Him all things were made.
> Without him nothing came to be.
> In him was life,
> And this life was the light of humankind.
> The light shines in the darkness,
> And the darkness has not overcome/understood it.
>
> He was in the world,
> And though the world was made by Him,
> It did not recognize/respond to Him.
> To his own he came.
> Yet his own did not receive Him.
> But all those who did accept Him,
> He empowered to become children of God.
> [Verses 12b–13 are the author's explanatory insertion about how one becomes such a child.]
>
> And the Word became flesh,
> And dwelt among us.
> And we beheld his glory.
> The glory of the only begotten Son of the Father,
> Full of grace and truth.

It has often been noted that this hymn is indebted to Genesis 1, but less frequently has it been recognized that in fact this hymn is indebted to the sapiential interpretation of Genesis 1 in places like Proverbs 3 or 8:1–9:6. Torah and Wisdom are seen as interrelated, the former being the consummate expression on earth of the latter, according to Wisdom literature (see Sirach 24). One needs also to keep in mind the interplay of Wisdom and Word in the Wisdom of Solomon. The two terms are used in parallel in Wis. Sol. 9:1–2; in 9:10 it is Wisdom that is said to be sent from God's throne by God; and in 18:15 God's "all powerful Word leaped from heaven, from the royal throne into the midst of the land. . . ." At the very end of this hymn we learn, however, that the Son or Word eclipses this Torah. Interestingly, in Sir. 24:8 Wisdom is said to tent in Israel in Torah. In other words, what has been previously said about Torah as the repository of Wisdom is now being said of Jesus. Phrases that were familiar in early Judaism are being used in this hymn. See, for example, 1QS 11:11: "All things come to pass by his knowledge. He establishes all things by his design, and without Him nothing is done [or made]." The phrase "full of grace and truth" is reminiscent of the idea in the Colossians hymn of Christ being the *plērōma,* or fullness, of God, another hint that all of these hymns likely came out of the same situation in life.

The very first verse is perhaps the most important verse of the prologue, and indeed of the whole Gospel. The author wants to make clear from the outset that the deeds and words of Jesus, God's Word and Son, are the deeds and words of a divine being. The *Logos* is not a created supernatural being, for he existed prior to all creation. The Son is said to be *monogenēs.* This may mean that he is unique, but more probably means that like produces like. The Son has come forth from the Father having the same nature, not like those other distinct beings who were made by the Father and the Word. Jesus, then, is seen as the natural Son of God, while others are the adopted sons and daughters of God through the new birth.

The Word is said to be involved in the whole scope of the divine work. Nothing was created and nothing is saved without him. Light and life are benefits of both the creation and the re-creation that come from and through the Word. There is great irony in what is said in stanza 3, namely, that the creatures rejected the one who created them when they rejected his offer of salvation. The real statement of the incarnation does not come until v. 14, when we are told that the Word took on flesh, or reached the human stage. The Word became more than he was before, not less, adding a human nature to his divine nature. There is no emptying language here. E. Käsemann has said that in this whole Gospel Jesus bestrides the stage like a God, and there is some truth to this claim.

Although the Word was on earth only for a limited time, so that only some saw his glory, nonetheless all have an opportunity to benefit from the Word's coming, all can received grace and truth at any time by believing. Truth in this Gospel always refers to saving truth, not simply accurate information. While Moses and Torah gave accurate information about God's will and plan, the Word gave the ability to perform God's will and to truly understand that plan. Though it is a bit of an overstatement, E. D. Freed was basically right when he remarked: "It may not be going too far to say that the writer of the *logos* verses in John has scarcely done more than add the technical term *logos* to a Christology which had already been formulated by Paul and others. . . ."[18]

We must now draw our discussion of the hymns to a close. The creators of these various hymns were concerned to make clear that the subject being discussed was a person, not merely a divine attribute or power of God. In each of these hymns, in one way or another whether through reference to death on a cross, making purification for sins, or being in the flesh, the author makes clear that he is talking about a real human figure who acted on the stage of history. In other words, there was an attempt to guard against these hymns being taken as mere myth making. When Jewish Christians composed these hymns, they were looking for exalted language and found it in their Jewish heritage. They used the language to give expression to their faith in Christ. They found particularly appropriate earlier hymnic material praising God's Wisdom, such as Proverbs 8–9, Sirach 24, or Wisdom of Solomon 7–9. It seems probable that these Christian hymns were first composed in Greek, especially in view of their indebtedness to Wisdom of Solomon. Thus, they may have originated in the Diaspora, but this is not necessarily the case. There were already Greek-speaking Christians in the earliest Jerusalem church, if we are to believe Acts 6–7. In any case, there is no reason to see any of these hymns as reflecting late Gentile thinking about Jesus.

The hymns are thoroughly Jewish in their concepts and phrases, and even in the V pattern they are indebted to earlier Jewish literature about Wisdom. The earliest Christians were groping for a way to adequately praise the divine Christ and at the same time not relinquish a belief in the one true God. The early Jewish discussion of the relationship between God and God's Wisdom facilitated this sort of christological development, and this surely transpired well before the Gospels were ever written. We must now look closely at another source used in the New Testament for what it shows about the christological reflections of the earliest Jewish Christians—the so-called Q material.

EARLY TEACHINGS OF AND ABOUT THE CHRIST

It is entirely possible that the Q material was collected before some of the christological hymns were ever composed, but we cannot be sure about this. The Q material is primarily, though not exclusively, sayings material. It includes also all the non-Markan material that Matthew and Luke share in common, including such major collections as the Sermon on the Mount. The Q material was not focused primarily on christological issues but rather on pedagogical ones. There are, however, texts in Q that depict Jesus as God's Wisdom.[19] In fact, I have argued elsewhere at considerable length that not just a few pericopes but the entire editing of Q was done with certain sapiential agendas in mind, part of which intended to portray Jesus not only as a great sage who told numerous parables and aphorisms but as God's Wisdom.[20] This is illustrated in the following table:[21]

A. The story of Jesus the Sage/Wisdom
   1. The Forerunner and the Announcement of the Sage's Coming (by John) (Luke 3:2–9/Matt. 3:1–10; Luke 3:15–17/ Matt. 3:11–12)
   2. The Anointing of the Sage with the Spirit (Luke 3:21–22/ Matt. 3:13–16)
   3. The Testing of the Sage (Luke 4:1–13/Matt. 4:1–11)
   4. The Sermon of the Sage (Luke 6:20–49/Matthew 5–7)
   5. The Wonder-working of the Sage (Luke 7:1–10/Matt. 8:5–10)
   6. The Questioning of the Sage (by John) (Luke 7:18–23/ Matt. 11:2–6)
   7. The Response of the Sage (Luke 7:24–38/Matt. 11:7–11)
   8. The Rejection of the Sage by "This Generation" (Luke 7:31–35/Matt. 11:16–19)
   PART ONE ENDS WITH THE REVELATION OF JESUS AS WISDOM— "Yet Wisdom is vindicated by her deeds" (Matt. 11:19).

B. Discipleship to Jesus the Sage—its Character and Mission
    9. Discipleship's Cost (Luke 9:57–62/Matt. 8:19–22)
   10. Discipleship's Mission (Luke 10:1–24/Matthew 9–11 [portions])
      a. The Mission Speech (Luke 10:1–12/Matt. 9:37–38/ 10:5–16)
      b. Woe on Galilean cities (Luke 10:13–15/Matt. 11:20–24)
      c. Authority of Missionaries (Luke 10:16–20/Matt. 10:40)
      d. Thanksgiving and Blessing (Luke 10:21–24/Matt. 11:25–27; 13:16–17)
   11. The Disciple's Prayer and Praying (Luke 11:2–4, 5–13/Matt. 6:7–13; 7:7–11)
      PART TWO ENDS WITH DISCIPLES URGED TO SEEK HELP FROM ABOVE.

C. The Wars and Woes of the Sage/Wisdom
   12. Struggling with Satan (Luke 11:14–26/Matt. 12:22–30, 43–45)
   13. Signs of Trouble (Luke 11:29–32/Matt. 12:38–42)
   14. The Light of One's Life (Luke 11:33–36/Matt. 5:15; 6:22–23)
   15. The Woes of Wisdom (Luke 11:42–52/Matthew 23 [portions])
      PART THREE ENDS WITH THE "Wisdom of God Said"—
      SEVENTH WOE ON THOSE WHO WOULD BE SAGES (cf. Luke 11:52/ Matt. 23:13).

D. The Revelations of Wisdom
   16. Hidden and Revealed (Luke 12:2–3/Matt. 10:26–27)
   17. Wisdom's Persecuted Followers (Luke 12:4–7/Matt. 10:28–31)
   18. Acknowledging the Sage and the Spirit (Luke 12:8–12/Matt. 10:19, 32–33)
   19. Wisdom in Nature (Luke 12:22–31/Matt. 6:25–33)
   20. The Treasures of Wisdom (Luke 12:32–34/Matt. 6:19–21)
   21. Preparation for Wisdom's Feast (Luke 12:35–40/Matt. 24:43–44)
   22. Preparation for Wisdom's Return (Luke 12:42–48/Matt. 24:45–51)
   23. Wisdom's Second Baptism (Luke 12:49–50)

24. Divisions over Wisdom and Her Demise (Luke 12:51–53/
    Matt. 10:34–36)
25. Signs of Trouble II (Luke 12:54–56/Matt. 16:2–3)
26. Time to Settle Accounts (Luke 12:57–59/Matt. 5:25–26)
27. The Lament of Wisdom for Jerusalem (Luke 13:34–35/
    Matt. 23:37–39)

PART FOUR ENDS WITH REJECTION OF WISDOM AT THE HEART OF
THE NATION. JERUSALEM'S HOUSE IS FORSAKEN AND WISDOM
WON'T RETURN UNTIL BEATITUDE IS PRONOUNCED ON WISDOM.

E. The Narrative Parables and Aphorisms of the Sage/Wisdom
    28. Seed and Leaven (Luke 13:18–21/Matt. 13:31–33)
    29. Gate and Door (Luke 13:23–27/Matt. 7:13–14, 22–23)
    30. East and West/Last and First (Luke 13:28–30/Matt.
        8:11–12/20:16)
    31. Wisdom's Banquet (Luke 14:15–24/Matt. 22:1–10)
    32. The Cost of Discipleship (Luke 14:5–27/Matt. 10:37–38)
    33. Old Salt (Luke 14:34–35/Matt. 5:13)
    34. Lost Sheep (Luke 15:3–7/Matt. 18:12–14)
    35. Lost Coin (Luke 15:8–10)

PART FIVE ENDS WITH WISDOM'S SEARCH FOR THE LOST.

F. Discipleship at the Turn of the Era
    36. Choosing Whom to Serve—God or Mammon (Luke 16:13/
        Matt. 6:24)
    37. The End of Torah's Era? (Luke 16:16–17/Matt. 11:12–13 [cf.
        5:18])
    38. The End of a Marriage (Luke 16:18/Matt. 5:32)
    39. Sins and Forgiveness (Luke 17:1–4/Matt. 18:7, 21–22)
    40. Mustard Seed Faith (Luke 17:5–6/Matt. 17:20)

PART SIX ENDS WITH ASSURANCE TO DISCIPLES THAT EVEN SMALL
FAITH CAN WORK GREAT MIRACLES.

G. The End of the Age
    41. Against False Hopes (Luke 17:22–23/Matt. 24:26)
    42. Like Lightning (Luke 17:24/Matt. 24:27)
    43. Like Vultures (Luke 17:37/Matt. 24:28)
    44. Like Noah's and Lot's Time (Luke 17:26–30/Matt.
        24:37–39)
    45. No Turning Back (Luke 17:31–32/Matt. 24:17–18)

46. Find Life by Losing It (Luke 17:33/Matt. 10:29)
47. Division of Laborers (Luke 17:34–35/Matt. 24:40–41)
48. Parable of the Talents (Luke 19:11–27/Matt. 25:14–30)
49. At Tables and on Thrones in the Kingdom (Luke 22:28–30/ Matt. 19:28)

PART SEVEN IS AN ESCHATOLOGICAL DISCOURSE, ENDING WITH PROMISE OF REUNION AND ROLES WITH JESUS.

A close analysis shows that the Q material is basically grouped into two kinds of data, oscillating between a focus on Jesus as sage or Wisdom and on discipleship, until the final section of Q, where we have an eschatological discourse.[22] It is in this discourse that we find the roles of Jesus and the disciples coming together, and we discover the moral results of rejecting or following Jesus. Sections B and F focus more on discipleship; A, C, D, and E more on the presentation of Jesus as sage or Wisdom. Notice that A, C, D, E all end with a personification of Wisdom or Jesus speaking as Wisdom.

The significance and preeminence of Jesus are established in the Q tradition in two ways: (1) by the identification of Jesus with Wisdom, who has already come and been rejected, and (2) by the identification of Jesus as Son of Man, in particular the future Son of Man who is yet to come. The two concepts often come together, for instance, in the Son of Man saying about nests.[23] If one takes all of this material together, the overall impression is that Jesus is a prophetic sage, one in whom the sapiential and prophetic/ eschatological traditions come together and come to full expression. He is one like, yet greater than, Solomon. He is anointed with the fullness of the Spirit, resists every temptation, and performs wonders and miracles that surpass what Jewish folklore predicated of Solomon. Most significantly, at the conclusion of several of the major sections of Q, Jesus is rather clearly identified as Wisdom come in the flesh, Wisdom who is vindicated by her deeds, Wisdom who seeks the lost or laments over Jerusalem as a mother over her children.

It is precisely the combination of the Son of Man and Wisdom that assures us that we are at an early stage in the thinking about Jesus, a stage in which this material is being handled by Jewish Christians steeped in the Old Testament and intertestamental prophetic and sapiential literature. It will be worthwhile to look briefly at some of the Son of Man material in Q a little more closely. First, in Q we find both the present Son of Man, who eats and drinks with sinners, and also the future Son of Man, who will intervene at the close of the age.[24] There is also considerable stress on sorting out the relationship between Jesus and John in collections of material such as Luke 7:18–35 and par. It is interesting that by the end of this collection of material John is clearly distinguished from Jesus as not the Son of Man, just as at the beginning of the collection he is distinguished from Jesus as not a miracle worker. G. N. Stanton points to the association of Isa. 52:7 and 61:1 in 11QMelchisedek, identifying the proclaimer of Good News with God's Anointed One. Reading the Q material in this light it suggests that the author of Q is also portraying Jesus as the Messiah who has finally come to bring in the New Age. In other words, this material tries not only to answer the question about the relationship of Jesus and John but also to make a statement about who Jesus was in himself. Thus, despite disclaimers by some scholars, Q does reflect an interest in important christological questions.

This conviction can only be strengthened when we examine the Q material on the baptism and temptation of Jesus, where the issue of whether Jesus is the Son of God is repeatedly raised. Notice that in the Q material the voice at Jesus' baptism is confirming Jesus as God's Son, even to the public in the Matthean form of the text (see Matt. 3:17 and par.), and there is no hint of adoptionist notions about the begetting of the Son at this point. In Luke's version (3:21ff.) John the Baptist's name is not even mentioned, and in the Matthean form of the text a clear attempt is made to portray John as a lesser figure, unworthy to baptize Jesus.

Another major emphasis in Q with christological implications is that in and with the ministry of Jesus the dominion of God is dawning. One may compare Matt. 12:28/Luke 11:20 with the Q beatitude in Matt. 5:3/Luke 6:20b. Most scholars regard Matt. 11:2–6/Luke 7:18–23 as the first Q pericope, and here we find the theme of Jesus bringing the eschatological and messianic blessings. The theme of Jesus as bringer of the climactic age or revelation or blessing is also apparent in Matt. 13:16f./Luke 10:23f.

Stanton sums up: "The Q material answers the questions 'Who was Jesus?' 'With what authority did he act and speak?' In other words it does contain Christological material—in the broadest sense of the term." Q also stresses "that the one anointed with God's Spirit, whose words and actions marked the dawn of God's age of salvation, was rejected by those to whom he was sent."[25]

It is not at all clear to me that we should talk about a Q community, if by that one means a community that had no traditions about Jesus except what we find in Q. Rather, we should likely think in terms of early Jewish Christian communities that used sayings collections such as we find in Q before the Gospels were written beginning in the late 60s. In view of the skillful sapiential arranging and shaping of the materials reflected in Q, it is believable that the collection was put together and edited by a Jewish Christian scribe (or scribes) who was something of a sage himself. This person was steeped in Jewish Wisdom material and sought to highlight the traditions that portrayed Jesus as sage and Wisdom. The lack of a Torah-centric orientation to Q does not discredit this notion, as there were many kinds of early scribes and not all were Pharisaic Torah scholars.

In order to show how Jesus differed from previous scribes or sages, the author of Q presented Jesus as not only sage but also Wisdom, as not only wise man but also Son of Man. In other words, the christological fruit in Q has not fallen far from the tree of Jesus' own self-presentation which bore it. Something greater than Solomon had come into Israel's midst. Indeed, something greater than just another son of man had come into Israel's midst. Wisdom, the Son of Man, had done so in person. This the editor or editors of Q brought to the fore.

THE EARLIEST CHRISTOLOGICAL USE OF THE OLD TESTAMENT

Our last clue to the Christology of the earliest Jewish Christians comes from a scrutiny of how they appear to have used the Old Testament in their christological reflections. This subject has frequently been addressed.[26] This christological use occurs in a variety of places, but here we will focus on some of the primitive material found in the first half of Acts. It is easy enough to point to midrashic or Jewish contemporizing treatments of the Old Testament, for instance, Psalm 2 in Acts 4:25–26 and 13:33 and Amos 9:11 in Acts 15:17. Especially to be noted is the use of *pais theou*, literally, "child of God." Is this to be taken as another way of calling Jesus Son of God, or, with another meaning of *pais*, is it as a reference to Jesus as Servant of God? In any case, the notion of the decree of God found in Psalm 2 is echoed in various places in the speech material in Acts, alluding to Christ as a royal figure. For example, in Acts 10:42 Jesus is called the one "decreed by God as judge of the living and the dead." Or again, the free use of the

verb "to raise up" in Acts 33:22–23, 26 and, 4:2 alludes to texts like
Hos. 6:2, used in the Targums to refer to resurrection, and quoting
texts like Deut. 15:18.

It seems clear that there were certain key terms or catchwords that
triggered the use of particular texts in application to Jesus. For
instance, Scriptures that contained the word "stone" were used
together to make a point about the rejection and acceptance of Jesus by
God's people and God, for example, combining Ps. 118:22 and Isa.
28:16 in Acts 4:11. The "this is that" or *pesher* use of the Old Testament is found in a variety of places in Acts, for example, in Acts 2,
where Peter indicates that what Joel spoke of was happening on Pentecost. Or notice the technique of transference, where in Acts 2:21 and
4:21, Joel 2:32 (Masoretic Text) is cited referring to "calling on the
name of the Lord." Of course in Joel "Lord" refers to Yahweh, but in
Acts the text is used of Christ (cf. Rom. 10:13), and it spawns other
allusions, for example, in Acts 3:16, where we find the peculiar phrase
"his name, through faith in his name" where Jesus' name is meant as
in other early Jewish Christian literature (cf. James 2:7).

When we examine some of the primitive christological material in
Acts, we find repeated instances of the Psalms and prophetic material
being drawn on to make points about Jesus (e.g., Ps. 2:7 used in Acts
13:33; Ps. 16:10 in Acts 2:25–28 and 13:35; Ps. 110:1 in Acts 2:34–35;
Ps. 132:11 in Acts 2:30; Isa. 53:7–8 in Acts 8:32–33; Isa. 55:3 in Acts
13:34; Amos 9:11–12 in Acts 15:15–17; Joel 2:28–32 in Acts 2:17–21).
More to the point, the *way* the texts are used reflects techniques found
in early Jewish material especially at Qumran and in some of the material in *1 Enoch.*

We may distinguish a good deal of this from Luke's preferred use of
Scriptures, for "one of his major concerns is to show that Jesus is truly
the fulfillment of the Scriptures, as is seen in numerous of his summary statements (Luke 24:25–26, 45–47; Acts 3:18, 24; 10:13; 17:2–3;
18:28; 24:14–15; 26:22–23; 28:23)."[27] There is no evidence that Luke
knew Aramaic—or for that matter the finer points about Jewish
exegetical and homiletical techniques—so a good deal of the material
we have examined must go back to the earliest Jewish Christians' handling of Old Testament material as a way to interpret the Christ-event.
Both M. Black and C. A. Evans have shown that a knowledge of how
these texts were handled in the Qumran literature or in the Targums
illuminates the use we find of these Scriptures in the early portions of
Acts.

We may also check our conclusions on these matters by way of cross-reference. For instance, two of the favorite texts used for christological purposes in Peter's speech in Acts 2—Joel 2:32 and Ps. 110:1 are alluded to not only elsewhere in Acts (Acts 8:16; 9:10–17; 15:26; 22:13–16) but also in the Pauline corpus in the hymn in Phil. 2:9–11. It is correspondences like this that reassure us that here we have yet another window on the christological reflections of the earliest Jewish Christians.

Finally, there are certain christological titles that crop up in the earlier speeches in Acts that seem to have a scriptural background but do not reflect Lukan tendencies or predilections (Luke tends to stick with the tried and true formulae—*christos* as a name and *kyrios*)[28] and so may also tell us about the christological reflections of the earliest Jewish Christians. I am thinking, for instance, of the use of *christos* as a title (e.g., Acts 3:18, 20; 5:42), the use of *pais* probably to refer to Christ as God's child (3:26; see above), and the reference to Christ as our leader (*archēgos*) and Savior (Acts 5:31). The latter title is uncommon in Luke-Acts, and the former we find in another early Jewish Christian document, the letter to the Hebrews (12:2). Another interesting early title found in the speech material in Acts is Righteous One (7:52). These data suggest that the christological reflections in Acts 1–15, including the use of the Old Testament, often reveal the views of Luke's sources and not necessarily Luke's views of the Christ.

CONCLUSIONS

We have analyzed, in all too cursory a fashion, a very wide range of data meant to give us a glimpse of the Christology—or, better said Christologies—of the earliest Jewish Christians. It seemed clear from analyzing the relevant Aramaic phrases in the New Testament that very early on Jewish Christians were worshiping not only God as *'abbā'* but also Jesus as the Lord, and praying for his return. They were also confessing "Jesus is Lord," by which they seem to have meant that he is the risen Lord and their Lord or Master since the resurrection. This christological evidence indicates that already the earliest Christians were expanding the horizons of what monotheism meant, for one did not pray to, worship, or confess as ultimate anyone less than God. This was a post-Easter development, for we saw clearly enough from a text like Rom. 1:3–4 that Christians were prepared to say some new and different things about Jesus as a result of the resurrection. He had assumed the role of Son of God in power since the resurrection and thus was appropriately called the (risen) Lord.

If we were looking for the origins of high Christology, it would appear that a good deal of it goes back to early Jewish Christian liturgy and worship, as is intimated not only by the prayers and confessions of the earliest Christians but also by their hymns. We noticed in these hymns the use of Wisdom traditions to discuss the preexistence of God's Son, Gospel traditions to refer to his earthly work, and then Old Testament Scriptures such as Ps. 110:1 to aid in the description of his exaltation. In each case it was not the Scriptures or traditions that suggested the Christology. Rather, the reflection on and worship of Jesus by early Christians caused them to go back and look at the Scriptures in a new light and to use these texts to express their new faith. The V pattern of the christological hymns seems clearly indebted to the early Jewish speculations about personified Wisdom. The application of these materials to Christ led to the discussion of such subjects as the Son's incarnation and his role in creation. The crucial point to be made about this material is that the very earliest of these hymns already implicitly suggests the incarnation of the Son by the way it discusses his preexistence. This earliest hymn, found in Philippians 2, also makes clear that there was no difficulty in using God's name of the Son or in discussing the universal worship of the Son, even by angels.

The subsequent hymns expanded on these ideas, further developing the understanding of the Son's role in creation, or his role in heaven, or the sacrificial character of his death, but so far as the issue of high Christology is concerned, we do not see any radical innovations or departures, even in John 1. The *logos* hymn has simply further developed ideas that were already latent in the earlier christological hymns, taking the use of the Wisdom material as a cue for how the expansion could and perhaps should go. These hymns stress that Christ is both the creator and the redeemer of his creation, but interestingly they say only the bare minimum about his earthly life—referring to his incarnation, his rejection, his death. Nevertheless, the latter was sufficient to make clear that the hymns were not simply exercises in myth making. Jesus was a recent historical figure, whom some people still remembered when the earliest of these hymns were created.

The Q material provides us with another window on earliest christological thinking, and here we saw how the Wisdom and Son of Man themes already present in the self-presentation of Jesus were further developed or unfolded. There was also a clear Son of God theology reflected in some of the early narrative material in Q, as well as implicit Christology to be gleaned from the way Jesus' relationship to John was discussed. In some respects, the Q material seems to stand closest to the self-expression of the historical Jesus, while the prayers, confessions, and hymns reflect more of the post-Easter situation.

Finally, we looked briefly at the christological use of the Old Testament and found a variety of Jewish techniques being implemented to make the material serviceable for christological reflection. Here too there was no difficulty in predicating God's name of Christ (or calling him "the Name"), as well as applying royal texts to him. We also saw a variety of titles that were not much used later in the first century by Christians, but these were being used of Christ in the early speech material in Acts.

Taken together this material presents a remarkable overview of how Jews could say so much about Jesus and still remain monotheists. There is nothing in the material we have discussed in this chapter that requires the theory that these christological reflections are impossible or alien to earliest Jewish Christianity, especially when the hellenization and sapientialization of early Judaism even in Israel are taken into account. Some of the highest christological material in the New Testament may be some of the earliest.[29] What we find when we turn to the works of that early Jewish Christian Paul is no radical departure from what we have already discovered, though it certainly is a fuller and fresh development of various christological possibilities. It is to the Pauline corpus that we must now turn.

NOTES

1. Though somewhat dated, in many ways the study of R. N. Longenecker entitled *The Christology of Early Jewish Christianity* (reprint, Grand Rapids: Baker, 1981) is still the most valuable of works that are in English. Even more dated, though still somewhat useful, is F. Hahn's, *The Titles of Jesus in Christology* (London: Lutterworth, 1969), esp. pp. 148–68. The basic problem with Hahn is that he assumes there was a normative or standard concept of a political Messiah that both Jesus and the earliest Palestinian church sought to avoid, and thus the early church did not think of Jesus in messianic terms before or immediately after the crucifixion.

2. See pp. 61ff. above.

3. Note, however, that ʾabbāʾ is clearly translated as "Father" here, which

may suggest that the Gentiles in the audience were told the meaning of this word early on, and in mixed congregations the translation became part of the form of address. It could also be that the translation is not part of the prayer, but in each case simply Paul's translation of the prayer for his audiences.

4. See C. F. D. Moule, *The Origin of Christology* (Cambridge: Cambridge University Press, 1977), p. 41.

5. R. H. Fuller rightly stressed this some time ago (*The Foundations of New Testament Christology* [New York: Scribner, 1965], pp. 156–58). This means that the older notion that there was a considerable period of time between Jesus as proclaimer and Jesus as the proclaimed, between implicit and explicit Christology, simply does not do justice to the data as we have it. Hahn tries unsuccessfully to avoid the conclusion that *marana tha* implies an exalted view of Jesus as the sort of being a Jewish person could worship (*Titles of Jesus*, pp. 95–98).

6. The fact that there was expectation even in this earliest period that Christ himself would return casts doubts on the older notions that originally Jesus spoke of someone else as the future coming Son of Man but that the church changed these sayings so that they would refer to Jesus himself. There is certainly no evidence of such a transformation and transference in the earliest New Testament documents, the Pauline letters, and this must cast serious doubts on the suggestion that there is implicit evidence of this in the Synoptics. See the discussion in Fuller, *Foundations*, pp. 144ff. Fuller rightly also notes that there is no clear evidence in Q of any "secondary" future sayings, but surely it is during the time Q was being formulated that this transformation took place, if at all. If there is no evidence in Paul or Q of such a transformation, the idea should be abandoned.

7. See Hahn, *Titles of Jesus*, pp. 103–17.

8. For a fuller discussion of this important text, see my *Paul's Narrative Thought World* (Louisville: Westminster, 1994), pp. 117–19. It is interesting that Paul, Mark, and the speeches of Acts reflect no knowledge that Jesus was born in Bethlehem, and yet all of these sources know of and affirm the claim that he was of Davidic descent. See Fuller, *Foundations*, pp. 164–65. This suggests that some scholars have made too much of these sources' silence about Bethlehem.

9. This way of describing the Spirit is not at all characteristic of Paul and likely indicates that he is drawing on an earlier Jewish Christian source that placed high stress on Jesus' Davidic descent in a way that Paul really does not.

10. One of the clearest signs of the datedness of Hahn's work is his overly neat distinctions between Palestinian and Hellenistic Judaism, on the one hand, and Palestinian and Hellenistic Christianity, on the other, in view of the degree to which Palestinian Judaism was hellenized in and after Jesus' day. The christological material in Paul's letters reflects Jewish thinking about Jesus, and largely Palestinian Jewish Christian thinking about Jesus. There is hardly anything in the Pauline corpus that can be called purely Hellenistic or pagan

in origin if we are discussing Christology. But see Hahn, *Titles of Jesus,* pp. 191–93.

11. Several of the speeches in Acts also reflect this primitive Christology; see Acts 5:31; 2:36. Acts 2:33 says that Jesus did not receive the promised Spirit to bestow until he was exalted. In these various so-called adoptionist texts it is not so much Jesus becoming something he wasn't before (a matter of ontology) but rather his assuming roles and tasks he had not assumed or done before (a matter of function in relationship to others).

12. See my discussion in *Jesus the Sage: The Pilgrimage of Wisdom* (Minneapolis: Fortress Press, 1994), pp. 249–94, and the literature cited there.

13. M. Hengel, "Christological Titles in Early Christianity," in *The Messiah: Developments in Earliest Judaism and Christianity,* ed. J. H. Charlesworth (Minneapolis: Fortress Press, 1992), pp. 425–48, here p. 443.

14. See N. T. Wright, *The Climax of the Covenant. Christ and the Law in Pauline Theology* (Edinburgh: T & T Clark, 1991), p. 116.

15. See pp. 17ff. above.

16. On which see below pp. 207ff.

17. See J. P. Meier, "Structure and Theology in Heb. 1.1–4," *Biblica* 66 (1985): 168–89.

18. E. D. Freed, "Theological Prelude and the Prologue of John's Gospel," *Scottish Journal of Theology* 32 (1979): 257–69, here p. 266.

19. See pp. 93ff. above.

20. See my *Jesus the Sage,* pp. 211–36.

21. This table appears in a slightly different form in *Jesus the Sage,* pp. 219–21.

22. We have followed the convention that Luke better preserves the order of Q. It is also my view that Luke has tended to edit the Q material more for the sake of his Gentile audience, and so often, but by no means always, we find the earlier, more Jewish form of a text or saying in the Matthean form of the material.

23. See pp. 56ff. above.

24. See G. N. Stanton, "On the Christology of Q," in *Christ and the Spirit in the New Testament* (Cambridge: Cambridge University Press, 1973), pp. 27–42.

25. Ibid., p. 41.

26. See, e.g., M. Black, "The Christological Use of the Old Testament in the New Testament," *New Testament Studies* 18 (1971–72): 1–14.

27. C. A. Evans and J. A. Sanders, *Luke and Scripture* (Minneapolis: Fortress Press, 1993), p. 211.

28. See my discussion of Lukan Christology in Acts in my forthcoming commentary on Acts with Eerdmans.

29. At the end of his survey of this pre-Pauline period Fuller characterizes the formulations of Palestinian Christianity as conveying "in terms of an explicit Christology precisely what Jesus had implied about himself through-

out his ministry" (*Foundations,* p. 173). This is in large measure correct, although as we have seen Jesus was at least occasionally more explicit about his self-understanding than some scholars have thought. Fuller in his later writings argues that Jesus had "something which comes pretty close to an incarnation consciousness. . . . Jesus understood himself as the one through whom God was uttering his last eschatological word to Israel, by which [hu]mans salvation or damnation would be decided. He understood himself as the one in whom God was decisively and eschatologically at work. The resurrection does not create this assessment of Jesus" ("The Clue to Jesus' Self-Understanding," in his *Christ and Christianity: Studies in the Formation of Christology* [Valley Forge, Penn.: Trinity Press International, 1994], p. 45). He thus stresses that the difference or discontinuity pre- and post-Easter in Christology is terminological, the difference between the implicit and the explicit.

4

Christ Crucified:
Pauline Christology

AULINE CHRISTOLOGY is for many such familiar territory that it
comes as a shock when it is discovered that among early Christians and even in the New Testament there were other significant ways of envisioning the Christ. Especially in Protestant circles
Christ has tended to be viewed through the eyes of Paul, and all other
presentations have been measured against the Pauline one and often
found wanting. This is unfortunate, but perhaps inevitable, because of
the depth and breadth of the Pauline material.[1] It would appear that
there were only a few early Christian writers or proclaimers equal in
brilliance to Paul. Perhaps we might mention the great mind behind
the Fourth Gospel or the author of Hebrews, but on the whole most
early Christians, rather than being in danger of surpassing Paul's brilliance, were struggling to come to grips with the profundity of the
Apostle to the Gentiles' writings (cf., e.g., 2 Pet. 3:15–16). We must do
our best to summarize here the major themes of Pauline Christology,
recognizing that we shall not be able to do the subject justice in the
next few pages.

It has been rightly emphasized that Paul's letters, including Romans
are not theological textbooks, but rather are mostly ad hoc letters
addressing specific situations and questions raised in various churches,
mostly the Pauline ones.[2] This means that the material of christological import is found in various places and differing forms. Of late,
Pauline scholars have been emphasizing the importance of treating
each Pauline letter and its substance individually,[3] but in a matter as
fundamental as Christology a broader and more synthetic approach is

103

called for, especially in a study like this. I have undertaken such a broad-scale study elsewhere,[4] and here must be satisfied with more limited synthetic remarks.

First, it would be wrong to underestimate how central and dominant Paul's Christology is to the rest of his thinking. Indeed, his thought revolved around the Son, whom he called with great regularity Jesus Christ.[5] Paul compares Christ to important human figures in the story of God's people (Adam, Abraham, Moses), but he also says quite a lot about Christ's relationship to the Father and to the Holy Spirit, without fully articulating a description of the Trinity. The former comparisons are only natural, since Paul thought of Christ as a truly human figure, but the latter ones are equally important, for Paul thought of Christ as divine, as part of the story of God, without violating his own vision of monotheism. In other words, Christology was a form of theology for Paul (without his thought being Christomonistic in approach), but it had much to do with anthropology as well.

THE NARRATOLOGICAL SHAPE OF PAUL'S CHRISTOLOGY

We may speak of a fourfold narrative that gives Paul's Christology its essential shape and contours. There is of course first the story of Christ himself. This story involves telling about the one who was in the very form of God (Phil. 2:6) but set aside his divine prerogatives and status in order to take the status of a human, indeed even a slave among humans, who died a slave's death on a cross and because of this was highly exalted by God. Much of this story of Christ Paul seems to have derived from his reflection on and elaboration of early Christian hymns, including the notion of the Christ as God's Wisdom.[6] Paul, however, does not think the story of Christ ends with the exaltation to the right hand of God, for he goes on to relate how Christ has an ongoing role in heaven, and how he will come again as a judge and triumphant Lord. Furthermore, for Paul, Christ's exalted state does not merely recapitulate his state when preexistent.

For Paul, the christological hymn in Phil. 2:6–11 indicates that it is the career of Christ that determined how he should be confessed.[7] Jesus is given the throne name of God ("Lord"), precisely because God exalted him as a result of his finished work on earth. We must take seriously the "therefore" or "that is why" in Phil. 2:9, which indicates that this happened to Jesus since his death and because of his prior life and death as God's and humankind's servant. The end result of this process is that Christ has now assumed the role of and is functioning as Lord over all.[8] In other words, the acclamation of Christ as Lord means that Jesus is the risen Lord (the Lord since the resurrection), but the term "Lord" is not viewed as merely honorific. A phrase that occurs with regularity in Paul's letters is "the Lord, Jesus Christ." If we compare this to the emperor's throne name, "Imperator, Caesar Augustus," it suggests that Paul could use "Christ" not only as a name but also as a title such that Christ's name rivals and surpasses that of the emperor.[9] In Paul's view, Christ is now functioning as Lord reigning from heaven.[10] It would appear from a text like 1 Cor. 15:28 that after Christ's work is done (which involves completing the job of placing everything under the divine dominion at and after the parousia), Paul believes that the lordship over everything and everyone (even the Son) will be returned to the Father.[11] One must ask what point on the time or career line of the Christ one is talking about if one is going to discover which titles are then appropriate to predicate of Christ. Christological titles are predicated to a significant degree on the basis of function or task being undertaken at the time.

A good example can be seen in the few times that Paul uses *christos* as something other than a second name for Jesus.[12] As an actual title, it describes the roles the Son assumed during his earthly career climaxing in the cross. This is why Paul can resolve to know nothing but Christ and him crucified (1 Cor. 1:23). This last striking and paradoxical affirmation is crucial for Paul in various ways. It shows that he, like other early Jews, saw the Christ as a human being, one who could be killed.[13] It shows also that the actual story of Jesus has caused Paul to reevaluate what it meant to be the Jewish Messiah, for it is probable that Paul was no different from other early Jews in that he did not expect a crucified Messiah. As W. Kremer points out, Paul is not content to use *christos* in the ways he found it used in his sources; rather, he also puts it to new and sometimes paradoxical uses.[14] For most early Jews, the phrase "Christ crucified" would not merely be a paradox; it would be a contradiction in terms. How could the Anointed One of God, God's most blessed one, at the same time be cursed by God, as demonstrated by such a hideous death (read in the light of Deut. 21:23)? If the story of Jesus was read in the light of Scripture, one could conclude that Jesus was not the Christ. But if the starting point was God's action through Jesus, and one then read the Old Testament in light of the recent events in the life of Jesus, another conclusion was possible. In short, the primary story for Paul is the story of the historical person Jesus, and it is this story that is seen as the key to all other stories, including all the ones found in the Hebrew Scriptures. Paul of course did not always use the term "Christ" in a purely historical manner; he used the term even to speak of the Son during his preexistence or even after his death and resurrection (see, e.g., 1 Cor. 10:4).[15] It is crucial to understand the Pauline titles for Christ within the story line and narrative framework that **Paul** presents to us.

A second, larger story, the story of Israel, also informs Paul's discussion of the Christ. For example, we are told in Gal. 4:4 not only that Jesus was born of woman but also that he was born under the law, which probably goes beyond saying simply that he was a Jew. For Paul this entailed God's sending of the Son to be the human Jesus, sending him to redeem those under the law. In other words, Jesus was specifically sent to redeem Israel. This of course presupposes the lostness of Israel. It was after all to Israel that the Messiah had been promised in the first place (Rom. 9:4–5), and it was through Israel that the Messiah would spread his benefits to others. One must take very seriously Rom. 1:16 and the whole discussion in Romans 9–11. Salvation and the Messiah who brings it are for Israel first but also for Gentiles. The Messiah, in Paul's view, brings the story of Israel to its proper conclusion and climax. For Paul, sonship was another way of speaking of the Jewish royal character of Jesus, who Paul is happy to affirm was born in the line of David (Rom. 1:3–4), even though this is not a major emphasis in Paul's letters and seems rather to be a quotation of a confessional statement of early Jewish Christians.[16] Paul's use of "Son" also shows that he understands the relational significance of the term—it implies a special relationship with the Father.[17] All the same, he uses this title far less often than he does *christos* or *kyrios*.

A further and larger story into which the story of Christ and Israel fits is the story of a world gone wrong. For Paul the world is clearly a fallen place (see Romans 1; 8) and for that matter is living on borrowed time, for the current form of this world is passing away (1 Cor. 7:31; Gal. 1:4). The fact of the world's gradual demise makes decisions about crucial issues in this life all the more critical. The world is hell-bent, headed for destruction, but longs for liberation. This is true not just of human beings, but in Paul's view of creation as a whole (see Rom. 8:20–22). It is not just that the world has fallen and can't get up, or is gradually decaying, the problem is also that there is active personal evil abroad in the universe. In other words, there are demons and Satan to reckon with, who are part of the present evil age (see 1 Cor. 10:20–21; 2 Cor. 2:11; 4:4). This is the dark backdrop against which the story of Christ and God's people, both old and new, is played out.

CHRIST AS *THEOS* IN PAUL'S LETTERS

Transcending yet involved in all of the stories just mentioned of Christ, of Israel, of the world, is the story of God. This is the story of the interrelationship of Father, Son, and Holy Spirit, and this story also informs Paul's Christology in important ways. For example, the christological hymn in Col. 1:15–20 (cf. 2 Cor. 4:4) says that the Son played an important role in the creation of all things and beings, even human beings. The role of redeemer that Christ plays is part of the story of God's attempt to win back that which God had created in the first place. Creation and re-creation are undertaken not by different actors in the drama, but by the same One, though in multiple personal forms. Furthermore, the incarnation is seen by Paul as part of the story of God. The story of the subduing and reconciling of the powers and principalities is also part of this larger story of God, but it is Christ who undertakes these tasks for the Father, and in the service of redeeming humankind (1 Cor 15:24). Whether one thinks Paul wrote Colossians or not, and probably most scholars, including this one, still do, the elements of this broad christological vision are already evident in 1 Cor. 15:24–26. For Paul, the big picture involves not just "in the beginning God" but also "in the end God." Only the eschatological action is undertaken by God in Christ or, perhaps better said, God as Christ, which leads us to comment more specifically about Christ's divinity in Pauline thinking.

It must first be said that this issue cannot be narrowed down to whether Paul called Jesus *theos* or not. We have already seen in the christological hymn in Philippians 2 that Christ is called Lord, which was one of God's names or titles in the Septuagint. Thus, even if we were to confine ourselves to titles, there are other titles that Paul uses of Jesus that suggest he saw him as divine in some sense. One must assume that the hymn source material Paul adopted and adapted he also endorsed and thus it tells us something about his own views as well as the views of those early Christians from whom he borrowed this material.[18] E. Schweizer has said that to a large extent Paul's importance lies in the way he brought together a wide variety of material (hymns, creeds, confessions, Old Testament formulae and catenae, doxologies and his own formulations) and focused them by his understanding of Christ's death and resurrection.[19] There is a large measure of truth in this, but Paul's letters are not just a repository of earlier Christian fragments that have now been focused. Paul's narratological approach to Christology provides him with a large framework in which many truths can be expressed and understood, and through it all Paul has made his source material his own so that we can rightly speak of Pauline Christology.

Our evidence is also augmented when we look at the examples where Jesus is called God's Wisdom and/or his agent in creation (1 Cor. 1:24, 30; 8:6; Col. 1:15–17). For example, the role Wisdom played in Wisdom of Solomon of providing water in the wilderness to God's people is said in 1 Cor. 10:4 to be undertaken by the preexistent Christ. Paul is grounding the story of Christ not so much in the story of Israel but in the archetypal story of God's Wisdom. It seems likely that the sapiential ideas found in 1 Cor. 1:24, 30 and 8:6 blossomed into Paul's concept of the cosmic Christ—not only Lord over land and universe but also involved in its creation. The full flower of this sort of thinking is seen in texts such as Col. 1:15–20. In that hymn Christ is said to be the image of the invisible God, the firstborn of creation, and the means and goal of creation, just as Wisdom is in Wis. Sol. 7:25–26. The point is that Paul is very happy to attribute divine attributes to Christ, so one must actually ask whether or not he would have gone so far as to call Jesus Christ God. We have already suggested that Phil. 2:6–7 says as much—he had the status of being equal to God, and the divine prerogatives he could have taken advantage of.[20]

Another crucial text is the much-debated Rom. 9:5. Before we deal with the particulars of this text it is important to set the discussion in the larger context of the use of *theos* in the New Testament in general. M. J. Harris has shown in detail that the term *theos* is not used of the Trinity in the New Testament, but reflects early Jewish Christian ways of thinking. In particular *theos* is used in the vast majority of cases for the one Jews called Yahweh and some early Jews and early Jewish Christians called Father. Indeed it is almost a proper name for the Father in some texts. Occasionally, however, the term *theos* is used in the New Testament of Christ in his pre-incarnate, incarnate, or post-incarnate states.[21] The texts Harris has in mind are Rom. 9:5; Titus 2:13; Heb. 1:8; John 1:1; 20:28; and 2 Pet. 1:1. We must now examine the first of these.

Rom. 9:5 comes at the beginning of Paul's discussion of the advantages enjoyed by the nation Israel. The sentence poses a problem in regard to its proper punctuation. The argument turns on whether the verse should be read as in the New Revised Standard Version (NRSV): "Messiah, who is over all, God blessed forever," with the NRSV's marginal reading: "Messiah, who is God over all, blessed forever," or with the New English Bible (NEB): "Messiah. May God supreme over all be blessed forever." In the lattermost example, v. 5b becomes a separate sentence from v. 5a, or at least a separate clause. The Jerusalem Bible (JB), New International Version (NIV), and the New King James Version (NKJV) all support the first of these readings, which makes *theos* a qualification of Christ. Both the grammar and the context favor one of the first two readings.

Notice that Rom. 9:5a has the phrase *ho Christos to kata sarka.* As the parallel in Rom. 1:3–4 suggests, we would expect a parallel following clause telling us what Christ was according to some other category. The language "according the the flesh" suggests an attempt to disclose one aspect of the truth, and it sets up the anticipation that more will be said; otherwise the phrase is unnatural. Furthermore, the Greek phrase *ho ōn,* translated "who is" is normally a way to introduce a relative clause, and here the parallel in 2 Cor. 11:31 is clear enough (where we find "who is blessed forever" with *ho ōn*).

The NEB translation unjustifiably fragmentizes things by starting an invocation with the word *theos* ("may God be blessed . . ."), but grammatically this is very difficult. Why should a participle agreeing with "Messiah" first be separated from the term and then be given the form of a wish with a *different* person (God rather than Christ) as the subject? This is most uncalled for. Furthermore, while we agree that Paul is offering a doxology of sorts here, elsewhere Paul's doxologies are always attached to an antecedent subject. Moreover, in both the Hebrew and the Septuagint doxologies tend to be "blessed be God," not "God blessed," in their form and word order. There is then a high probability that Paul calls Christ God here in a doxological statement, which shows the degree to which Paul is willing to qualify his monotheistic remarks, something already evident in statements like 1 Cor. 8:6. There is a certain naturalness to speaking of the Messiah as someone blessed forever (by the Father), since he is the Anointed One.

As for the meaning of the use of *theos* here, Harris makes an important distinction between the examples such as here and in John 1, where *theos* is used without the definite article, and the other texts mentioned above, where the article is present. *Theos* without the article is a generic reference indicating that Christ belongs to the class or category of being called God or Deity. When the article is present the titular aspect comes to the fore.[22]

Thus far we have noticed that Paul predicates both divine attributes and divine titles or names to Christ (Wisdom, Lord, God), but there is other language he uses that makes equally clear that he sees christological language as God language. For example, one of the most prevalent phrases throughout the Pauline *corpus* is *en Christō* ("in Christ"). As Moule has pointed out, though some of this usage means no more than that one is a Christian, there are numerous examples where it is actually being used to say something about the Christian's condition or religious location, and only about an omnipresent being can one suggest that in some sense *that* being is the place where and the person in whom believers dwell.[23]

This picture can be further enlarged by examining what Paul says about Christ's relationship to the Spirit. Of course it is well known that Paul closely identifies Christ and the Spirit. For example, in 1 Cor. 15:45 Christ is said to be life-giving Spirit, and in Rom. 1:3–4 it is made clear that without Jesus' resurrection the Spirit would never have come to believers in the first place, but also that it was through the Spirit's power that Jesus was enabled to be Son of God in power. Being in Christ is often simply another way of speaking about being in the Spirit as is shown by the following: (1) Believers are righteous in Christ (Phil. 3:8–9) but also in the Spirit (Rom. 14:17). (2) Believers have life in Christ (Col. 3:4) but also in the Spirit (Rom. 8:11). (3) Believers have hope in Christ for the life to come (1 Cor. 15:19) and in the power of the Spirit to give them eternal life (Gal. 6:8). (4) Believers are sanctified in Christ (1 Cor. 1:2) but also in the Spirit (Rom. 15:16). (5) Believers are sealed both in Christ (Eph. 1:13) and in the Spirit (Eph. 4:30). 2 Corinthians 3:17 does not likely mean that Paul is simply equating the Lord and the Spirit but rather that he is dealing with Exodus 34 so as to explain that "the Lord" in the text means the Spirit. Nevertheless, 2 Cor. 3:17 shows the close connection between the two in Paul's mind. Notice that in Rom. 8:8–9 the Spirit of Christ = the Spirit of God = the Spirit of the Lord. Of course Paul does distinguish the two as well—only Christ came in the flesh, died on the cross, and rose again. Christ sent the Spirit to believers on earth, while he in his resurrected body remained in heaven. The point of all the above, however, is that this identity in function and effect between the Spirit and Christ

surely at least implies the deity of Christ. From an Old Testament perspective it is only God who can send or be a life-giving Spirit. In sum,
in the church age Christ and the Spirit are not one but two in identity,
but they are often one in function and effect because the Spirit is
Christ's agent on earth.

Pauline Christology has to do not only with the divinity of Christ
but also with his humanity. The terms Son of David, last Adam, or
human being all have to do with aspects of Jesus' tasks on earth as a
human being, as does the term Messiah. It must be remembered that
Paul does not use the phrase "Son of Man" at all, and the phrase "Son
of God" is relational in character and seems to have been kept for
exceptional use at the climax of certain key statements both about
Christ's work as a human being and also as more than human. We will
consider the phrase "Son of God" first, as a transition to our discussion
of Christ's humanity.

In Rom. 1:3–9 we are informed that the Son is the theme of Paul's
Gospel, and elsewhere he is the content of what God revealed to and in
Paul in his Damascus road experience (Gal. 1:16). In statements such as
Rom. 5:10; 8:32; Gal. 2:20; and Col. 1:13f. Paul emphasizes the supreme
value of Christ's death by stressing that it was God's Son, the one who
stood closest to God who died on the cross. The humanness is thereby
stressed. It is the Son who is descended from David as well as come
forth from God (Rom. 1:3–4), and he is also said to become Son of God
in power since the resurrection. In other words, he is Son not just on
earth but also in heaven beyond death. If we take the sequence Col.
1.13-15 seriously it suggests also that Paul has no problem calling the
pre-incarnate One the beloved Son for whom or through whom all
things were created.[24] The term "Son" and the phrase "Son of God,"
perhaps more than any other similar terms or titles except Christ, binds
together the narrative of the career of the Redeemer in Paul's thought
and stresses Christ's unique relationship with the Father, which in turn
allows him to have a unique relationship with God's people.

THE HUMAN FACE OF CHRIST

It is not an accident that when Paul discusses Jesus' humanity in various ways he stresses his Jewishness. For example, in Gal. 4:4 Jesus is
not merely said to be born of woman but also is said to be born under
the law. His appearance in this world came in the form of a normal

birth from a human Jewish mother. This text implies nothing peculiar or unusual about his birth. Notice too that Paul stresses that Jesus was born under the law to redeem those under the law; in other words, his ministry was directed to Israel.[25] In Paul's thought there is an interesting paradox: salvation is of God, but it could come to human beings only in and through a human being, the man Jesus Christ, in fact a particular sort of human being—a Jew. For Paul, the heart of the matter is that salvation comes in the form of Christ crucified, which in turn means that the humanness of the savior is a necessity, as well as his more-than-humanness.

There are various texts ranging from Phil. 2:7 to Rom. 8:3 that stress that the Son was born in human likeness. Probably the carefully worded phrase "in the likeness of sinful flesh" is meant to indicate that Jesus did not look any different from any other human being, but Paul wishes to avoid saying that he was a sinner or was born with a sinful nature. This comports with what we find elsewhere in the metaphorical statement that Jesus was the Paschal Lamb (1 Cor. 5:7), who had to be unblemished and spotless to be an appropriate sacrificial offering to God. In other words, like Adam, Jesus was born with an unfallen nature that had a capacity to sin, but unlike Adam he was obedient to God even unto death (cf. Philippians 2) and so in due course became an unblemished sacrifice.[26] It is interesting that the only other event besides Jesus' death that Paul mentions that Jesus did as a human being is the reference to his participation in the Last Supper. Jesus was one who broke bread, poured wine, shared in fellowship with his disciples, but even here Paul is interested not simply in these mundane facts but in their soteriological import. He mentions only events in the life of Jesus that are of prime theological weight.

By far the most common term that Paul uses for Jesus is Christ, usually as a name, but occasionally as a title as in Rom. 9:5. For most Jews it appears that *māšîaḥ* was a term referring to an especially anointed and singled out human being, usually a king or sometimes a priest.[27] It is thus not surprising that in the context where Paul mentions Jesus' messianic character there is stress on his humanity—he is born of the seed of David (Rom. 1:3–4). Paul's use of the term "Christ," then, probably especially stresses the humanness of the Messiah. This also is clearly implied in the phrase "Christ crucified" (1 Cor. 1:23). Of course, the story of Jesus brought about a redefinition of Paul's understanding of the Davidic Messiah in various ways, but it did not cause Paul to drop the Davidic terminology or categories altogether.

Paul says very little about Jesus' humanity in general; the subject of anthropology does not intrigue him when applied to Christ, except insofar as it has christological significance. This is seen not only because of what we have already said about Paul's presentation of Christ's humanity, but it can be further noticed when we examine Paul's presentation of Christ as the Last Adam. This concept comes up in more than one Pauline letter, and so obviously it was of some importance to Paul. When Paul thought of Jesus' true humanness he thought in terms of a comparison with the first human being.[28] In fact he thought typologically on this subject.

In Romans 5 in the midst of his comparison and contrast between Adam and Christ he says in v. 15 that just as death came by "the one" Adam, so God's grace and the gift that accompanied it (righteousness, 5:17) came by "the one" Jesus. This point is reiterated in 1 Cor. 15:21, only here the last half of the statement speaks of resurrection coming through a human being. In the later and disputed Paulines, in particular in 1 Tim. 2:5, these notions are further developed when we hear about Christ as the one mediator between God and human beings, and again he is said to be "the human being Christ," but there is more emphasis here on Jesus being both God and human being, standing at once on both sides of the fence in order to experience and know and represent both sides of things. Why all this stress on grace, righteousness, reconciliation, and even resurrection coming by a human being? Presumably part of the answer is that sin was a human problem that had to be resolved for humankind by and through a human being. While it has sometimes been stressed that the efficacy of salvation was due to Jesus' divinity, Paul in fact emphasizes the opposite. If Jesus had not been human, humans would not have ever received God's grace. God of course, apart from an incarnation, is not subject to death, and thus for one who stresses Christ crucified, there must also be stressed Christ's humanity.

The "last" Adam motif in 1 Cor. 15:21–23, 44–49 deserves a more extended comment. Here we have the responsibility for sin and its consequences placed squarely on Adam's shoulders. It is interesting that in this context Ps. 8:6 is applied to Jesus (in v. 27), which has suggested to some that Last Adam is Paul's substitute for the phrase Son of Man. Adam and Christ are seen to be both like and unlike each other. Both were truly human; both are representative heads of a human race; and both had a dramatic effect on their physical/spiritual progeny. However, in some ways the differences outweigh the similarities. The powerful effect of Adam's act on humanity was death (1 Cor. 15:21) but Christ's act produced life in the very specific form of resurrection from death, a far greater and more surprising effect. The parallelism here is not perfect, for while all did indeed die in Adam, Paul does not appear to think all will rise in Christ. For example, both in 1 Corinthians 15 and in 1 Thessalonians 4:16 Paul makes it quite clear that elsewhere when he speaks of resurrection it is of those who are in Christ. Paul strengthens this impression in 1 Cor. 15:23 when he speaks of the resurrection of those who belong to Christ.

The following chart shows how Paul compares Adam and Christ in 1 Cor. 15:44–49.

15:45	The First Adam	The Last Adam
	A Living Being	A Life-Giving Spirit
15:47	The First Human Being	The Second Human Being
15:47–48	From Earth's Dust	From Heaven

Paul relies on the concept of representative headship. In one sense Adam sinned for all humankind, and so the human race died in and because of him. To put it another way, because humankind's representative sinned, the whole race felt the effects. Adam is a corporate head of a body of people who are affected when he acts for all (compare Rom. 5:12 with Col. 1:14).

The second key to understanding the Adam–Christ analogy or typology is that salvation comes only "in Christ." A person must be in Christ to receive the benefits of Christ's work, and when they are in Him they both die to sin and rise to newness of life, becoming new creatures (compare Rom. 6:3–4 with 2 Cor. 5:17). The idea of representative headship when applied to Christ the last Adam means that Christ performed deeds that subsequently shaped that race. He died in a believer's place as his or her corporate head, just as Adam sinned for and in the place of humankind. Calling Jesus the last Adam or second human being involves an eschatological claim—Christ as the first-fruits of the new creation is himself the beginning as well as the progenitor of a new race. Yet paradoxically in another sense he is the end and goal of the human race, bringing in the last age, the end of God's plan, which means the new creation.

There is a further difference between Adam and Christ. Adam was strictly an earth creature, not only made from the earth but returning to dust. His body and life were natural and physical. Insofar as humankind is indebted to him, humankind is also earthly, physical, contingent, fallen, and has only a natural life in the body. Christ by contrast was from heaven and of heaven, in that he was a life-giving Spirit.

Several points of importance come out of this analogy. Christ is not merely living like Adam; he is a life-giving Spirit, whereas Adam in fact gave us death. Paul also likely does not mean that Christ had no body in heaven but that he lived in the spiritual realm and that he was the one who dispensed the Spirit, and life thereby. Equally, the phrase "a spiritual body" for Paul means not a body made out of immaterial substance but a body totally empowered by the Spirit. It is interesting that Paul, in contrast to Philo, does not see the Adam of Genesis 1 as the model or ideal human. Rather, it is the last, not the first, founder of the race that is seen as the ideal human being in Paul's thought.

Turning back to Rom. 5:12–18 for a moment, we notice that not only death but also sin entered the world through Adam. In fact, death enters the picture because of sin, so that for Paul human death at least is not a natural phenomenon but a consequence of evil in the world. It appears that Paul accepted Genesis 1–3 as a straightforward historical account, but as always his concern is with its theological and soteriological significance. It is interesting that Paul takes a both/and approach to sin. Whatever believers may have inherited from Adam, whatever effect his sin had on the race, nonetheless Paul believes that it is also true that each individual digs his or her own grave, has personal responsibility for his or her own sin. God has not unjustly punished any with death simply because of original sin, though of course none of the race would be dying if Adam had not done what he did. Thus, we have an interesting dualism. On the one hand, Paul can say in Rom. 5:15, "many died by the trespass of one man," or through Adam death reigned, but on the other he can also insist on personal responsibility. It is similar when we discuss salvation. It is clearly from God in Christ and happens to those in Christ because of what the one man Christ did for us, especially on the cross. Yet the individual does not automatically get this benefit; it must be appropriated by faith, which includes the faith response of confessing Jesus as Lord (Romans 10).

In Paul's view, God's antidote in Christ for sin is not merely an equal and opposite reaction to the trespass. The gift is far greater than the trespass and can affect far more in the believer than the trespass could (Rom. 5:15). While the death penalty followed just one sin, grace came after very many sins and quite apart from what humans deserved. Rom. 5:17 makes apparent that the life lived in Christ is not merely more powerful than the death Adam passed on to humankind; it is of an entirely different order—coming from heaven, from the Spirit, from the realm that transcends and transforms nature and can even overcome death. But none of this comes to pass without the christological facts that make this all possible. In particular, for Paul it is Christ's righteousness which includes his sinlessness and obedience even unto death which made possible the undoing of all that Adam's disobedience and sin inflicted on the human race. Salvation is not a self-help program in Paul's thought. It is a gift available only because of the finished work of Christ.

CHRIST—THE CENTER OF PAULINE THOUGHT

A way to demonstrate the importance and centrality of Christology for Paul is to examine the impact it had on other areas of his thinking of which we will discuss four briefly—eschatology, soteriology, ecclesiology, and God. The encounter of Christ on Damascus road caused a Copernican revolution in Paul's thinking about all these matters and much more.[29]

First, Paul's eschatological outlook most certainly changed when he encountered Christ on the Damascus road. There is little or no evidence that early Jews expected two comings of a Messiah,[30] yet that is precisely what both Paul and the other early Jewish Christians who prayed *marana tha* believed. This bifurcation of the Christ-event affected how Paul viewed the future and the life of believers. For Paul, because Christ had already come in the "fullness of time" (Galatians 4), the eschatological age could be said to have already dawned, though it was not yet completed. Redemption was already available in part—now in the spirit but later in the body as well when Christ returned. In other words, redemption had yet to be completed.

The coming of the eschatological age had relativized everything, such that the form and institutions of this world, while still extant, were nonetheless already passing away (1 Cor. 7:31) and should not be adhered or clung to in some sort of ultimate fashion. Powers and principalities still existed and menaced the world, but they could not separate believers from God's love. Colossians 2:15 in fact makes clear that Christ had disarmed the powers and principalities insofar as their being able to dominate or rule believers was concerned. Further, the inner life of believers had indeed changed. A believer was now a new creature, part of a new creation begun by the Last Adam (2 Cor. 5:17), a new creature that had righteousness and joy and peace in the Holy Spirit. This was a major part of what it meant in Paul's mind that the kingdom had already come (Rom. 14:17). The full redemption of the body at resurrection was yet to come, so that not only the world but also the believer's very existence was in an already-and-not-yet state of eschatological affairs, which had been initiated by Christ's coming and would be brought to consummation only when he returned.

There is no early Jewish evidence that a resurrection of the Messiah, much less an isolated resurrection of the Messiah apart from other believers, was expected in the midst of history, yet on the basis of the life and story of Jesus, this is precisely what Paul proclaimed. It must be understood that for a Pharisee like Paul, resurrection was perhaps the clearest piece of evidence that the eschaton had arrived.[31] Again, it was what happened to Christ that made Paul rethink and reshape his eschatology. Paul managed to continue to see resurrection as a unified thing, by using the concept of Christ being only the firstfruits of the resurrection of all believers.

Paul's concept of salvation was equally reshaped because of what he came to believe about Christ, in particular about his death and resurrection. Unless new finds from Qumran change the picture, and I see no evidence thus far that suggests this, early Jews were not expecting a crucified Messiah.[32] In fact, Paul tells us this message of a crucified Messiah was a scandalous one in the eyes of Jews (1 Cor. 1:23). The message here is deliberately paradoxical; to the factionalized Corinthians Paul depicts a Christ who on the surface appears to create more divisions than he heals, being a stumbling block to Jews and a scandal to Gentiles.[33] Deuteronomy 21:23 does not speak directly to the matter of crucifixion, much less crucifixion of God's Anointed One, and could not have generated such a belief. Nor is there any early first-century evidence that Isaiah 53 was really understood to refer to a crucified Messiah (though cf. the later *Targum of Isaiah* 53). Because of the bifurcation of the Christ-event, salvation also came in more than one stage or part. Paul speaks of large numbers of Gentiles already being saved, but God had not completed his plan for saving Jews yet (cf. Romans 11). Already a believer had right standing with God and even peace (Rom. 5:1), but the same believer was not yet fully sanctified and glorified, as is clear from the ongoing tension between flesh and the Holy Spirit in the believer's life (Gal. 5:16–26).

Without a doubt, Paul's thinking about God's people was changed because of the coming of Jesus. This is especially so in regard to the issue of the basis for inclusion in God's people. In Paul's view, God's people were Jews and Gentiles united in Christ (Gal. 3:28), and they could even be called the Israel of God (Gal. 6:16). Neither heredity, nor obedience to Torah could secure one a place in true Israel or in God's coming Kingdom (cf. Rom. 3:23–4:8). In Christ, the law, at least as a basis of obtaining or maintaining right standing with God, was at an end (Rom. 10:4). Paul also states clearly in Rom. 14:14 that it was no longer necessary for him, or other Jewish and Gentile Christians to continue to keep the laws of clean and unclean. This means that in Paul's mind, the Christ-event had changed the very basis of fellowship among God's people, and also changed the badges or markers of identity which singled God's people out.

If Torah, Temple, and Territory were three of the great pillars or landmarks of early Judaism, in Christ these landmarks had undergone a remarkable transformation. We have already said a bit about Paul's view of the law, but when we examine what he says about sacrifice and Temple, things are also radically different. For one thing, Christ is seen as the paschal lamb who was sacrificed once for all, thus making any further such literal sacrifices unnecessary and not even useful (1 Cor. 5:7) . Henceforth, only the sacrifice of presenting one's self wholly to God in devotion and for service was required (Rom. 12:1–4). It is also Paul's belief that the new temple is on the one hand Jew and Gentile united in Christ and in which body the Holy Spirit dwells (1 Cor. 6:19); on the other hand the individual believer's body is seen as the temple (1 Cor. 3:16–17).

It is also notable that the territorial doctrine of Israel nowhere comes up for real discussion in the Pauline letters, *even though* Paul wrote when such a doctrine was still a critical part of Israel's hope, before 70 C.E. It is possible that Paul made room for such a doctrine as feasible when Christ returned and "all Israel" was saved (Rom. 11:23–25). It is remarkable, however, that in the list of things Paul says God promised Israel according to the flesh, nowhere is land mentioned (Rom. 9:4–5, unless the vague reference to the promises involves such an idea). It would appear that the territorial doctrine also was transformed by Paul's understanding of the Christ-event such that he could speak of an inheritance or possibly even a commonwealth or citizenship in heaven (Col. 1:12; Phil. 3:20).

We have seen evidence of how Paul's christological monotheism changed his thinking about God, but further evidence can certainly be produced. In 2 Cor. 5:10 and 1 Thess. 5:4–10 it is not Yahweh but Christ who will come to judge the world, and this is not because the Father decided to send someone less than divine to accomplish this task. Paul is quite happy to speak about Christ assuming a variety of functions previously predicated only of Yahweh in the Old Testament. Though Paul certainly did not articulate a full trinitarian theology, the raw stuff of trinitarian thinking surfaces often in his letters, especially in doxological texts when Paul is thinking about who he worships or in prayer texts (cf. 1 Thess. 1:2–5; 2 Cor. 13:13). Paul only invoked blessing in God's name, but now God had three names by which the Lord could be called.

CHRIST IN THE LATEST PAULINES

We have not said much in this chapter about the Pastoral Epistles for two reasons. They do not add much new christological data, being mostly letters of practical advice about ethical and social matters. Furthermore, most scholars think that these letters are post-Pauline. An adequate survey of Pauline Christology can in fact be given by leaving the Pastorals out of account. Nevertheless, the Pastorals are at least a further development of Paulinism, if not by Paul himself, and so the Christology there deserves some attention at this point.[34] Among the faithful sayings in the Pastorals, two have some christological substance. In 1 Tim. 6:13 Christ's witness is made before Pilate, thus making clear that the life of Jesus prior to his execution had christological significance. In 1 Tim. 1:15 Christ came into the world for the purpose of saving sinners. This may allude to Christ's preexistence, as the hymn fragment in 1 Tim. 3:16 seems to do.[35] The stress on Christ's humanity is certainly clear in 1 Tim. 2:5. It is also noteworthy that the Pastorals reflect a predilection for the particular phrase Christ Jesus (in that order) or sometimes Christ Jesus our Lord. The Pauline letters seem to avoid the juxtaposition Lord Christ because it was known that ultimately this would be placing together two titles without a personal identification such as the name Jesus.

There is one text of special importance in Titus. In Titus 2:13 Christ is identified as God (here *theos* with the definite article, thus indicating a title for Christ). The text refers to Christ as coming Savior who will manifest himself in glory. The entire verse seems to be an anti-emperor-cult polemic, now predicating of Jesus what elsewhere was predicated of the emperor.[36] The immediately following verse stresses the previous work of Christ on the cross, which provides and makes possible redemption from iniquity and impurity and the creation of a people zealous for good deeds. Titus 2:13 is interesting especially because in the salutation to this same letter God and Christ are distinguished (1:1, 4).

Perhaps more significantly, when one takes the Pastoral Epistles together as by the same hand we find the same shared sacred story, the same narrative framework and logic informing the christological discussion as we find in the undisputed Paulines. Thus, these letters speak of the preexistence of Christ (1 Tim. 1:15: he came into the world to save sinners), his Davidic descent (2 Tim. 2:8), his ministry (1 Tim. 6:13), his saving work (1 Tim. 2:5–6; 2 Tim. 1:9–10), his resurrection (2 Tim. 2:8), his future coming and reign (1 Tim. 6:14; 2 Tim. 2:11–12; 4:8, 18), and deity (Titus 2:13). There is an effort to make clear that the teachings in these documents have a christological basis in salvation history (1 Tim. 3:16; Titus 2:11–14).[37] Again, there is nothing really new or surprising here except the occasional new turn of phrase. The substance seems to be the familiar Pauline christological thought.[38]

Before we draw this cursory discussion to a close, it is important to say something about what characterizes Paul's Christology. There is hardly anything in Paul's writings about Christ that is totally without analogy elsewhere in the New Testament.[39] The notions of the pre-incarnate existence, the divinity, and the humanity of Christ can all be found outside the Pauline corpus. In addition, the stress on Christ crucified is not uniquely Pauline either, being found in the Synoptics, in Hebrews, and in 1 Peter as well as elsewhere in the New Testament. The focus on Jesus' Jewishness is not unprecedented, nor is his resurrection. Furthermore, the idea of Jesus as God's Wisdom has already been seen to be present in the Q material (to give but one example). I stress this because all too often scholars have treated Paul as an anomaly or an aberration, instead of the prime example or main articulator of a rather widespread approach to Christology and a variety of other important subjects.

We have noted that Paul does not use the phrase "Son of Man" to characterize Jesus, perhaps because of the predominant character of Paul's audience. In this regard, Paul of course stands apart from the Gospel writers. One could argue, however, that the most distinctive aspect of Paul's Christology is his idea of Christ as the Last Adam, which has some similarities to Son of Man Christology. On the whole, though, this Adamic Christology is not an attempt to transpose Son of Man Christology into a new key for Gentiles. Genesis 1–2, not Daniel 7, provides the scriptural matrix for Paul's thinking on the Last Adam, which is compared to what Paul already believed about Jesus Christ. Moreover, the Son of Man Christology has nothing to do with someone being the founder or progenitor of a new race of human beings; it refers rather to a representative of and for Israel who comes before God and is given dominion. My point is that Paul has chosen a more universal mode of discourse than one finds in Son of Man Christology, and this is surely deliberate. By going back to Adam, Paul could talk about starting the whole race and its relationship with God over from scratch, not merely restoring Israel. He came up with a concept that could include Jews and Gentiles in the same fellowship simply because they were human and needed salvation.

Certainly, Paul's use of the formula "in Christ" is remarkable, when it refers to the real spiritual union between the exalted Christ and his followers. The Pauline notion transcends what we find in 1 Peter, though the phrase occurs there as well.[40] This formula more than any other describes how Paul viewed the position and condition of believers—they were in Christ. This idea goes well beyond the notion that believers are conformed to the pattern of Jesus' death and resurrection (Rom. 6:3–11), which is also a notion we find elsewhere (1 Peter). The burial with Christ was a one-time event occurring at conversion, but being "in Christ" is an ongoing phenomenon. So real was this union with Christ in Paul's mind that it excluded other forms of union that would be spiritually antithetical to it (1 Cor. 6:15–17). Being "one spirit" with Christ provided the basis for Paul's exhortation to imitate the sacred story of Christ, an appeal we find in various places (Phil. 2:5; 1 Cor. 11:1). "In Christ" is a crucial concept for Paul which is developed in ways and to a degree that is unprecedented elsewhere in the canon. Paul's Christology is not neatly summed up by the usual titles. A larger narrative framework and a grappling with profound and penetrating ideas are required, not least because the whole is much greater than the sum of the parts in this case. One must grapple with the foundational stories of Christ, Israel, Adam, Moses, Abraham, and God to get an adequate understanding of Pauline Christology.

THE WIDER IMPACT OF PAULINE CHRISTOLOGY

The compelling force and impact of Pauline Christology were felt in a variety of places and ways. The homily we call Hebrews seems especially to know and draw on Pauline modes of thought about Christ and other matters.[41] The author of that document seems to have been especially familiar with Galatians, but perhaps also with 1 Corinthians and Romans (compare 1 Cor. 15:24–28, 45–49 with Heb. 2:6–13).

Another place where Pauline Christology seems to have had some impact is in the Johannine community, particularly the Fourth Evangelist. Not only does this Gospel have a christological hymn at the outset, which has various similarities to the christological hymns found in Paul's letters, but this Gospel also presents a notion of being incorporated into Christ that is very similar to what we find in Paul, though under the image of the vine and the branches (but compare John 15 with Romans 11 on this point). We also find in the Fourth Gospel the notion of Jesus as the Passover lamb (John 1:29; 19:28–31), which we saw already in Paul's letters. Further, the concept of the Holy Spirit having close ties to the death and resurrection of Jesus finds its only full New Testament parallel in Paul's letters (compare John 14:1–21 with, e.g., Rom. 1:3–4). It is not beyond belief that this influence came from Paul himself during his several years in Ephesus, which according to tradition is also where the Johannine community was located. Other evidences of Pauline influence may be found in the formula "in Christ" in 1 Peter and also in the use of the phrase "the Lord Jesus Christ" in that document (1 Pet. 1:3, 13; 5:10), which seems especially close to what we find in Philippians. This impact of Paul's christological thought upon the author of 1 Peter and also upon the Petrine community is well attested in 2 Pet. 3:15–16.

For the most part, the similarities in Christology between Paul and other New Testament writers come from the fact that they all share the sacred story of a Jesus who was born of a woman under the law, took on a human nature, died on the cross, and rose from the dead for the salvation of the world. Not only did they all share this story; it appears from the prayers and confessional and hymn fragments that they all confessed and sang it as well. Christ crucified and risen, both human and yet more than human because he could be worshiped, was the touchstone for all these early Christian writers and missionaries and informed their preaching and writing throughout the New Testament era. There does not appear to have ever been a form of Christianity that did not know about and celebrate the death and resurrection of Jesus as the saving event. Thus, the shared sacred story of Christ, not direct influence in most cases, accounts for the numerous similarities in themes, titles, and concepts in the various New Testament Christologies. Yet it would be doing Paul an injustice to ignore that his writing appears to have made a significant direct impact on other New Testament writers as well, as we shall see, particularly in the case of Hebrews.

NOTES

1. And yet in spite of the depth of the Pauline material it is also true to say with Jerome Neyrey that "Paul is not interested in so wide-ranging a portrait of Jesus who discourses on *all* the issues of the day. Paul, rather, has already made a selection of what he thinks Jesus means and stands for vis-à-vis each church. It is not Jesus' attitude to many issues, but his relationship to a specific, topical issue that interests Paul" (*Christ is Community: The Christologies of the New Testament* [Wilmington, Del.: M. Glazier, 1985], p. 198).

2. Romans is of course not addressed to a church founded by Paul, and Colossians is probably not either, though in the latter case it seems to have been started by a Pauline co-worker.

3. See, e.g., *Pauline Theology, Volume I, Thessalonians, Philippians, Galatians, Philemon,* ed. J. M. Bassler (Minneapolis: Fortress Press, 1991); and *Pauline Theology, Volume II, 1 & 2 Corinthians,* ed. D. M. Hay (Minneapolis: Fortress Press, 1993).

4. See my *Paul's Narrative Thought World* (Louisville: Westminster/J. Knox, 1994).

5. In fact some 270 of 531 uses of the term Christ in the New Testament occur in the Pauline corpus.

6. See pp. 79ff. above.

7. Another form of this argument is found in my article "Christology," in *The Dictionary of Paul and his Letters,* ed. G. F. Hawthorne, R. P. Martin, and D. G. Reid (Downers Grove, Ill.: Inter-Varsity, 1993), pp. 100–115.

8. It is right to stress, as W. Kremer does that Paul often uses this title to enforce parenetic material or practical advice or in ethical instruction (*Christ, Lord, Son of God* [London: SCM Press, 1966], pp. 181–82). For example, Paul

advises in 1 Corinthians 7 that Christians are free to marry but that such marriages should take place "in the Lord."

9. Another thing that points in the direction of Paul's sensitivity to Christ as a title is that he never simply combines the two titles Lord and Christ ("Lord Christ"). See E. Richard, *Jesus: One and Many. The Christological Concept of the New Testament Authors* (Wilmington, Del.: M. Glazier, 1988), p. 326.

10. E. Schweizer rightly points out that since the contrast to "Jesus is Lord" is "Jesus be cursed" (1 Cor. 12:3) it becomes clear that the acclamation "Jesus is Lord" in the main refers to his lordship over the church, over those who confess and submit to him (*Jesus Christ: The Man from Nazareth and the Exalted Lord* [Macon, Ga.: Mercer University Press, 1987], pp. 15–18). Pointing also to Rom. 1:3–4 Schweizer adds: "His human existence was a preliminary stage in which he was designated, but not yet ruling king. Again, resurrection is installation to lordship over the church."

11. It is thus correct to say that Christ's lordship looks to the ultimate lordship and reign of God the Father. See Richard, *Jesus: One and Many*, p. 330.

12. In general it can be said, as Kremer notes, that Paul tends to use familiar titles for Christ repeatedly because those he addressed would naturally be expected to assent to such formulae (*Christ, Lord, Son of God*, p. 186).

13. See the discussion of 4 Ezra on pp. 15ff. above.

14. See the discussion in Kremer, *Christ, Lord, Son of God*, pp. 133–50, here p. 150.

15. I am assuming that when Paul says "the rock was Christ," he means that Christ actually existed during Old Testament times and aided God's people then, but that he did so in the same fashion that God the Father did, from heaven. In other words, in 1 Cor. 10:4 Paul is not discussing an earlier incarnation of the Christ on earth as a rock!

16. See pp. 73ff. above.

17. See Kremer, *Christ, Lord, Son of God*, p. 189.

18. See pp. 79ff. above.

19. Schweizer, *Jesus Christ*, p. 27.

20. The "divine" language would have been all the more striking in Paul's day because the language here that Paul or his source is co-opting was also being used of the emperor—namely, that he was divine but yet humbled himself to be a public servant. But the deity Paul has in mind performs his public service by dying on the cross and producing peace with God and between humans, while the emperor performs his public service by erecting a few more crosses, and so creating a very different sort of peace—the *pax Romana*.

21. See M. J. Harris, *Jesus as God* (Grand Rapids: Baker, 1992), pp. 298–99.

22. See ibid., p. 298.

23. See C. F. D. Moule, *The Origin of Christology* (Cambridge: Cambridge University Press, 1977), pp. 62–65.

24. Richard readily admits that there is a discussion of the preexistent

Christ in Colossians 1 which affects the rest of the christological discussion in the letter (*Jesus: One and Many*, pp. 344–45), but because he denies that we find such discussions in the undisputed Pauline's, he sees this as another indicator that this is a post-Pauline letter.

25. This fact, coupled with the fact that Paul is the missionary to the Gentiles, may go some way in explaining why Paul does not say more about Jesus' earthly ministry—namely, that Jesus' ministry was to a largely different audience than his own.

26. One of the real problems in dealing with the christological material in Philippians 2 is that there is a tendency to either over- or underestimate the degree to which the image of Christ as the last Adam is guiding what Paul says here. In general the parallels are confined to what is said by way of contrast: (1) Unlike Adam, Christ really was equal to God and had divine prerogatives. (2) Also unlike Adam, he was obedient even unto death. The hymn focuses on choices made by Christ, both before and during his earthly career, as a model for choices Christians must make,and thus the conclusion that Christ's pre-existence and incarnation are not referred to here is incorrect (*pace* Neyrey, *Christ is Community*, pp. 219–20 and others). The text does not say that Christ was merely like God in some one particular respect; it says he had the status and condition such that he was equal to God. See my discussion of this hymn and how it functions rhetorically in my commentary *Friendship and Finances in Philippi* (Valley Forge, Penn.: Trinity Press International, 1994).

27. See pp. 11ff. above.

28. This may in fact partially explain Paul's use of the phrase in Romans 8: "in the likeness of sinful flesh."

29. See the discussion in S. Kim, *The Origin of Paul's Gospel* (Grand Rapids: Eerdmans, 1982).

30. I find unconvincing J. H. Charlesworth's arguments about *Pss. Sol.* 18:5 meaning "to bring back the Messiah" in "From Messianology," in *The Messiah*, ed. J. H. Charlesworth (Minneapolis: Fortress Press, 1992), p. 30.

31. See Richard, *Jesus: One and Many*, p. 326: "Paul sees the Christian reality from the perspective of the risen Lord, the one whom God raised from the dead."

32. See pp. 13ff. above.

33. See Neyrey, *Christ is Community*, p. 205.

34. I have treated Colossians and Ephesians in the context of the main discussion because I am thoroughly convinced they are Pauline, as are most New Testament scholars, at least in the case of Colossians. Even cosmic Christology is already hinted at in the undisputed Paulines, particularly in 1 Corinthians, and texts like Eph. 1:22 or 5:32 seem to be just a further development of christological thinking as it impacts ecclesiology. Christ rules the universe for the sake of the church, and the great mystery has to do with the relationship of Christ and the church.

35. On this text see pp. 83ff. above.

36. See pp. 108ff. above.

37. See rightly E. E. Ellis, "Pastoral Letters," in *The Dictionary of Paul and his Letters*, pp. 658–66, here p. 665.

38. Richard fails to draw attention to the high christological elements in these letters which results in a skewing of the assessment of the overall portrait found in these letters (*Jesus: One and Many*, pp. 360–61).

39. Note Kremer's conclusion: "So it is not in his christology that we find Paul's own theological achievement, but rather in the way in which he works up his subjects, drawing upon already existing propositions about Christ, Lord, and Son of God" (*Christ, Lord, Son of God*, p. 194). In his view, Paul largely adhered to the christological conceptions and formulae he inherited from the pre-Pauline church. There is much truth in this conclusion, although Paul is more creative in some respects than Kremer allows, perhaps especially in his use of *theos, kyrios,* and Wisdom language of Christ.

40. See pp. 208ff. below.

41. See pp. 213ff. below.

5

Seeing with One Eye:
The Synoptic Christologies

T HE TERM "SYNOPTIC" means with one eye, and it is used in New Testament studies to refer to the first three canonical Gospels—Matthew, Mark, and Luke. The term was used chiefly because of the great similarities in content in these three Gospels, including many passages of christological significance. Yet it is equally important, indeed perhaps more important, to recognize that Luke and Acts share not merely a common vision but also a common author. Accordingly, we will treat only two of the Synoptic Gospels in this chapter, the ones generally believed to be the first two Gospels written—Mark and then Matthew. In the next chapter we will examine Luke and Acts in some detail. This approach makes sense because Matthew takes well over 90 percent of Mark's content into his own Gospel, including over 50 percent of Mark's exact words and clearly is very dependent on his Markan source, whereas Luke uses much less of his Markan source. In spite of this heavy dependence of Matthew on Mark, as we shall see, the First Evangelist does not simply repeat Mark's christological material but edits, expands, and adds new insights. The "evangelists did not put together their picture of Jesus from individual traditions; rather they began with the overall picture of Jesus and incorporated the individual stories as illustrations of their faith. They did not want to create a mosaic but to offer a portrait of the whole."[1]

THE SUFFERING AND SILENCE
OF THE SON OF MAN: MARKAN CHRISTOLOGY

In recent years, the christological interpretation of what most scholars believe is the earliest of the canonical Gospels has been bedeviled by both old and new factors.[2] Certainly one of the most enduring theories used to explain what we find in Mark's Gospel is W. Wrede's idea of the messianic secret. Another factor that has loomed larger and larger is of more recent vintage. I am referring to the theory that the original ending of Mark's Gospel is 16:8 and that other endings, which we usually find in brackets or in the margins of modern translations, were added by later scribes. If the Gospel ended at 16:8, it did not record any resurrection appearances of Jesus. This raises the question of how Mark understood what happened to Christ after his death and what its importance was for the Good News about Jesus Christ, which Mark 1:1 says he is offering to his audience.

Let us consider first the theory of the messianic secret, which continues to haunt the discussion of Christology in this Gospel.[3] W. Wrede's theory was that Jesus' ministry was nonmessianic and that Mark or perhaps his source created the messianic secret motif to cover up or smooth over this embarrassing fact for his church audience, who believed Jesus was the Christ. There are, however, some severe problems with this theory, not the least of which is all the evidence we dealt with in chapters 2–4 of this study which suggested that Jesus did leave a messianic impression on his audiences and the earliest Christians believed in and elaborated on this significance.

There are also problems that arise from a close analysis of Mark. For one thing, there is no unified messianic secret motif in Mark. By this I mean that the secrecy motif does not have to do exclusively with Christology. In Mark 4:10–12 the secret has to do with God's dominion, and in 5:43 it has to do with miracles. In 1:24 it does have to do with Jesus as the Messiah, but in 3:11 it has to do with Jesus as God's Son. Moreover, it is awkward for Wrede's theory that in 10:46ff. Jesus is clearly called by a Davidic royal label (Son of David) and Jesus does not silence the one calling him by this title. There is in fact a tension in this Gospel between secrecy and openness, and both tendencies must be taken into account.[4]

It was always the heart of Wrede's case that this motif could be seen in the exorcism stories in Mark. But even in these stories (see 5:1–20;

7:24–30; 9:14–29) the command to silence is not always found. J. D. G. Dunn in fact turns the tables on Wrede's argument by noting a publicity theme in the exorcism story in Mark 5 (see vv. 19–20, where the former demoniac is told to go and tell what the Lord has done for him). It is then difficult to argue that either Mark or his source consistently imposed a secrecy motif on these exorcism stories.[5] Furthermore, there is also a publicity theme in some of the healing stories (2:12; 3:3ff.), which differs from stories where a privacy motif is brought to the fore in order to show Jesus' compassion and his attempt to protect a family from unnecessary attention (5:43).

There is also the more puzzling issue of why Mark records the disobedience to Jesus' command to silence in 1:25–28, 43–45 and 7:36–37 if he was really trying to impose a messianic secrecy motif on his material. Are we to think that Mark is simply a bad editor of his source material, despite considerable evidence to the contrary (see below)? It is better to conclude that Mark was not trying to impose a messianic secret motif on his source material, for neither the healing texts that call for privacy nor the kingdom secret material really fits under this conceptual umbrella and the publicity and disobedience motifs both move in the opposite direction. Further, the fact that the disciples are taught in private probably has nothing to do with a messianic secret motif. Some of these texts are about Jesus revealing the kingdom's secrets to his disciples, and some are about in-house teaching of the disciples about divorce and other nonchristological issues (see 10:10–12).

We have pointed out that Jesus' main form of public discourse was Wisdom speech in the form of aphorisms, parables, riddles, and the like.[6] There is an inherent veiledness or indirectness to this form of metaphorical speech, and if Jesus spoke in this fashion about the coming of the kingdom, he could just as well have spoken in this fashion about the coming of the king. It is still easier to believe that because of the volatility of Jesus' environment he might silence or reject certain kinds of acclamations of him to prevent misunderstanding without this implying he had no messianic self-understanding.[7] That Jesus rejected the notion of his being a political pretender does not imply that he rejected all messianic ideas when applied to himself. I thus must conclude that something else is going on in Mark's Gospel and that it involves neither an attempt to veil Jesus' nonmessianic ministry nor to reconcile two dueling Christologies, one that suggested Jesus became the Messiah at the resurrection (something the Markan outline gives no hint of—notice the lack of titles in 16:6) and another that suggested he was the Messiah all during his ministry.

The second misleading discussion has to do with where Mark's Gospel originally ended. Some scholars have suggested that 16:8 is a perfectly appropriate ending in a Gospel that presents a semiveiled and enigmatic portrait of Jesus, and that this ending is quite possible grammatically, even if it seems abrupt to moderns, who tend to expect happy endings with all loose ends neatly tied up. This reasoning in turn sometimes leads to the conclusion that Mark did not see the recording of the resurrection appearances in this Gospel as crucial to the audience's Christian faith in Jesus as Son and Christ (either they already knew about the appearances, or the appearances simply weren't critical in Mark's view) or that Mark thought they were not crucial to understanding or revealing Jesus' identity. There are at least three major problems with this whole line of reasoning.

First, it is clear enough from the textual history of this Gospel that more than one early Christian in the second century (the author of the long ending, and also the author of the so-called Freer logion) did not feel that 16:8 brought the Gospel to an adequate closure. It is far more likely that the earliest readers would understand the literary conventions of documents such as Mark's Gospel than we do at almost two thousand years remove, and that they would know when a narrative did not have an appropriate closure.

The second point has to do with the Markan outline itself. As we shall see shortly, the Gospel is not interested simply in silence but also in key moments of disclosure or revelation in regard to Jesus' identity. In particular, 14:28 and 16:6–7 both set up an expectation in the reader's or hearer's mind that there will be at least one appearance account at the end of the Gospel, an appearance in Galilee to Peter and the others in the inner circle of disciples. Further, the disclosure accounts, which are carefully placed at the beginning (1:9–11), in the middle (8:27–30; 9:2–8), and toward the end of the book (14:61–62), set up an anticipation in the reader that the book will close with a final climactic disclosure of Jesus' identity to the very disciples that we are told in 14:28 and 16:6–7 will receive such a disclosure. It is clear enough that after 14:62, keeping the messianic secret is no longer the order of the day, not even in a hostile public setting.

The appropriateness of modern abrupt endings should not lead us to think that such an approach was equally accepted in the case of ancient biographies. Anyone who has read Plutarch's *Lives* or other ancient biographical literature knows that it was widely believed that how a person's life ended revealed a person's true character. It must be doubted that the final impression Mark wanted to leave in readers' minds about the Jesus he believed in as the Son of God and Christ was his cry "My God, my God, why have you forsaken me," or the final impression of the disciples was that they were cowards, either dispersed and in hiding (having betrayed, denied, or deserted Jesus, 14:50) or, in the case of the women, as in fright and in flight and silent (16:8). Silence was not golden after Good Friday, as is made very clear in 16:6, and Mark's failure to flesh out what this latter text points to would have been seen as a significant omission by ancient readers of biography.

Third, though there is some evidence for a Greek sentence or even a paragraph ending with *ephobounto gar* ("for they were afraid"), I know of no evidence whatsoever for this being an appropriate ending for a whole document of the biographical sort that we have in Mark's Gospel. Mark knew very well that there was a better way to conclude a Greek sentence that spoke of a group of persons' being afraid than to leave a *gar* dangling at the end (see 5:15, cf. 6:50), even if one wanted to use a *gar* phrase about fear to end a sentence (cf. 9:6, *ekphoboi gar egenonto!*). There is also the problem of the verb tenses and structure of 16:8. The two key verbs are in the imperfect tense, and there are two *gar* clauses, not one. The structure suggests that because the women were possessed with fear and trembling, they fled from the tomb, and because they were afraid, they said nothing to anyone. Both "fleeing" and "speaking" are aorist verbs indicating a particular and punctiliar action, motivated in each case by fear. The text surely also implies that the fleeing and the silence went on only for a specific period of time, namely, for the period while the women were afraid. This combination of verbs seems to set up an expectation for a sequel when the women are no longer scared to death and no longer fleeing and silent, a sequel in which they presumably are finally obedient to the angelic command. It is hard to believe that Mark wanted to leave his audience with a picture of the women's disobedience and denseness *after* Easter, whatever may have been appropriate before Easter. I thus must conclude that 16:8 is not the original ending of Mark's Gospel and that it does not reveal the christological cards Mark was playing with all along.[8]

A better clue to Mark's purposes is found in examining the structure of Mark's Gospel and its narrative flow. That Christology is of paramount importance to Mark is shown by the very first verse of the book, where we are told that the book will be about the beginning of the Good News about Jesus Christ, the Son of God. This way of announcing the subject matter of the book at the very beginning strongly suggests that we are meant to see this book as falling into the genre of ancient biography, which focused on presenting a vivid portrait through the chronicling of words and deeds of some great person—in this case Jesus.[9] This in turn means that the question of identity was very important for Mark. The main character's personality and identity must be revealed, and we should look for this especially at key or climactic junctures in the story. As we shall now see, the story in the first half of the Gospel especially is structured around certain key christological moments.

In the first half of this Gospel a variety of questions are brought, the function of which is to begin to raise the issue of Jesus' identity. For example, we may list the following:

1:27:	The crowds ask, "What is this?" and the scribes, "Who can forgive sins but God?"
2:16:	The scribes ask, "Why does he eat with sinners?"
2:24:	The Pharisees ask, "Why are they doing what is not lawful?" But the question is ultimately meant to raise questions about Jesus and his practices.
4:41:	The disciples ask, "Who then is this that even wind and water obey him?"
6:2	The hometown folks ask, "Where did this man get his wisdom?"
7:5:	The Pharisees ask, "Why do your disciples not live by the tradition?" But again the question is ultimately directed at Jesus.
7:37:	In preparation for the key answer to these questions, particularly the identity question, the crowds say, "He has done all things well."

These questions lead up to 8:27–30, where the question of identity is raised by Jesus himself and is answered in a way that Jesus does not reject. It is only *after* this juncture that the Son of Man's mission of suffering is announced in a threefold way in 8:31; 9:31; and 10:32. Thereafter follows the passion narrative, where the fulfillment of the prophecy of the Son of Man's suffering is chronicled. In other words, in short form, the structure of this Gospel is as follows, clearly revealing that Christology has dictated how the material has been handled:

> THE GOSPEL'S SUBJECT MATTER: ABOUT JESUS CHRIST, SON OF GOD (1:1)
>
> THE QUESTIONS (1:2–8:26)
>
> THE QUESTION OF IDENTITY IS ANSWERED: PETER'S CONFESSION "YOU ARE THE CHRIST" (8:27–30)
>
> THE MISSION OF THE CHRIST IS STATED: A MISSION OF SUFFERING (8:31; 9:31; 10:32)
>
> MISSION ACCOMPLISHED (chapters 11–16)

This structure reveals several key points about Markan Christology. First, in Mark's view until you have a grasp of who Jesus is you will not understand why he had to suffer and die on the cross. The understanding of the identity leads to an understanding of Jesus' mission. Second, Mark believes that Jesus is the Christ and the Son of God, but the terminology he reveals to have been on Jesus' own lips most frequently if not exclusively is Son of Man, a phrase that is particularly linked to the tasks Jesus must undertake first in Jerusalem by going and dying and then at the eschaton when he must return for judgment (14:62).

There are in fact at least four christological disclosure moments in the narrative: (1) at the baptism (1:9–11), but this is a private and visionary disclosure to Jesus himself that he is God's Beloved Son; (2) at Caesarea Philippi (8:27–30), where a disciple reveals and learns something about Christ's identity; (3) in 9:2–8, where the inner circle of three disciples receive a visionary disclosure of Jesus' identity as the Beloved Son; (4) in 14:61–62, where Jesus is finally asked publicly and point blank by the Jewish authorities whether he is the Christ, to which he responds affirmatively but immediately qualifies his remarks by referring to his coming tasks as Son of Man, just as he did for the disciples in chapter 8. In short, Mark has revealed not only that Jesus' preferred self-designation was Son of Man, but that the church's belief in his being the Christ and Son of God, the two titles mentioned in Mark 1:1, is vindicated by climactic christological disclosure moments in the story.

A failure to recognize the narrative flow of the Markan outline and the importance of the climactic christological disclosure moments has sometimes led to various skewed readings of Mark's purposes, including the theory that this Gospel presents a polemic against the earliest disciples. To the contrary, the point is that no one could understand Jesus, even the disciples, unless the secret of his identity and mission was revealed to them (see 4:10–12; 9:2–8 on the importance of disclosure or revelation even to the disciples). With this framework, we can examine some of the christological details a bit more closely.

There was a time earlier in this century when many scholars saw Mark as almost pure unvarnished narrative, with little theological profundity or depth. It is safe to say those days are now long gone. Wherever Mark got his Gospel material, he has shaped it in such a way as to present a very striking portrait of Jesus as Christ, as Son of God and as Son of Man—the man destined to die, the Beloved Son destined to save and be raised from the grave. This last point, which is clearly announced in 16:6 and coupled with the pointing out of the empty tomb, makes evident that Mark is concerned to proclaim the Easter message, but in a way that is not open to misunderstanding.[10] In particular, Mark is concerned that royal titles such as Christ or Son of God or King are not misinterpreted to suggest that Jesus was some sort of political figure and aspirant.

To fully understand Mark's use of titles such as Christ, Son of God, King, and Son of Man, it is crucial to take into account the matter of point of view. As 1:1 indicates, Mark shares with his audience a Christian viewpoint about Jesus' character, but individuals within the narrative almost never (some scholars would say never) have this understanding, and even when, as in the case with Peter in Mark 8, some glimmering of comprehension breaks through, it immediately becomes clear that partial insight is still blended with partial misunderstanding requiring further correction. J. D. Kingsbury has made an excellent case that the theme of Jesus as Son of God is the red thread tying together the christological reflections of Mark in this Gospel. The theme is announced in 1:1,[11] revealed privately to Jesus at baptism, known by demons and spirit beings, revealed to Peter, James, and John on the Mount of Transfiguration, but not understood and disbelieved by Jesus' adversaries at his trial, and finally announced at the point of Jesus' death by the centurion, a Gentile.[12]

A closer look at the way the phrase "Son of God" is used shows that in 1:11 the announcement reflects a combination of Ps. 2:7 and Isa. 40:1. What unites these allusions is the royal or kingly character and power of the one spoken about. This suggests that we should see Jesus' baptism as his enthronement by God as king, but in the Markan outline this is only revealed to Jesus himself at this point.[13]

If we compare this to what we find in Mark 9:2–9, we discover that while here Jesus is announced as God's Son to the disciples, they are told not to tell anyone until after the Son of Man rises from the dead, and clearly enough the disciples don't understand this latter reference. Mark seems to be making clear that during the ministry of Jesus there was indeed a necessary and intentional veiling of Jesus' true identity until after Easter. Even the demons are silenced during the ministry when they call Jesus something like Son of God (1:25, 34; 3:12). The reason is probably not disclosed before Mark 15, where Jesus is repeatedly called King. During the ministry, there were certain kinds of messianic expectations that Jesus wanted nothing to do with, including particularly the more overtly political ones, and as things turned out this is seen by Mark as a wise move. With the command to silence, Jesus was free to continue to minister until such time as God, not popular expectations, led him up to Jerusalem to suffer as the Son of Man. Mark's Gospel is written with a knowledge of the volatile and dangerous potential of certain kinds of royal claims. Jesus is not to be publicly acknowledged as God's Son before he is lifted up on the cross; at and after that point it will be appropriate.[14] It is also right to note that the title Son of God is presented at the beginning of Mark's Gospel without definition, in order to allow the story to reveal its proper content and to critique misunderstandings of the use of the title.[15] "The title *Son of God* fulfills for Mark a summary view of the Jesus who is at work on earth, is equipped by God with the Spirit and power, yet goes his way obediently to the cross. In every realm of activity . . . the secret of the Son of God who is close to God is visible, although still veiled and incomprehensible to witnesses."[16]

The title Christ also occurs in 1:1 and crops up at crucial junctures in Mark's narrative structure. The first public announcement within the narrative of this title is in 8:27–30, but Mark stresses that on this occasion Jesus, while not rejecting the title, qualified it dramatically by speaking of the coming suffering of the Son of Man. The idea that the Christ would be immune to suffering is seen as a misunderstanding about what God's Anointed One would do and be. Indeed, the suggestion that the Christ must not suffer is seen as satanic and to be rebuked. Here in Mark 8, as in Mark 1, the various titles and their content flow into one another and must in the end be evaluated together for their overall impact.

Son of Man is the most frequently used title, and with one probable exception (2:10, where it is apparently part of the author's aside) is found solely on Jesus' lips. Moreover, there is only one exception to this rule elsewhere in the Synoptics, so it seems that Mark is conveying a historical fact about Jesus' self-disclosure. When we combine insights from examining 8:31 and par. with what we learn from 14:61–62 we discover that the author is drawing on allusions and overtones from Daniel 7 (this is particularly clear in Mark 14). The roles assigned to the Son of Man in Dan. 7:13–14 are in fact royal roles: he will have dominion, glory, and kingship.

In other words, Son of Man terminology in Mark is not an alternative to royal phrases being used of Jesus; it is another way of putting the point about Jesus' kingship with new nuances and connotations. Jesus is a king all right; Peter's confession is not to be rejected, but it must be qualified three times in 8:31; 9:31; and 10:32 to make clear that he is to be a suffering king, a Son of Man who must go up to Jerusalem and die. Notice too how the allusion to Daniel 7 in Mark 14:62 is combined with an allusion to Ps. 110:1—the Christ who is also the Son of Man will be seated at the right hand of God before he comes on the clouds. "Thus Jesus' public confession in Mark points to the equivalence of the three titles used Christ, Son of God, and Son of Man with their one common element the reference to kingly power."[17]

This overall royal impression is only further confirmed by Mark 10:46–52, where Jesus is publicly addressed as Son of David, and not Jesus but the disciples silence the man.[18] Also of importance when one examines a text like Mark 10:45 is that Son of Man theology includes the elements of both Jesus' humility during his ministry, coming to serve others, and his self-sacrifice: ultimately he came to present himself as a ransom for many.[19]

R. Schnackenburg has urged that we see in 14:61–62 a summary or condensation of Markan Christology. Mark presents the two titles Son of God and Son of Man as coming together at this juncture with both being affirmed, but Son of Man being used to correct or further define what an affirmation of being the Son of God means.[20]

> Jesus answers the high priest affirmatively, but at the same time his answer corrects the Jewish concept of Messiah: he is the one sitting at the right hand of God and the Son of Man coming on the clouds of heaven (14.62). Here the "Son of God" appears in yet another light. He is the one

exalted to God and the Son of Man coming again in power. The Son of God Christology is connected with Son of Man Christology.[21]

While the conjunction of these two titles comes at the climax of Jesus' ministry as he makes his final public utterances, it is also illuminating to consider what we find at the beginning of the ministry as well. As is well known, Mark does not record the substance of Jesus' temptation by Satan in the wilderness, only the fact of it, and he alone mentions that Jesus was with the wild beasts (1:13). Mark goes on to affirm that angels waited on him. This has suggested to Schnackenburg that Mark is portraying paradise restored, with Jesus being an Adam who did not succumb to temptation. Thus, humankind's place in the hierarchy of being is restored—ruling over the animals and served by the angels. This is a possibility, but Mark does not make much of the matter, and in fact the text does not say that Jesus subdued or ruled over the animals while in the wilderness; he is simply with them.[22]

It should not be seen as puzzling that the title King does not appear in Mark until chapter 15. Our author has been carefully nuancing the christological discussion up to this point so that his audience would not misunderstand what was meant when Jesus is repeatedly called King at the end of his life.[23] This is a clear case of Markan irony, for while the acclamation is true, Pilate and others misunderstand what it really means when applied to Jesus. A crucified king would seem a contradiction in terms to the authorities, but not to Mark. Pilate asks Jesus point blank if he is the king of the Jews (v. 2), and then uses the phrase again in vv. 9 and 12. In 15:18 it occurs on the lips of the Praetorian guard, and both here and already in vv. 9 and 12 we have a public announcement of Jesus as the king of the Jews, which is set down in a sort of legal proclamation on the *titulus* or placard that was to go on Jesus' cross (15:26). In all these cases Gentiles speak of Jesus this way, even though they are insincere. This is finally followed by what appears to be the climactic confession by a human being in this Gospel, again by a Gentile who sincerely recognizes Jesus in his noble death as Son of God in some sense (15:29). Before this juncture, perhaps only Peter has been given this insight that leads to a true confession, but, unlike Peter, the centurion is not silenced or rebuked. In this way Mark makes evident that it was not until after Jesus' death and by precisely reflecting on that death, that Jesus was seen to be who he really was—Christ, Son of God, Son of Man, and even King of the Jews.

This is why even the disciples in the Markan story never quite get things completely right before Easter. This is also why it is unlikely that 16:8 was Mark's originally intended ending. The post-Easter acclamation and even the empty tomb, if not also accompanied by post-Easter appearances, did not in Mark's view transform the disciples into true Christians, and Mark is writing to a Christian audience that would have needed confirmation that the original disciples, like Mark's audience themselves, had indeed been so transformed, not left out of the kingdom as those who feared and fled, or denied, deserted, or betrayed. This Gospel is not just about how the proclamation of Jesus as Christ and Son of God was the Good News for Mark's disciples, but also how it came to be Good News for the first disciples. Mark's attempt at biography means that by and large he is happy with a narrative Christology that is revealed indirectly through the words and deeds of Jesus, but occasionally also in moments of divine disclosure.

It seems probable that Mark's Gospel, as the earliest Gospel, retains a key historical element from the actual ministry of Jesus, namely, that Jesus' self-disclosure came in an indirect manner involving sometimes hiddenness and revelation to certain persons. Occasionally the light partly dawned during the ministry, though rightly Mark suggests that there were no full-fledged Christians before the death of Christ.

At the end of the day, there is something to be said for a messianic secret (or sonship secret) being both Markan and historical. Jesus was an enigmatic and forceful figure, and Mark, probably more than any other Gospel writer, has given us the flavor of what it might have been like to encounter him in a world with a wide variety of hopes and dreams about redeemer figures. Jesus did not wish to be defined by others but rather to redefine the christological categories. Mark would also have us know that spiritual things are spiritually discerned—only by revelation can the Christ be truly comprehended. But once comprehended he could be confessed with a variety of royal titles—Christ, Son of God, Son of Man, King, Son of David.

JESUS AS IMMANUEL AND SAGE: THE CHRISTOLOGY OF MATTHEW'S GOSPEL

Having discussed the Gospel of Mark, which is supposed to, and does in general, have lower and more primitive christological formulations than we find in the other Gospels, we turn now to a Gospel, called Matthew's Gospel, which scholars almost unanimously agree has a high and rather overt Christology, including conveying the idea that Jesus is deity or divine. While recognizing the high Christology in this work, scholars do not agree why this is the case. It is my view that perhaps the major reason we find high Christology not only in Matthew but also in John is that both of these evangelists portray Jesus not merely as a sage but as God's Wisdom come to earth, or as Matthew prefers to put it, as God's Presence on earth, Immanuel. In other words, a sapiential portrayal in both of these Gospels leads to the predication of some remarkable things of Jesus. It will be well to flesh out the similarities and differences between Matthew and John at this point since they reveal something of the christological focus of each Gospel.

On first blush, the First and Fourth Gospels seem to be distinctively different from each other. The Gospel of Matthew has no *logos* prologue, I-am discourses, or sign narratives, and John has no birth narrative, human genealogy, Sermon on the Mount, or parable collections. Matthew follows Mark very carefully and takes over 90 percent of Mark's substance into his own Gospel. John could never be accused of doing that.

On closer inspection, however, these two Gospels have much in common. Both begin with a statement about the origins of their central character, Jesus.[24] Both of these Gospels have a notable emphasis on Jesus as teacher, which in both cases takes the form of several discourses.[25] Both Gospels conclude not only with a full presentation of the passion events and the resurrection appearances but also with a recommissioning and regathering of some of the inner circle of disciples. Furthermore both Gospels were written by Jewish Christians in the last quarter of the first century to communities that had ongoing controversies with the synagogue but were clearly separate from it, at least at the points of origin of the respective Gospels. Thus, in both Gospels the Jewish disciples of Jesus can be separated from "the Jews" (Matt. 28:15; John 10:19–24), which seems to mean primarily those Jews and Jewish authorities opposed to the Jesus movement. Both Gospels seem to have arisen out of a context of conflict and controversy and are shaped not only by whom they are written for but also by whom they are written against.

It is also arguable that both of these Gospels arose out of, or at least for, a school setting and were meant to be used in Matthew's case as an aid for Jewish Christian teachers to use with their flock, and in John's case as a tool for Johannine evangelists and teachers to use in presenting the Gospel to outsiders. It is no accident that Jesus is most clearly presented as a teacher with learners (the meaning of *mathētēs*, which we translate as disciple) in these two Gospels. For example, the term *mathētēs*, which occurs only in the first five books of the New Testament, is used some seventy-three times in Matthew, some seventy-eight times in John, but only forty-six times in Mark, and thirty-seven times in Luke (with twenty-eight more instances in Acts). It is also not a chance happening that in both Matthew and John discipleship is defined as keeping Jesus' commands or words (compare Matt. 18:19 with John 14:14 and Matt. 28:18–20 with John 14:15–26; 15:10). It is obvious enough that Matthew's Gospel focuses on instructions for disciples, but there is clearly an interest in portraying Jesus' followers in John also as disciples in general (and not particularly as the Twelve, which group hardly receives notice in the Fourth Gospel). Thus, we find Jesus' followers doing the things that disciples of early Jewish teachers did—spending time with the Master (3:22), calling him rabbi (or some variant thereof, 1:38, 49; 4:31; 9:2; 11:8; 20:16), buying food for him (4:8, 31), and baptizing others for him (4:2). Both Gospels end with stories about how the disciples both doubt and believe even after Jesus is raised from the dead.

The First and Fourth Evangelists, both deeply steeped in Jewish Wisdom literature and lore adopt different sapiential strategies in their presentations of Christ. Matthew focuses on Jesus as a Jewish sage and concentrates on his public forms of wisdom teaching—parables, aphorisms, riddles, and beatitudes. John follows the discourse form we find in Proverbs 8 or Sirach 24, where one subject is treated and developed at some length; thus he portrays Jesus as Wisdom in person.

Matthew and John are also similar in the sapiential way they highlight the use of Father language for God or Father–Son language. In Matthew, Father is used of God some forty-two times, but in John we find a remarkable 115 instances. This is compared to only five times in Mark (none of which occurs before 8:38) and only fifteen times in Luke, some of which come from Q. This usage is closely tied in both these Gospels to an understanding not only of Jesus as *the* Son of God but also of disciples as sons and daughters of God. Furthermore, a close study of the way both the First and Fourth Evangelists qualify the use of Father by the possessive modifiers "my" or "his" when Jesus is speaking reveal that the authors are trying to stress that Jesus had a unique relationship with God.[26] Theology, Christology, and discipleship are linked in both of these Gospels through the use of Father language. When one believes that Jesus is God's Son, one can come to relate to God as Father, as Jesus did. Matthew stresses this in a text like Matt. 11:27b, where it is made clear that one can come to know the Father truly only through the Son. An adequate comparison of the Christologies of Matthew and John would show that Matt. 11:27–28 is no anomalous meteorite fallen from a Johannine sky but rather evidence that both Gospel writers are deeply steeped in Jewish Wisdom and this affects how they present christological matters. We must turn more exclusively to Matthew's presentation at this point.

The First Evangelist carefully constructs his Gospel as a word to the wise (or at least to some Jewish Christians, who probably were already teachers), using three primary sources—Mark, Q, and M. Matthew 13:52 should probably be seen as a clue to how Matthew views both himself and his audience. He is a scribe trained for the kingdom who brings forth both old and new treasures from the Jesus tradition for other Jewish Christian teachers to use. Matthew does not see himself as like later rabbinic scribes, but rather as standing in the tradition of the sapiential scribes described in Sir. 39:1–3: "He seeks out the wisdom of all the ancients, and is concerned with prophecies; he preserves the sayings of the famous and penetrates the subtleties of parables; he seeks out the hidden meanings of proverbs."

The evangelist alludes to himself not as a sage but as a scribe, as is probably the case with his audience. This distinction is important to the First Evangelist because he wants to portray Jesus as the great sage and master teacher, but himself and his audience as only recorders and passers down of the tradition. Scribes are not the originators of the tradition but rather the transmitters, interpreters, and appliers of it. It is not an accident that Peter, the first key disciple of Jesus, is portrayed in Matt. 16:17ff. as the one given the authority to bind and loose in the sense of making decisions and giving certain commandments about what one is bound to do and what one is free to do. In other words, Peter is portrayed as the disciple given the task of interpreting the Jesus tradition for the church. There is a deliberate contrast between his teaching and that of the Pharisees, who, instead of using (hermeneutical) keys to open the gate to the kingdom as Peter does, do not allow people to go into the kingdom (Matt. 23:13, 15). The commissioning of Peter in this role provides the climax of the first main part of Matthew's narrative. Of course the climax of the whole work may be compared to Matthew 16, for Matt. 28:18–20 indicates that it is the duty of disciples to make other disciples and this involves teaching them. In Matthew, but not in Mark, Jesus instructs his disciples on

the dos and don'ts of being teachers (5:19). The whole point of mentioning the scribes' and Pharisees' righteousness in 5:20 is that they are
rival teachers. Again in 10:24–25a, a passage not paralleled elsewhere,
a disciple is said not to be above his master teacher (Jesus), but rather
is called to be like his teacher.

Thus, Matthew edits and arranges his material in careful fashion to
present a certain kind of portrait of the central character in the narrative—Jesus. In general, as was common in ancient biographies, the
method of portraiture is indirect, allowing words and deeds and relationships to reveal the identity and character of the main character. A
close examination of the editorial work shows the type of pedagogy the
author has in mind. Strikingly, in Matthew's Gospel, while the disciples repeatedly address Jesus as Lord (see, e.g., 8:21, 25; 14:28; 16:22),
when a stranger or a Jewish leader addresses Jesus it is as rabbi or
teacher (see, 8:19; 12:38; 19:16; 22:16, 24, 36). Notice that it is only the
betrayer Judas among the disciples who calls Jesus rabbi (26:25, 49).
What this tells us immediately is that the First Evangelist does not see
titles or terms of respect like rabbi or teacher as adequate to describe
Jesus. This is not to say that such titles are inaccurate, for indeed texts
like Matt. 23:8–10 make plain that Matthew does want to say Jesus is
a sage or teacher, indeed *the* teacher of the disciples. Thus, the disciples, who will in turn disciple others, should not seek to label themselves as rabbi or use the customary term of endearment ʾabbāʾ or
Father sometimes used of Jewish teachers or wise men.[27] Further, in
Matt. 26:17–19 near the end of Jesus' earthly ministry Jesus calls himself "the teacher" with the assumption the audience will know immediately who this is. The setting apart of Jesus as sage, and more than
sage, from other potential teachers is also seen in the contrast found at
the end of the Sermon on the Mount in chapter 7, where Jesus, who
teaches with independent authority, is contrasted with *their* scribes.
The point here is twofold: Jesus is no mere scribe and the problem is
not with scribes in general but with *their* scribes.

The image of Jesus as sage or teacher is so crucial for Matthew that
in redactional summary passages he cites teaching ahead of preaching
and healing as Jesus' chief task (see 4:23; 9:35; 11:1). This is all the
more striking when one compares the parallel Markan summary in
Mark 1:39, where there is no mention of teaching, and when one compares Matt. 11:1 to Luke 7:1, where in the Lukan passage there is no
use of the term "teaching." The content of this teaching is seen repeatedly to be parables, aphorisms, and Wisdom discourses. This image of

Jesus as sage or teacher and his disciples as scribes or teachers is crucial and gets at the heart of some of things that make Matthew's contribution to the christological discussion distinctive.

Much has been made of the idea that Matthew's central idea is that
Christ is the New Moses, offering five great discourses, the first even
from a mount. Without discounting this idea, probably too much has
been made of it. For one thing it is not clear whether there are five or
six discourses (depending on what one does with Matthew 23 in relationship to chapters 24–25). Moreover, the evangelist seems as interested in contrasting Jesus with Moses as in comparing the two. After
all, Moses did not ban oath taking, all killing, or adultery of the heart!
Even in the birth narratives where a Moses motif has sometimes been
detected it is surely a secondary motif because Matthew 1 is by and
large about how Jesus can be called Son of David and Matthew 2 about
how he can be called Son of God (see below). Moses is not a Son of
David or of God, and he is certainly not a Son of Man figure, and these
are the three primary titles Matthew applies to Jesus. We must conclude that the "New Moses" idea, if it exists at all in Matthew, is at
most a minor theme, and so one must look elsewhere to discern
Matthew's distinctive contribution to the christological discussion. I
would argue that he makes his most distinctive contribution by showing that (1) Jesus is a messianic Son of David, like but greater than
Solomon, offering even greater Wisdom; (2) he is Wisdom come in person and so embodying and conveying the very presence of God to God's
people (Immanuel); (3) he is Son of God, whose characteristic intimacy
with the Father is modeled in part on the relationship of Wisdom to
God in Jewish sapiential literature; and (4) he is the great eschatological sage, offering God's final teaching for salvation.

What then happens when an early Jewish Christian wishes to portray Jesus as like Solomon but even greater, being the very embodiment of Wisdom on earth? For a largely Jewish audience such as
Matthew's, one would stress that Jesus is *the* Son of David in a way the
source did not (the phrase is found eleven times in Matthew but only
four in Mark and Luke and *none* in John).[28] The Jewish tone of this
Gospel is set from the very beginning, where Matthew expands on his
Markan source by adding the birth narratives, which stress that Jesus
is the Son of David, the seventh son of the seventh son.[29]

It was also the case, however, that in Jewish tradition ultimately
Wisdom was *the* teacher of God's people (see Prov. 1:20–30; 8:10–16;
Sir. 4:24; Wis. Sol. 6:14; 8:4). This role of Wisdom as *the* teacher is

assigned by Matthew to Jesus himself, which explains how Matthew can portray Jesus as both sage and Wisdom. In calling Jesus *the* Teacher, a sapiential Christology would be implied to those steeped in Jewish Wisdom material (cf., e.g., Wisdom of Solomon, where the teacher is ultimately Wisdom, who inspires Solomon, but also Solomon as great sage).

Various scholars have attempted to make one or another of the more familiar christological titles the key to Matthean Christology (e.g., J. D. Kingsbury choosing Son of God).[30] This appears to me to be a fundamental mistake for two reasons. First, it neglects the sapiential character of the Gospel as a whole, which helps to explain how all the titles are used. Second, a comprehensive approach must be taken because there is overlap in meaning between some of the titles. Consider, for example, Matthew's use of Son of Man when compared to his sources. We find the title Son of Man thirty-two times in Matthew, twenty-one of which come over from Mark or Q, but nine of which are found in special Matthean material. Six of these nine are in apocalyptic contexts that stress the future roles of the Son of Man, and in some of these—for example, Matt. 13:41—the Son of Man traditions in Daniel 7 stand in the background here.[31] In Matthew, as in Mark, Son of Man is Jesus' chief phrase of self-identification (see Matt. 16:13–20). During his ministry Jesus is Son of Man, representative of his people and one endowed with kingdom power, but he is also the one coming as Son of Man to be the apocalyptic judge.[32] But Jesus' ministry roles and roles at the eschaton can also be described in other terms and with other titles (e.g., the use of Son of David of Jesus' ministry).

Another title that has led to misunderstandings of Matthew's Christology is the title *kyrios*. Too often it has been assumed that *kyrios* necessarily implies the divinity of Christ in this Gospel. This overlooks the fact that when it is used in the vocative, such as in 7:22 or 25:11 it seems to mean no more than "respected sir," or "master." It is certainly arguable that this is the meaning in 8:2, 6, 8, 21; 25:14; and 28:30, where an appeal to Jesus and not a confession is being made. In short, this title cannot be used as the quintessential proof that Matthew has imposed a high Christology on more primitive material.

Of course the title Christ is very important to the First Evangelist. He does wish to argue that Jesus is the Jewish Messiah (see 11:2), the one who sought out the lost sheep of Israel. Christ's messiahship is furthermore closely connected with his role as acting for and perhaps even in some sense as Israel, fulfilling the roles Israel had failed in (see

2:13–15, where what was said of Israel is now said of Christ). There is a definite Jewish flavor to how Matthew uses the term, though there is also the additional Christian twist of speaking about Christ as one who must suffer and die on the cross. It is interesting that it is often in healing contexts where Jesus is revealed to be the Christ in this Gospel (see 10:1, 8; 11:2). Jesus in these contexts speaks of his fulfilling of Isaianic prophecies. Yet with all this Christ is not an omnibus term that explains or provides the essence of the christological reflections of Matthew.

For one thing, messiahship is primarily a theme in chapters 1–4, and not surprisingly it is intertwined with the material about the Son of David and Jesus as Israel (2:15; 4:3, 6). Furthermore, it is also precisely in these early chapters, perhaps particularly chapter 2, that we are introduced to Jesus as Son of God, though the title occurs also at crucial junctures of the Gospel (4:3, 6; 14:33; 16:15–16). Jesus is said to be Son of God from birth and so by nature because of the virginal conception (on which see below),[33] whereas he is Son of David through Joseph by legal adoption. It is also true that Matthew more than the other evangelists emphasizes that Jesus is king, in particular king of the Jews (1:1, 6, 17, 18–25; 2:6, 15; 9:27; 12:22–24; 21:1–14).[34] *All* of these titles, then, are ways of showing Jesus to be not only the fulfiller of Old Testament prophecy but also the fulfiller of Israel's mission on earth. In Jesus, Israel's history is recapitulated and climaxes. These titles are woven into the fabric of the discussion, and no one of them really explains the author's christological orientation and perspective in the way focusing on Jesus as sage and Wisdom does.

In a moment we will attempt to show how following the flow of Matthew's narrative and doing a sapiential interpretation of the material best gets at Matthew's Christology. It is in order to point out, however, that it is not just in the overt statements about Jesus as Wisdom that we find a high Christology but that there are other hints as well. The use of the term Immanuel or the idea behind it to frame the Gospel (1:23 and 28:20–21) is likely to indicate not just that Jesus brought the presence of God to God's people while he was on earth, but, as the Matthew 28 reference suggests, he continued to be, even after his death and resurrection, the divine presence with them forever. This concept likely has ontological overtones suggesting the omnipresence of Jesus after his exaltation. Notice also Matthew's modification of the Markan saying "Why do you call me good? No one is good but God alone" (compare Mark 10:17–18 with Matt. 19:16–17).

Matthew avoids the possible interpretation that Jesus might be neither good nor God by having Jesus say "Why do you ask me about the good? There is only One who is good." This says something significant about Matthew's christological outlook.

One may also consider Matt. 22:14ff./Mark 12:35ff. as further evidence that Matthew is comfortable even calling Jesus David's Lord in a way that suggests that that Lord existed before David. Matthew is the only one who states explicitly that this Son of David is Lord. Here Jesus is revealed as Lord, Son of David, even Christ, but most importantly in this text Lord is not used in an honorific way or as a vocative. Rather, something ontological, something about Christ's essential nature, seems to be implied. This is in no way surprising in a Gospel that begins by calling Jesus Immanuel and predicating of him a divinely caused conception, and throughout uses Scriptures that the author thinks Jesus fulfilled or is described by, including Scriptures that previously were taken to be about Yahweh and his activities (see, e.g., Matt. 21:15–16, drawing on Ps. 8:2). It is interesting to see how Matthew has modified his source at the crucial point of Jesus' trial. Matthew 26:63 has Jesus' answer to the high priest as "You have said so," which may be an affirmation ("you have said it"), but if so it is certainly a less clear one than what we find in Mark (see above). Schnackenburg suggests that this modification may be related to the fact that Jesus is mocked at the cross as Son of God in this Gospel (Matt. 27:40, 43). "The mockers hang on to the high priest's question and want to carry it *ad absurdum.*"[35] There is, then, a good deal to be learned by looking at the traditional titles in Matthew, but this does not do full justice to Matthew's christological approach, as we shall now see.

The Gospel begins with the announcement that it will present Jesus the Messiah, the Son of David, in other words. Jesus the King, and so it begins where one ought to start with a story about a king, with his royal pedigree. Jesus' genealogy has some surprises in it, but then so did Solomon's, and it is the desire of the evangelist to show that Jesus is indeed a Solomonic figure, only greater than Solomon—*the* archetypal Son of David.

Kings were often said in antiquity to have miraculous births, and Jesus is no different. Not only is Jesus born of a virgin but he is to be called Immanuel, one of the throne names for the king mentioned in Isa. 9:6.[36] It must be kept steadily in view that the precise title Son of David is not really attested before the time *Psalms of Solomon* was written. In other words, our author's frequent use of this title throughout his Gospel reflects a late sapiential perspective, not an Old Testament one. The term Immanuel at the least implies that God is present with his people through Jesus, but the discussion of the form this presence takes is held back until Matt. 11:19, where Jesus is specifically called Wisdom—in other words, God's presence come in the flesh.[37] Again in Matt. 13:42 the old categories, the old titles don't fully capture Jesus—one greater than Solomon is present, one who is more aptly described as Wisdom, who is divine and yet who can be distinguished from the Father.

But if Jesus is the great king, *the* Son of David long awaited, one would expect signs in the heavens to announce his coming, and would expect king's counselors and seers to announce his coming and visit him, and would expect that he would be in power struggles with other great kings. This is of course precisely how things are portrayed in Matthew 2. The birth of Jesus is signaled by a great star; he is visited by Magi; he is presented with gifts fit for a king; and he is the subject of a plot by King Herod and forced to flee the country.

Great kings are foretold by prophets, and when kings traveled anywhere they had heralds going before them announcing their approach and arrival. This is clearly the role John the Baptist plays in the first Gospel. He is said to fulfill Isa. 40:3 and speaks of the greater one coming after him in a way that plays down his own status (Matt. 3:11). Later in the story John sends his own disciples to find out about the royal or messianic deeds of Jesus (11:2). Jesus at that point recites his deeds and in a statement paralleling 11:2 says that Wisdom is vindicated by her deeds.

Of course Jewish kings, like most ancient kings, had to be anointed before they could act or speak as royal ones, and so Matt. 3:13–17 records the anointing ceremony and the public pronouncement, "This is my Beloved Son with whom I am well pleased." Here our evangelist not only is drawing carefully on his Q source but is re-presenting it with a sapiential twist drawing on material from Wisdom of Solomon. It was expected of a king that he would "fulfill all righteousness" (see Wis. Sol. 1:1ff.) and that the endowment of God's Spirit poured out on the king also included the endowment of divine wisdom to make decisions and help the people. Matthew has added the phrase "with whom I am well pleased" in 17:5 to make clear the parallels between the baptismal and transfiguration scenes. At the Matthean transfiguration we hear that Jesus' face shone like the sun and his clothes became dazzling white, a description extremely reminiscent of the description of

Wisdom in Wis. Sol. 7:26–29. The point is that Jesus is being portrayed early and late in this Gospel as the royal one, the Son of David, as the one who manifests the very properties of Wisdom precisely because he is Wisdom come to earth.

In the Wisdom of Solomon, what follows the discussion of the investiture of the king with spirit and wisdom is the discussion of the testing of the king (Wis. Sol. 2:12ff.). This passage in fact illuminates the two major testing scenes in Matthew 4 and 26–27 and deserves to be quoted in part: "Let us lie in wait for the righteous man, because he is inconvenient to us and opposes our actions. . . . He professes to have a knowledge of God and calls himself a child of God . . . he calls the last end of the righteous happy, and boasts that God is his father." This portion informs our reading of Matthew 4, but what follows it informs Matthew 26–27: "Let us see if his words are true, and let us test what will happen at the end of his life; for if the righteous man is God's child, he will help him, and will deliver him from his adversaries. Let us test him with insult and torture him, so that we may find out how gentle he is [see also Matt. 11:29], and make trial of his forbearance. Let us condemn him to a shameful death. . . ." Jesus thus is being tested first and last as the righteous king, the true Son of David like Solomon. He resists by relying on God's Word or wisdom to resist temptations.

At the beginning of the account of Jesus' ministry in Matt. 4:12ff. another quotation from Isaiah (9:1–2) is offered. This text is part of a longer passage lauding the coming great Davidic king with numerous throne names, and then is added in Isa. 9:6–7: "his authority will grow continually, and there will be endless peace for the throne of David and his kingdom." When Jesus goes forth preaching and healing and teaching, he is meant to be seen as a king going forth bringing righteousness and healing and proper rule to the land.

It is not necessary to go over in detail the sapiential material in Matthew 5–7, which would be better called the Teaching on the Mount. What is striking is that when one examines the topics broached in this so-called sermon it reads like the standing topics discussed in Proverbs 2–6, after the introduction of Wisdom herself at the outset of Proverbs, topics dealing with dealing with the narrow path, with beatitudes, with warning against sexual impurity, with acknowledgment of God's wisdom revealed in nature, and exhortations to guard one's speech. Nor is it an accident that the discourse in Matthew 5–7 ends in 7:24ff. with the parable about the wise man. The one who hears and heeds this discourse will become such a person.[38] Matthew is portraying Jesus as the king greater than Solomon and beyond that even as Wisdom offering her teaching. Thus, the reader will not be jolted when shortly after this Jesus is simply identified as Wisdom.

The miracles stories in Matthew 8–9 also fit into this sapiential presentation of Jesus as one greater than Solomon/Wisdom because Jesus heals as the Son of David, as a Solomonic figure, and Josephus reminds us in *Antiquities* 8:45–47 that God granted Solomon knowledge of the arts to use against demons and the wisdom to cure illnesses. In every instance after the birth narratives, the phrase Son of David arises in Matthew in a healing context. Jesus is a healer like Solomon; therefore, he should be appealed to using the Solomonic title. Elsewhere we have offered a more detailed analysis along these lines of all Matthew's material, but what we have said above should suffice to show that all the different kinds of ministry teachings and narratives are read through a sapiential filter by this evangelist in the service of his presentation of Jesus as both royal Son of David like Solomon, as the ultimate Jewish sage, and also as the one greater than Solomon—namely, Wisdom come in the flesh.[39]

Matthew's presentation is not partial and piecemeal; it is systematically approached and cannot be limited to the passages more obviously indebted to Wisdom material such as 23:37ff., where Jesus is seen as Wisdom trying to gather her Jewish children in Jerusalem, or 11:28–29, where Wisdom offers her yoke, drawing on Sir. 6:19–31 and 51:26. The matrix of the whole presentation of Christ in this Gospel is sapiential, and the other titles and terms are fitted into this wider context. This is why focusing on the traditional titles is inadequate, even when it includes the title King.

For Matthew there is one great sage, one great teacher, one final Son of David, one Wisdom of God, one person who can be called Immanuel. This person is Jesus. He was a nonpareil who could be both David's Son and yet also David's Lord, both Son of Man and yet also Son of God. It is indeed hard to imagine a much higher Christology than is conveyed in this Gospel, which begins with a person who is Immanuel and ends with his being given all authority in heaven and earth to empower and send out disciples for the task of replication. The yoke to which Matthew beckons his listeners is at once the yoke of Jesus' wisdom and the yoke of Jesus as Wisdom, who says "take up your cross and follow me" as well as "take my yoke upon you."

We have reached the apex of canonical christological development with these statements, for it is clear that Jesus is seen as both human and divine, both sage and Wisdom, even if Matthew nowhere directly uses the term *theos* of Jesus. For this evangelist, the one who was Wisdom and Immanuel was of course not less than divine and yet fully human. In his view it was wise to say this much, but perhaps unwise to try to say more. There was, however, one Gospel writer who dared to say more, as we will see when we turn to the Fourth Gospel, after we have examined Luke-Acts.

NOTES

1. R. Schnackenburg, *Jesus in the Gospels: A Biblical Christology*, trans. O. C. Dean (Louisville: Westminster/J. Knox, 1995), pp. 321–22.

2. See H. C. Kee, "Christology in Mark's Gospel," in *Judaisms and their Messiahs at the Turn of the Era*, ed. J. Neusner, W. S. Green, and E. Frerichs (Cambridge: Cambridge University Press, 1987), pp. 187–208.

3. The issue still receives significant play and is given fresh life in books such as *The Messianic Secret*, ed. C. Tuckett (Philadelphia: Fortress Press, 1983).

4. See my discussion in *The Christology of Jesus* (Philadelphia: Fortress Press, 1990), pp. 261–67.

5. See J. D. G. Dunn, "The Messianic Secret in Mark," in *The Messianic Secret*, ed. Tuckett, pp. 116–31.

6. See pp. 53ff. above.

7. See pp. 24ff. above.

8. In other words, I think Mark's ending was lost, probably because Matthew's Gospel, a much fuller and complete Gospel quickly became the church's favorite in the second century. Moreover, since Matthew contained 95 percent or more of Mark (and half of that is a verbatim copy of Mark), Mark's Gospel was quickly eclipsed and fell into disuse in most circles. It is quite easy to see how the original ending could be lost, because ancient documents tended to be left with the end edge exposed to the elements. Even in ancient times people were lazy about rewinding things. Perhaps only one vertical column of the original document was lost, and perhaps we may see the substance of what it looked like in Matt. 28:9–10, 16–20.

9. See R. A. Burridge, *What are the Gospels?* (Cambridge: Cambridge University Press, 1992).

10. See the discussion in Schnackenburg, *Jesus in the Gospels*, pp. 17–73.

11. There is some textual uncertainty here since some manuscripts don't have the phrase "Son of God," but it is supported by a wide array of early and important manuscripts including Aleph-a and B, and D and is probably the original reading.

12. J. D. Kingsbury, *The Christology of Mark* (Philadelphia: Fortress Press, 1984).

13. It is not convincing to argue, as Neyrey does, that the use of "Son of God" in this Gospel has no overtones of divinity because the term was used in the Old Testament of God's chosen people as a whole (Exod. 4:22; Deut. 14:1; Hos. 2:1). This logic overlooks two important factors: (1) Jesus alone is being singled out at the baptismal and transfiguration scenes (and elsewhere) as God's unique Son in a way that echoes the material in the Psalms, where the king is singled out in this fashion; (2) Jesus' disciples as a group are never called the Son of God or the sons of God in this Gospel.

14. See the discussion of P. J. Achtemeier, "Mark, Gospel of," in *The Anchor Bible Dictionary*, ed. David Noel Freedman (New York: Doubleday, 1992), 4:551–53.

15. See E. Richard, *Jesus: One and Many. The Christological Concept of New Testament Authors* (Wilmington, Del.: M. Glazier, 1988), p.117.

16. Schnackenburg, *Jesus in the Gospels*, p. 52.

17. Achtemeier, "Mark," p. 553.

18. I personally would not see Mark 12:25–37 as evidence that Mark thought Jesus denied that he was David's Son. Rather, he is denying a false understanding of that sonship that considers the Messiah only David's human heir and not also someone much greater than David.

19. See Schnackenburg, *Jesus in the Gospels*, pp. 58–59.

20. Ibid., p. 39.

21. Ibid., p. 52.

22. But see ibid., pp. 48–49.

23. Richard rightly points out that in Mark there are only two instances where Son of Man is used of Jesus as he acts in the present on earth, while the vast majority of instances have to do with the coming suffering of the Son of Man or his future return from heaven (*Jesus: One and Many*, pp. 110–11). This must count against the suggestion that the earliest Son of Man sayings were noneschatological in character and were simply an oblique form of self-reference, something like "a person in my position."

24. It is my view that both Matthew and John, like Mark, should be seen as examples of ancient biographies, with Jesus as the central subject matter. This distinguishes these Gospels from Luke's, because his purposes are more specifically historical. Luke does not follow biographical conventions at the beginning of his Gospel, offering instead a historical prologue followed by a chapter not on Jesus but on the Baptist and his family. This was not how biographical works were meant to begin. Luke's interest is more broadly in salvation history; the other Gospels in Jesus as savior, Lord, etc. This is why, I submit, that there is not as much christological substance or development in Luke's work as we find in the other Gospels.

25. A fuller version of this discussion can be found in my *Jesus the Sage: The Pilgrimage of Wisdom* (Minneapolis: Fortress Press, 1994), pp. 335–80.

26. Richard, for example, rightly notes that in Matthew Jesus refers to God as my Father some sixteen times, and all but two of these instances are unique

to Matthew and reflect his editing of Mark, Q, or other sources (*Jesus: One and Many*, p. 151).

27. On ʾ*abbāʾ*, see pp. 61ff. above in regard to its use of mere mortals.

28. Here we have a salient difference between Matthew and John. The latter's primary target audience may well have been Gentiles (by which I mean that Gentiles were the ones with whom the Christian teachers were to share these Johannine traditions), unlike Matthew—hence the more universal and less Jewish approach to a host of matters, including the Jewishness of Jesus in John. Jesus is seen in John as the universal Wisdom that made the world, in Matthew as the embodiment of God's revelation to God's people Israel, as *the* Son of David.

29. See Schnackenburg, *Jesus in the Gospels*, pp. 75–76.

30. See J. D. Kingsbury, *Matthew: Structure, Christology, Kingdom* (Philadelphia: Fortress Press, 1975).

31. See Schnackenburg, *Jesus in the Gospels*, p. 101.

32. It is possible that Son of Man did not become a prominent title used to confess Jesus even in Jewish Christian circles because it did not really describe his role now in heaven, but rather only his roles on earth, either at his first or at his second coming. In other words, it did not describe his present relationship with the church, which is what many of these titles such as Lord do describe.

33. As in Luke, Son of God does say something about Jesus' nature, not just his roles or tasks.

34. The spread of the term throughout Matthew distinguishes this Gospel from both Mark and Luke, which do not really use the term until the climax of the Gospel in the passion material.

35. Schnackenburg, *Jesus in the Gospels*, p. 99.

36. Certainly part of the significance of the virginal conception story is to make clear that God alone is Jesus' Father, and thus that Jesus has divine parentage, which must affect how one evaluates Jesus' character and career. See Richard, *Jesus: One and Many*, p. 150

37. Richard rightly stresses that the Immanuel terminology is no mere label but indicates God's actual existential presence in the life of Jesus (*Jesus: One and Many*, p. 154).

38. Matthew is careful not to call such a person a *sophos*; rather, he uses the phrase *andri phronimo* lest it be thought that Jesus' disciples could be sages just like Jesus. No, their wisdom is of a derivative sort, depending on the teaching of the Master.

39. See *Jesus the Sage*, pp. 349–68.

6

Lord and Savior:
The Christology of Luke-Acts

I F THERE IS A CASE to be made for one of the New Testament writers
being both a Gentile and an ancient Greco-Roman historian that
case must be made for Luke. These factors seem to have affected
Luke's christological perspective, but it is also likely that we must add
to the discussion of Luke's Christology the probability that Luke's
audience was Gentile. We may see these factors coming into play
when Christ is designated Savior of both Jews and Gentiles in Luke-
Acts (see, e.g., Luke 2:11, 30–32), but there are other ways these factors
affect Luke's presentation of Jesus. For example, it has been widely
noted that Luke deals with his christological titles with some historical sensitivity.[1] Thus, for example, while Luke himself calls Jesus
"Lord" in the narrative framework of his Gospel in the full Christian
sense of the term (see Luke 7:13), he is careful to avoid placing such a
full Christian usage on the lips of his characters in the Gospel narrative (see below). These factors need to be taken into account as we
examine the christological material in Luke-Acts.

There was a time when it was thought of Acts as it has been thought
of Mark, that at most one could find a rudimentary Christology here.
In more recent years C. H. Talbert, I. H. Marshall, and others have
shown Luke to be a masterful theologian as well as a historian even
though he does present us with various examples of primitive christological reflection, especially in Acts. I will begin my discussion of
Lukan Christology with Acts for two unrelated reasons. The first is
that I think C. K. Barrett is likely right that Luke's Gospel has been
revised or smoothed out through the editorial process in a way that is
not true of Acts. If this is so, it means we are more likely to find prim-

153

itive Lukan Christology in Acts than in Luke's Gospel. This approach
of beginning with Acts of course has its limitations, not least because
there is a certain narratological and chronological approach that Luke
seems to take to matters, such that he tries hard to avoid anachronism
in the dialogues in his Gospel and tries to show the differences
between how Christ was discussed before and after Easter and Pentecost. There is also the very real possibility that by beginning with Acts
we may be able to find some pre-Lukan theology that goes back to an
earlier stage in the Christian thinking about Jesus (though perhaps not
back to Jesus).

JESUS THE EXALTED LORD: CHRISTOLOGY IN ACTS

Certain things immediately stand out when one examines Acts in
comparison to Luke's Gospel. For instance we may contrast the plentiful use of the phrase Son of Man in the Gospel with the singular use
of the term in Acts 7:56. Yet even the single reference to the Son of
Man in Acts is significant, as this is the *only* use of this phrase outside
the Gospels other than when Daniel 7 is quoted in Revelation. There
the use is not titular but involves an analogy ("one like a son of man").[2]
Clearly there were various titles or terms with a Jewish and/or Old
Testament background that soon fell into disuse once the Gospel was
increasingly shared with Gentiles, and the phrase Son of Man seems to
have been a victim of this process. It is interesting that in Acts 7:56
there are differences in the way the phrase is used compared to what
we find in Luke's Gospel.

First, there is the fact that in the Gospel Son of Man and glory are
discussed purely in future terms, unlike in Acts. Second, here the Son
of Man is standing, not merely seated at the right hand of God. Clearly
both here and in Luke's future Son of Man sayings in his Gospel,
Daniel 7 lies in the background. What we see here is the way the time
frame affects the christological expression. Stephen speaks believing
that Jesus has already ascended and is at God's right hand, for the
church exists in the era after Jesus' resurrection and ascension. In other
words, the image we find in Acts 7:56 would be out of place in the
Gospel unless Jesus was speaking of someone other than himself when
he referred to the future coming of the Son of Man. C. F. D. Moule has
made the case eloquently that this is but one example that Luke uses

christological terms and titles with a clear historical perspective on the differences between the pre- and post-resurrection situation and the pre- and post-resurrection community of Jesus' followers. From a historian's point of view, the resurrection has decisively changed things for and about Jesus, and so too for and about the community that spoke of him.[3]

It is in fact an integral part of Luke's very spatial and temporal approach to things including Christology that we find at the end of Luke's Gospel (Luke 24) and throughout Acts what Moule calls an exaltation Christology—a Christology that Jesus is up there in heaven, exalted to the right hand of God. It is not an accident that both the Gospel and Acts include the ascension, which event makes clear Christ's bodily absence.[4] This too is a reflection of Luke's attempt to think historically about what happened to Jesus and his body. Jesus, then, in Luke's view left nothing behind but his followers. This is also why the sending of the Spirit is so crucial in the Lukan scheme of things. If Jesus is absent, the church must have some source of divine power and direction, and the Spirit provides both.

Probably too much has been made of the fact that only Luke gives us a doctrine of the ascension, for it may well be alluded to in the Fourth Gospel when we are told that Jesus must return to the Father, and texts like John 20:17 suggest that this has some bearing on Mary and others clinging to Jesus' body. The notion may also be implied in the christological hymns that refer to Christ's exaltation to God's right hand, and, more to the point, texts like 1 Corinthians 15 assert not only a bodily resurrection of Jesus but also a definite limited period of time after Easter when Jesus appeared in the body to his followers, after which Jesus' bodily presence on earth ceased. In other words, while only Luke articulates the notion of the ascension, it seems to be presupposed in other New Testament sources, and so is probably not an idea conjured up by Luke as a sort of theologoumenon or non-historical theological idea. To the contrary, the early christological hymns assume a descending and ascending Christ, a notion found in Eph. 4:8 as well when Paul applies Ps. 68:18 to Christ. For a Gentile audience, the ascension of Jesus would have reminded them of ancient heroic figures that were approved by the gods and taken up into heaven.

It is right to stress that for Luke the ascension implies a sort of absentee role for Christ in heaven, with the Spirit now acting on earth as Christ's agent. Texts such as Acts 2:33; 3:21; 9:3; 22:6 and 26:13

stress that Christ is in heaven, even if he appears to some on earth such as to Stephen or Paul (see, e.g., Acts 7; 9; and 23:11). In almost all instances in Acts it is by the Spirit or an angel that God acts on earth (see 8:26, 29, 39; 11:28; 12:7; 13:4; 15:28; 16:6; 20:23; 21:11; 27:23). Notice as a corollary of this that we do not really find the "in Christ" or corporate Christ theology in Luke-Acts as we do in Paul's letters. Nor is there any ongoing Immanuel Christology in Acts such as we find at the beginning and end of Matthew's Gospel. In other words, Luke's Christology seems simpler and more primitive than what we find in Paul's letters or in the incorporation theology in the Fourth Gospel.

The historical perspective of Luke is in full evidence if we compare and contrast the use of the term Lord in Acts and in Luke's Gospel. Luke calls Jesus "Lord" in the narrative portions of both his volumes (compare Luke 7:13 with Acts 23:11), in a way the other Synoptic writers refrain from doing in the narrative sections of their Gospels. Jesus even calls himself Lord obliquely once in Luke 19:31–34, but this usage is found in the other Synoptics as well and may mean little more than "master" or "owner." However, no other being calls Jesus Lord in Luke's Gospel unless a person is under inspiration (1:43, 76) or the term is found on the lips of an angel (2:11). Once we get past the resurrection of Jesus, various people can and do call Jesus Lord in the ordinary course of things (compare Luke 24:34 with Acts 10:36–38).

The same phenomenon can be found in the use of sonship language. In the Gospel, Jesus is called Son by other than human voices (Luke 1:32, 35; 3:22; 4:3ff.; 8:28), but in Acts in both 9:20 and 13:33 Paul openly calls Jesus Son. Moreover, words about Jesus as Savior or as one who saves are found only on superhuman lips in the Gospel (2:11, 30; 3:6), but after the resurrection and ascension such talk is an essential part of the church's confession (Acts 4:12; 5:31; 13:23). Luke is supremely conscious of the difference the resurrection made in terms of what Jesus did and what he could become for his followers. He could not have truly fulfilled his christological role, nor could his followers have confessed him as Christ if he had not risen from the dead. The resurrection is for Luke the watershed event for both Christology and ecclesiology.

It is not entirely surprising that in these two volumes, which are so firmly grounded in historical considerations, there is no clear preexistence language applied to Christ, though some texts might imply the notion. It is interesting, however, that Acts 2:31 implies that David saw Jesus' resurrection coming in the future but says nothing about David seeing or foreseeing Jesus himself. In any event, Christ's preexistence (which does not deal with his historical manifestation) is not a subject Luke chooses to debate or even really to address. Luke's concern is with Jesus from his birth to his present and ongoing exaltation in and reigning from heaven as Lord over all. He also refers to Christ as the coming judge (Acts 3:20ff.; 17:31), though this is also not a central concern of his in either of his volumes. Notice the focus of Peter's description in Acts 2:22–36, where the whole scope of Jesus' ministry is chronicled from birth as a man (2:22) to his exaltation and coronation in vv. 33–36. The humanness of Jesus is stressed in Acts by the repeated reference to Jesus as "of Nazareth" (3:6; 4:10 et al.), just as it was stressed in the Gospel as well.[5] This is often emphasized in conjunction with the name Jesus Christ, not simply Jesus. Acts 10:36ff. is in various ways one of the more important texts in Acts for christological discussion, for here we not only see the exalted Christ, the one who is Lord over all, but in the same text we find the so-called low christological notion of God being with Jesus and anointing him with Spirit and power while he was on earth. The point is that Luke wishes to stress Jesus' humanness but at the same time reveal his divine roles.

E. Schweizer has amply shown that Luke is also concerned to reveal that Jesus was the Davidic Messiah and Son of God, a connection made through Ps. 2:7, among other texts. Acts 2:30 and 13:33 bring to the fore a "Messianic figure, God's Son of Davidic descent who rules over Israel in the latter days."[6] This is not a major image in Acts, but it is significant in that it makes clear that Luke has no desire to portray Jesus as simply a man or a generic savior, but rather as a Jew, and indeed the Jewish Messiah. This comports with the use of the Isaianic material in Acts (Acts 3:13; 4:27–30), which reveals that Jesus is the servant of whom the prophet spoke. It is material such as this that gives no aid to those who think Luke is simply inserting a Christology of his own throughout Acts rather than trying to present a variety of Christologies which he found in his sources. This likely also explains why we find both the titular and nominal use of "Christ" in some of the early Petrine speeches in Acts.[7] Luke does not iron out all the variations he finds in the sources he uses in Acts, and this is why some primitive material can still be found in Acts.

It has often been asserted on the basis of texts like Acts 2:36 (where it is said that God has made Jesus Lord and Christ) that Luke is adoptionist in his Christology. This overlooks that Luke is operating in a historical and narratological mode and discusses such things from a functional perspective. The issue for Luke is not who is Jesus before and after the resurrection, for it is "this same Jesus" in both cases, but rather what roles or functions he assumes after Easter that he could not, or could not fully, assume before Easter. Luke's point is that only as the exalted One could Jesus truly assume the tasks of Lord over all and be Messiah and Savior for all. In other words, Luke is not given to ontological speculation; such texts are about roles and functions and what tasks Jesus did when.

Although there is not a great deal of reflection on the atoning nature of Christ's death in Luke-Acts, there is certainly some. One form this takes is found in the problematic text of Acts 20:28 on the lips of Paul, which probably reads "the blood of His own," referring to Christ's blood. Another form is in the discussion about Christ suffering in order to release people from their sins, or to provide forgiveness (compare Acts 13:38 with Acts 2:38). This is not an insignificant theme, for as D. P. Moessner has stressed: "It is, however, the suffering or death of Jesus that is the fulfillment of Scripture tied most closely to 'the plan of God' which results in the release of sins."[8]

Before we turn to some of the distinctive and interesting christological elements in Luke's Gospel it will be well to look a bit more closely at two of the key titles in Acts—*kyrios* and *Christos*. The former is by far the most frequently used title in all of Luke-Acts, occurring almost twice as often as *christos*. In fact, the majority of all references to Christ as *kyrios* occur in either Luke-Acts (210 times) or in the Pauline letters (275 times) out of a total of 717 instances in the New Testament. The basic concept Luke has of *kyrios* seems to be one who exercises dominion over the world, and particularly over human lives and events. In other words, the term is always used relationally, for if one is to be a lord, one must have subjects.

The term *kyrios* occurs in Acts 104 times, of which only eighteen are references to God the Father and forty-seven definitely refer to Jesus, with most of the rest referring either to Jesus or to God, though it is not always clear which is meant in some of these texts. A clear reference to Jesus is evident in some texts because *kyrios* is combined with the name Jesus (1:21; 4:33; 8:16; 15:11; 16:31; 19:5, 13, 17; 20:24, 35; 21:13), or the name Jesus Christ (11:17; 15:26; 28:31). It is also clear that where *theos* and *kyrios* are combined it is not Jesus that is being discussed (2:39; 3:22). In Acts 2:34, which draws on Ps. 110:1 both God and Jesus are called Lord. It would be wrong to conclude from such a text that Luke sees Christ as only the believer's Lord, for Acts 10:36 makes such an assertion impossible.

Probably when we encounter various Old Testament phrases such as the Day of the Lord (2:20), the angel of the Lord (5:19; 12:11, 23), the fear of the Lord (9:31), or the hand of the Lord (13:11), it is proper to assume that God and not Jesus is meant. There are, however, two probable exceptions to this rule. In view of Christianity being called "The Way" in Acts it is probable that the "way of the Lord" in Acts 18:25 involves a reference to Christ. In addition, the phrase "the Word of the Lord" would appear to refer to the Word about or from Jesus (see 8:25; 13:44, 49; 15:35–36). It is, in any case, important not to underestimate the significance of transferring the term *kyrios* from God the Father to Jesus. "In using *kyrios* of both Yahweh and Jesus in his writings Luke continues the sense of the title already being used in the early Christian community, which in some sense regarded Jesus as on a level with Yahweh."[9] Luke does not directly call Jesus God, but he stands in the tradition of those who found it appropriate to worship Jesus as the Lord and so as divine. He is well aware that the early church's confession was that Jesus was the risen Lord (Acts 10:36; 11:16; 16:31; 20:21). It is to Jesus the risen and exalted Lord that one must turn to be saved (5:14; 9:35; 11:17), and to whom a believer must remain faithful (20:19), and Jesus as Lord commissions people for ministry (20:24).

Luke, even within Acts seems conscious that as time went on the Lord terminology was used of Christ more and more frequently. It is striking that the vast majority of references where God and not Jesus is called Lord are found in Acts 1–10 (2:39; 3:20, 22; 4:26; 7:31; 10:4, 33) or on the lips of Jews or proselytes to Judaism. The further one gets into Acts, the more Christians speak for themselves; and when they do, Lord almost always means Christ. After the council in Acts 15 only one text seems clearly to use *kyrios* of God rather than Christ—17:24. Luke does not shy away from the paradox of speaking of a risen Lord (Luke 24:34); indeed, it is said to be the resurrection that makes Jesus Lord in some sense (Acts 2:36). What this suggests is that Luke uses the term sometimes to indicate when Jesus began to function as Lord and sometimes simply as the Christian way of referring to Christ in Luke's Gentile environment.[10]

More univocal is Luke's use of *christos* in Acts. The term occurs some twenty-six times, and in every case, not surprisingly, it refers to

Jesus. Texts such as Acts 3:18 or 4:26, which have the qualifier "his," make clear that Luke knows the root meaning of the term *christos*, and also understands the term's relational character. If one is "the Christ," one must have been anointed by someone else, namely, God. Hence, in Acts Jesus is God's Christ or Anointed One, but the believer's (and all other creatures) Lord. The full phrase "our Lord Jesus Christ" (15:26) implies both of these relationships. Luke makes explicit in two places that being a Christian involves confessing Jesus as "the Christ" (9:22; 17:22). It is in the witness to the synagogue that this issue is pressed. By way of generalization we may say that "Christ" mainly functions as a name when the audience is Gentile, but can serve as a title when the audience is Jewish (though texts like 2:38; 4:10; 8:12; 10:48; 15:26 make evident that this is not always so). What was critical for Jews to confess was that Jesus is the Christ, the Jewish Messiah (5:22; 7:3), while for Gentiles what was paramount was confessing Jesus as Lord (15:23–26). Luke also emphasizes that it was God's plan for the Christ to suffer (17:2–3) and be raised (2:31, citing Ps. 16:10). Finally, baptism in the name of Jesus Christ is seen as the characteristic entrance ritual for Christians (see Acts 2:38; 10:48).

JESUS THE SPIRITED MESSIAH: CHRISTOLOGY IN LUKE'S GOSPEL

Turning to the Christology of the Gospel, we may mention the unique title (in terms of the usage in the Synoptic Gospels) Savior (see Luke 1:47; 2:11; Acts 5:31; 13:23).[11] This title is found elsewhere in the Gospels only in John 4:42. This term was of course a common one in the Greek-speaking world, but it is not common in the New Testament except in Luke-Acts and in the Pastorals (see 1 Tim. 1:1; 2:3; 4:10; Titus 1:3; 2:10; 3:4, using the term of God and Titus 1:4; 2:13; 3:6; 2 Tim. 1:10 of Christ).[12] For instance, we find it on an inscription about Julius Caesar dating to 48 C.E., where he is called "God manifest and the common savior of human life." Thus Luke, at the inception of his Gospel (here at 2:11), wants to stress to his Gentile audience who the real savior is. As Luke uses the title, it refers to Jesus right from his birth and relates to the Old Testament promises of salvation (see Acts 13:23). In Acts he argues that there is salvation found in no other name (Acts 4:12—such as the name of the emperor). Some of this emphasis may reflect Luke's use of the Septuagint, for God is called Savior (*sōtēr*) fairly often in the Septuagint (see, e.g., Isa. 45:15).[13]

It is interesting that it is Luke alone among the Synoptic writers who combines the title Christ or Messiah with reference to Jesus' suffering (Luke 24:26, 46; cf. Acts 3:18; 17:3; 26:23).[14] In view of the fact that such an idea was probably not found in early Judaism,[15] and Luke himself does not overly stress the point, it is likely this idea goes back to Jesus in the form of the Son of Man suffering.[16] Notice Luke's careful use of *christos* mostly in the titular sense in his Gospel (2:11, 26; 3:15; 4:41; 9:20; 20:41; 22:67) but more often as a name in Acts (2:38; 3:6; 4:10, 33; 8:12).

There is at the climax of Luke's Gospel a rather clear repudiation of the idea that when Jesus is called King it has a political connotation. In Luke's Gospel as in Mark's the title on the cross is King of the Jews, thus Jesus is crucified for insurrection. Of course ironically Jesus shows his kingship in weakness by suffering. The soldiers mock Jesus, assuming that king means political ruler (Luke 23:37), but the thief on the cross understands that Jesus' kingdom is not of this world (see 23:42). Thus, in his passion narrative Luke juxtaposes the two different attitudes toward kings and ruling. Notably it is only in Luke that Jesus is praised as king as he enters the city on Palm Sunday (Luke 19:38), and it is also only in Luke that at the Last Supper Jesus explains that in his realm servanthood, not lording it over people, is the way leaders should act, and he is conferring this sort of leadership role and kingdom on his disciples (Luke 22:25–30). We may compare this to Acts 17:7, where again we find controversy over a misunderstanding about Jesus. The early Christian proclaimers are heard to have proclaimed a king other than Caesar, which is both true and false in different ways. In other words, the irony and sense of double meaning found in the Gospel passages about Jesus as king are seen also in this Acts passage.

In regard to the use of sonship language in the Gospel, Luke is exercised to show that Jesus is Son not by adoption or by obedience but by birth, hence the emphasis on the virginal conception in Luke's birth narrative. Luke 1:32–35 states plainly the truth that Jesus is born God's Son. Luke is happy to refer to Jesus as Son of God, or Son of the Most High, or my Son. It is probable that Son is not exactly synonymous in Luke's mind with king or Messiah, perhaps because in the Old Testament the phrase "Son of God" is never directly used of the coming

Davidic Messiah (but cf. 2 Samuel 7). For Luke, Son implies a unique relationship between Jesus and the one whom he calls Father, as the birth narrative makes clear (see, e.g., Luke 2:49), even though Jesus' disciples may also address God in this fashion (see Luke 11:2). Texts such as Luke 6:35 make evident that the sonship of believers is not on a par with that of Jesus. This is also apparent from Acts, where Son of God is something Christ is confessed to be uniquely (Acts 9:20; cf. 8:37 in the Western text).[17]

The use of Son of Man in Luke's Gospel is very much the same as what we have found in Mark's Gospel—namely, that Son of Man is used to describe the earthly ministry, the suffering, and also the future coming and judging activities of Christ.[18] Luke always uses the definite article before the phrase Son of Man. Luke finds this title important, for in his Gospel he uses the phrase at least three times when it is not found in the parallel (compare Luke 6:22 with Matt. 5:11; Luke 9:22 with Matt. 16:21; Luke 12:8 with Matt. 10:32), and in each of these cases the phrase is on Jesus' lips, as is true in all its other uses in this Gospel. There are of course other titles or terms applied to Jesus that are found only in the Gospel and are only used during Jesus' ministry, such as doctor (Luke 4:23). These titles do not, however, amount to major motifs in Luke's christological presentation. Coupled with the abundant language and discussion of healing in Luke-Acts, however, the reference to Jesus as doctor appears to be part of a theme that is more important for Luke than for the other Synoptists.[19]

Perhaps a further piece of evidence pointing to the primitive character of the Christology in Luke-Acts is that more than many New Testament writers, Luke places a rather notable emphasis on Jesus as a prophet, indeed perhaps as the great prophet like Moses whom God would raise up.[20] As such he is seen as the last great eschatological and messianic prophet or, to put it the other way around, a prophetic Messiah. Perhaps the easiest point of entry into this form of christological thinking is to examine Acts 2:22–24: "Jesus of Nazareth, a man attested to you by God with mighty works and wonders and signs which God did through him in your midst . . . this Jesus you crucified. But God raised him up." This must be compared to Deut. 34:10–12: "There has not arisen a prophet since in Israel like Moses, whom the Lord knew face to face, none like him for all the signs and wonders which the Lord sent him to do." This prophecy is given in the context of statement about Joshua (in Greek, Jesus) that he was "full of the Spirit of wisdom, for Moses had laid his hands upon him." In early

Judaism it was thought that Joshua had not completely fulfilled what Deut. 34:10–12 predicted and so an eschatological fulfillment in a latter-day Moses/Joshua figure was looked for (cf. 4QTestim 1–5; John 1:21; 4:19; 6:14). In the Acts passage cited above the deeds of Jesus during his ministry coupled with his being "raised up" (in a nonmetaphorical sense) by God are seen as clear evidence that the prophecy in Deuteronomy has come to fulfillment in Jesus. Once one recognizes that this is one of the ways Luke is portraying Jesus, it is then possible to go back to his Gospel and make sense of other details.[21]

For example, like Joshua, Jesus is said not only to have received the Spirit bodily (Luke 3:22) but also to have been "full of the Spirit" when tempted (4:1), and he began his preaching "in the power of the Spirit" (4:14). The paradigmatic sermon in Jesus' hometown (Luke 4), which sets the agenda for what follows in the Gospel, depicts Jesus as reading from Isaiah and claiming not only that he understands prophecy but that he fulfills it (4:21). Jesus is the one anointed by God with the Holy Spirit and power (Acts 10:38; cf. Acts 4:27) to prophesy great things, do mighty works, and even bring to fulfillment God's eschatological promises.[22] Luke-Acts is written with the understanding that something fundamental is being revealed about Jesus' prophetic character in Luke 4. Indeed, he calls himself prophet in 4:24. Near the end of the speech in Luke 4, Jesus compares himself to Elijah and Elisha in his deeds (4:25–27).

In Luke 7 this comparison is fully fleshed out when Jesus heals a Gentile centurion in response to Jews' interceding for him (Luke 7:1–10), just as Elisha healed a foreigner in like fashion in response to the intercession of a Jewish girl (2 Kgs. 5:1–14). Further, just as Elijah raised a widow's son from the dead (1 Kgs. 17:17–24) Jesus, raises the widow of Nain's son (Luke 7:11–15), after which the response to these deeds is that a "great prophet whom God raised up" is in their midst and through him "God is visiting his people" (7:16).[23] It is precisely at this juncture that Jesus sends word to the Baptist that "the poor have good news preached to them," fulfilling the prophecy announced in Luke 4.[24]

Equally important to the discussion of this christological theme in Luke-Acts is Luke 13:33–34. The lament over Jerusalem which begins in 13:34 is Q material also found in Matt. 23:37–39. But Luke has prefaced this with 13:33, which is found only in his Gospel: "Yet today and tomorrow and the next day I must be on my way, because it is impossible for a prophet to be killed outside of Jerusalem." Here Jesus is not

merely called a prophet; he calls himself a prophet as he nears the climax of his ministry, and he looks to suffer a prophet's fate. This theme
becomes even more explicit in Acts, where in Stephen's speech in Acts
7, Stephen, himself a prophetic and visionary figure, speaks of a twofold sending of Moses to God's people, first in weakness then in power
with two offers of salvation to God's people (7:23–43). Those who
reject Moses after the second offer of salvation and the great signs and
wonders he worked are themselves to be rejected by God. Stephen
makes the connection with Jesus crystal clear in Acts 7:35–37 especially when he says: "This is the Moses who said to the Israelites, 'God
will raise up for you a prophet from your brothers as he raised me up.'"

But as it turns out, Jesus is not only a prophet; he is the one in the
church age who sends the Spirit of inspiration and prophecy to Christians so they may offer prophetic witness as well. Thus, as L. T. Johnson says, "the power active in their prophetic witness is the Spirit of
Jesus (Acts 2:33; 3:13; 4:10; 13:30–33),"[25] or, perhaps better said, the
Spirit Jesus sent.[26] This image, therefore, of Jesus as the eschatological
or Mosaic prophet who is also therefore the prophetic Messiah is an
important one for Luke, and it serves to bind his christological presentation in Luke-Acts together to some degree. Luke stresses that Jesus
is not only prophet but also Messiah throughout his earthly career and
beyond (at birth [2:11; cf. 1:35]; during the ministry [4:21, 41; 7:20–23;
9:20]; at his death [24:26, 46; Acts 3:18; 17:3; 26:23]; at the resurrection
he becomes both Lord and Messiah [Acts 2:36]; as such he is the object
of the proclamation [Acts 5:42; 8:5; 9:22; 18:5, 28]; and he will come
again as Messiah one day [Acts 3:20; cf. 1:11]).[27] It is understandable
why he might highlight this theme if he wrote to Gentiles, among
whom there was a great respect for and interest in prophecy, including
especially Jewish prophecy.[28]

Another way Jesus is portrayed in Luke's Gospel which was likely
meant to get the attention of Gentiles is the portrayal of Jesus as a sage
or wise man. We see this image especially at the beginning and end of
Luke's Gospel. Thus, in Luke 2:46–48 the boy Jesus astounds the Jewish teachers with both his questions and his answers and overall
understanding, and after this episode Luke stresses that Jesus grew in
wisdom and stature (Luke 2:52). The alert reader is thus prepared for
what follows, for example, in Luke 6; 8; and 10–18, where Jesus is
revealed as a great sage who offers sapiential speech in the form of
beatitudes and woes, aphorisms and parables, riddles and pronounce-
ments, but never prefaces his teaching with the prophetic formula

"Thus says Yahweh" or with a citation of human authorities; he chooses instead to speak on his own authority in a metaphorical way.

As he draws his Gospel to a close, Jesus is portrayed as the ideal wise man, like a Socrates who, with perfect self-control and freedom from fear, goes to his death and is proclaimed a righteous man (23:47) by an independent, unbiased Gentile witness. It is also part of this portrayal that Luke turns the Last Supper into something of a farewell address at a Greco-Roman banquet and a handing over of authority to his successors (Luke 22:29–30).[29]

In summing up, we note two major factors that seem to affect Luke's christological presentation. The first is Luke's historical consciousness, which causes him to be careful about what titles and ideas he predicates of Jesus at what point. He avoids having ordinary persons or disciples call Jesus Lord during the ministry, but finds this characteristic of Christians after the resurrection. Second, it is also important to Luke to distinguish who Jesus is and what he is called. The titles often seem to have more to do with what particular roles, functions or tasks Jesus assumes at particular points in time (e.g., after his baptism, or after his resurrection) than to do with ontology, though there are exceptions to this. Jesus is God's Son from birth in Luke's presentation, but he is not in any full sense Lord until he completes his earthly mission, dies, and is raised and exalted by God so he may take on such roles. It is also true that though Jesus is Son from birth he is not really called this by a group of his followers until some time later. Luke is aware of the disparity between truth's presentation and the recognition of that truth.

Most of these titles indicate relationships—Jesus is God's Christ or Anointed One or God's Son, but the believers' Lord and Savior. In general, what Jesus is in relationship to God is constant from first to last, but what Jesus is in relationship to other human beings, in particular believers, changes along the way depending on a variety of factors such as whether Jesus is raised from the dead yet or not. The phrase "Son of Man" seems to bridge the ontological and functional titles and refer to both who Jesus is (the human being who represents God's people), and what he does (exercise dominion and power, bring in a kingdom). Luke is cautious to make clear that Christ was not merely a second name for Jesus. In both Luke and Acts he uses the term with the article to indicate this fact, though also he increasingly uses it as a name as Acts develops.

R. H. Fuller has offered a useful summary of what we find in Luke-

Acts. He stresses that at Jesus' birth he is destined (and, we would add, made able by nature and pedigree, being Son of God and Son of David) to be the Messiah for God's people. At baptism he is invested as the eschatological prophet and equipped for ministry with the Holy Spirit. At death he is king and suffering Messiah, though the latter is not revealed until after the resurrection, and it is revealed by Jesus himself (Luke 24). Yet Jesus does not completely fulfill any of the major titles (Lord, Son of Man, Savior, Son of God) until he is exalted to the right hand and can truly and fully offer inspiration and salvation by the Spirit he sends to those who accept him on earth. Then he assumes these roles openly and fully. [30] This is Luke's portrait of the Christ.

NOTES

1. See, e.g., R. Schnackenburg, *Jesus in the Gospels: A Biblical Christology,* trans. O. C. Dean (Louisville: Westminster/J. Knox, 1995), pp. 131–33.

2. See pp. 193ff. above.

3. See C. F. D. Moule, "The Christology of Acts," in *Studies in Luke-Acts,* ed. L. E. Keck and J. L. Martyn (London: SPCK, 1968), pp. 159–85.

4. The ascension is depicted in the Gospel as a closure event, bringing to an end Jesus' earthly ministry, but in Acts it is seen as the essential presupposition and preparatory event for Pentecost. See my discussion in my forthcoming Acts commentary for Eerdmans.

5. See the discussion in Schnackenburg, *Jesus in the Gospels,* pp. 181–90. As Schnackenburg says, Luke makes an effort to portray Jesus as not merely human, but humane, full of compassion for the oppressed and disenfranchised, including women and the poor.

6. E. Schweizer, "The Concept of the Davidic 'Son of God' in Acts and its Old Testament Background," in *Studies in Luke-Acts,* ed. Keck and Martyn, pp. 186–93, here p. 191.

7. See pp. 155ff. above and the discussion of S. S. Smalley, "The Christology of Acts Again," in *Christ and the Spirit in the New Testament,* ed. B. Lindars and S. S. Smalley (Cambridge: Cambridge University Press, 1973), pp. 79–84; and cf. his "The Christology of Acts," *Expository Times* 93 (1961–62): 358–62.

8. D. P. Moessner, "The 'script' of the Scriptures in Acts," in *History, Literature, and Society in the Book of Acts,* ed. B. Witherington (Cambridge: Cambridge University Press, 1996), pp. 218–50, here p. 249.

9. J. A. Fitzmyer, *The Gospel of Luke I–IX,* Anchor Bible 28 (New York: Doubleday, 1981), p. 203.

10. See Schnackenburg, *Jesus in the Gospels,* pp. 150–51. He rightly notes

that Luke does not shy away from calling Jesus Lord even in his infancy. See Luke 1:43; 2:11; and perhaps 1:76.

11. Luke's more primitive Christology compared to Matthew's is probably in part the result of his historiographical perspective and his attempt to hellenize the narrative somewhat for his Gentile audience. It is not clear whether Luke's Gospel was written before or after Matthew's, or even whether the date makes a difference in the christological presentation.

12. This is one more piece of evidence that Luke may well have been the one who wrote the Pastorals, perhaps at Paul's behest.

13. See Schnackenburg, *Jesus in the Gospels*, pp. 146–47. He is right that "one must assume that the 'Savior' [usage] has connections with both Jewish tradition and Hellenistic conceptions" (p. 147).

14. As Jerome Neyrey points out, Luke also frequently links the title Christ with Lord, indicating that Jesus is the unique Lord of the covenant, God's anointed agent (*Christ is Community: The Christologies of the New Testament* [Wilmington, Del.: M. Glazier, 1985], p. 133). Cf. Luke 2:11; Acts 2:11, 36; 20:21; 28:31.

15. But see pp. 11ff. above.

16. Servant language is occasionally applied to Jesus in Acts (3:13, 26; 4:27, 30) and there are a few places where the suffering servant notion seems to be in the background; certainly Acts 3:13 alludes to Isa. 53:12. It is not, however, a major motif. See Schnackenburg, *Jesus in the Gospels*, p. 153.

17. See Schnackenburg, *Jesus in the Gospels*, pp. 152–53.

18. Although Luke uses Son of Man less often than for instance Matthew when the parousia is in view, Luke does not omit the idea; see, e.g., Luke 21:27–28. See the discussion by Schnackenburg, *Jesus in the Gospels*, pp. 171–72.

19. See Schnackenburg, *Jesus in the Gospels*, pp. 186–87.

20. J. D. Kingsbury thinks that prophet is not a christological title for Luke, even though Luke casts Jesus' ministry in a prophetic light. Kingsbury prefers the term "prophetic Messiah." The reason for this seems to be that Kingsbury rightly recognizes that to call Jesus prophet, even the Prophet, was insufficient from Luke's perspective. See Kingsbury's "Jesus as the 'Prophetic Messiah' in Luke's Gospel," in *The Future of Christology: Essays in Honor of Leander E. Keck* (Minneapolis: Fortress Press, 1993), pp. 29–42.

21. E. Richard rightly stresses that on the whole, in his Gospel Luke follows Mark's use of titles with only minor modifications, though these modifications are not insignificant (*Jesus: One and Many. The Christological Concept of New Testament Authors* [Wilmington, Del.: M. Glazier, 1988], p. 179. For example, the title Son of God is extended into Jesus' childhood (1.32, 35).

22. See Richard, *Jesus: One and Many*, p. 185.

23. Here I am following the helpful discussion of L. T. Johnson, "Luke-

Acts, Book of" in *The Anchor Bible Dictionary*, ed. David Noel Freedman (New York: Doubleday, 1992), 4:412–15.

24. Neyrey points out that there is overlap between the images of Jesus as Son of Man and prophet in Luke-Acts, particularly in the depiction of Jesus as judge (*Christ is Community*, p. 137).

25. L. T. Johnson, *The Gospel of Luke* (Collegeville, Minn.: Liturgical Press, 1991), p. 18; cf. pp. 19–20. Throughout this section on Jesus as prophet I am indebted to Johnson's discussion.

26. This comports with Luke's major emphasis throughout his two volumes that it is the Spirit that brings salvation as well as its announcement. Jesus, like his disciples, must be full of the Spirit to perform his ministry. Jesus himself provides the paradigm of the Spirit-anointed and appointed and empowered person. It is not, however, true to say as Schnackenburg does (*Jesus in the Gospels*, p. 138) that Jesus is the only Spirit-filled and driven person during Jesus' life. This overlooks Mary, Anna, Simeon, John the Baptist, and others. Luke's view of the Spirit, like his view of prophets and prophecy, owes much to the Old Testament presentation of these matters.

27. See Schnackenburg, *Jesus in the Gospels*, pp. 150–51.

28. Consider, for example, the famous story of Josephus saving his own life by prophesying that his captor Vespasian would become emperor, which in fact did happen.

29. See Johnson, "Luke-Acts," p. 414.

30. R. H. Fuller and P. Perkins, *Who is this Christ?* (Philadelphia: Fortress Press, 1983), pp. 81–95, here pp. 93–95.

7

The First and Last Word:
The Christology of the
Johannine Corpus

THE GOSPEL OF WISDOM

A NY STUDY OF JOHANNINE CHRISTOLOGY has inevitably had to come to grips with the differences between the Synoptics and the Fourth Gospel in their portraits of Christ. Some scholars have seen such a marked difference between the Fourth Gospel and the other three in this matter that it has been said that in John Jesus bestrides the stage of human history like a colossus or God, not at all like the human and more approachable Jesus of the Synoptics. While this assessment is certainly a caricature, especially if one is comparing the Jesus of Matthew and of John, there is enough perceived and perceivable difference between the portrait of Jesus in the Synoptics and that in the Fourth Gospel to require some explanation. I have suggested in another context that one of the major reasons for the differences is that the Fourth Gospel is intended to provide the resources for Christian evangelistic work, especially the christological resources, and so is much more explicit and extensive in its treatment of Christology.[1] This is of course not the only major reason for the differences.

Another reason for the differences in approach between the Synoptics and John is that the discussion of two levels in the Fourth Gospel reflects and is part of a vertical eschatology, which may be contrasted with the more horizontal or end-time eschatology found in the Synoptics. By this I mean that the Fourth Evangelist sees reality somewhat dualistically such that on one side of the divide is heaven and all that comes with it (God, God's Son, the Spirit, power, eternal life) while on the other side stands earth and all that comes with it (space, time, flesh, world). Obviously our author is not an absolute dualist, because he believes that the material universe is made by God and can and is being remade through Christ. Furthermore, our author seems more concerned with a moral dualism of good and evil than an ontological one. Our author also believes that the two realms of heaven and earth can be and have been bridged in God's Son, who through the incarnation has become the mediator between the two, with one foot in each realm throughout his earthly career. Flesh, earth, and world become the indispensable medium through which heaven, light, life, and the Spirit are mediated to human beings. Christ has come from above to bring salvation and has returned above to complete the salvific work he began on earth. Heaven and earth co-inhere through the Son. Unlike the Synoptics, which focus on kingdom, final salvation, and judgment being *out there* in the future, John focuses on these things being *up there* in heaven.[2] This perspective does not tell the whole tale, especially since there is also obviously a vertical dimension to eschatology in the Synoptics as well, but it goes part of the way to explain some of the differences. In particular it helps to explain the language of above and below, descending and ascending, and even before and after, when before has to do with the preexistence of God's Son (before the Baptist and even before Abraham).

A third, and perhaps the most significant, reason for the differences between John and the Synoptics, especially Mark and Luke, is that John intends to portray Jesus as God's Word and Wisdom incarnate throughout the Gospel, in a way that goes well beyond even what we find in Matthew's Gospel.[3] R. Schnackenburg has put the matter thus: "Whereas the Synoptic Gospels offer, on the basis of Jesus' earthly appearance, a view of his salvific significance as a person, in the Gospel of John everything is revealed on the basis of his original being with God, his preexistence."[4] It is the Wisdom factor, which generates the preexistence language, on which we will concentrate in this chapter.

It appears the Fourth Gospel was written to an audience that was expected to understand the sapiential orientation of the work, signaled by the prologue. In particular, the audience was expected to understand that the *logos* hymn conditions and prepares for all that follows. Knowing that God's Son/Word/Wisdom has come down from above and returned above is the key to understanding not only his identity but also his words and work while on earth. This hermeneutical key is provided up front for John's audience so they will have a christological understanding of the story that the characters in the narrative for the most part do not. The *logos* hymn will state in one way what will be reiterated throughout the work—Jesus is the juncture between earth and heaven, being both God and human being. This is why, for instance we see angels ascending and descending on him in John 1:51. He is the gate of and to God and of and to humankind.

We have already dealt with the *logos* hymn when we studied the christological hymns,[5] so it is not necessary to go into detail about the sapiential character of the hymn.[6] It will be useful, however, to say something about the christological meaning of the very first verse (v. 14) and also v. 18, which occurs right after the hymn and comments.

In John 1:1 we have one of the few instances in the New Testament where the one who took on flesh and the name Jesus is called *theos*. This is by no means likely to be the first instance (chronologically) of this phenomenon in the New Testament books. Romans 9:5 is certainly earlier, and Heb. 1:8 and Titus 2:13 probably are as well. Here, as in Rom. 9:5, *theos* occurs without the definite article, which emphasizes the generic side of things (the *logos* is of the *genus* or species called *theos*). The word order and structure in the Greek of the first verse are such that the translation "the Word was a god" is surely inappropriate. *Theos* without the article here is surely the predicate of the sentence. It emphasizes the kind of being the Word is or the Word's true nature rather than the Word's personal identity (which is indicated by either the name Jesus or by a relational term such as "Son"). It also makes clear that the Word does not exhaust the Godhead. In other words, we don't have the reverse proposition here "God was the Word," or "the Word was *the* God" (i.e., all there is to God).[7] This is also made clear by the fact that in this same verse the Word is said to be *with* God, which thereby distinguishes the Word from the one that our author usually calls *theos*, namely, the Father.

The attempt by some commentators to argue that there is no comment on a personal preexistence of the Son here, but that the author is talking about an abstract idea or quality of God up until v. 14, is, quite frankly, incorrect. The things predicated of the Word in this christological hymn are also predicated of Jesus Christ, the Son who has seen God and made God known and is in the bosom of the Father (vv. 17–18). This is why later in this Gospel the statement "before Abraham was, I am" is seen as blasphemy by outsiders, but in the Fourth Evangelist's view is a true statement about the personal existence before the incarnation of the one speaking. It is precisely because our author believes that the Son truly is and was *theos* even before the universe began, as the very first verse asserts, that what he says in the rest of the book about Jesus is assumed to be appropriate and within the bounds of the Christian monotheism he affirms. The one who is the redeemer is also the one who was the creator.

Verse 14 affirms that the Word took on flesh, or, as some have preferred to translate, "came on the human scene." The essence of the idea of incarnation is that a personal being who already existed added a human nature to that identity. There is nothing here to suggest that the Word turned into flesh in some sort of kenotic process where the former state is left behind and a new one taken up. Indeed, the statement "we have seen his glory, the glory of the Father's only Son full of grace and truth" surely indicates that while on earth the Word retained the divine presence and attributes that were his by nature. It is the divine preexistent Word whose glory has been seen. This leads us to John 1:18.

Unfortunately there is a textual problem here. Does the text read "the only Begotten," "the only begotten Son," "the only begotten God," or simply "only begotten God"? Though the arguments are complex it seems probable that the appropriate reading here is the last one mentioned above, with the second reading listed being the second most likely.[8] The key term in this phrase is *monogenēs*. Like texts such as Tobit 3:15, it refers to an only child. More important in view of the Wisdom background of the christological hymn in John 1 and indeed of this entire book is Wisd. of Sol. 7:22, where Wisdom is said to be *monogenēs*, which we may translate "alone in kind" (a translation that suits *1 Clement* 25:2 as well).

What is being emphasized here is not merely the Son's personal uniqueness but his pedigree—he is the sole natural descendant of the Father. The issue here is not means or manner of birth but lineage and family connection. The term does not merely mean "beloved," as is shown by the expanded form of the phrase in 1 John 5:18 (see below on this text). In short, the word *monogenēs* means the only member of a kin or kind and when coupled with *theos* has the expanded sense of the only kin of God who is also God or the sole divine descendant of the Father or, as M. J. Harris translated it, "the only [natural] Son who is God." It is no accident that in both the Fourth Gospel and in 1 John Jesus alone is called Son of God (*huios Theou*) while believers are called children of God (*tekna Theou*).[9] John 1:18 reflects this distinction. The Fourth Evangelist not surprisingly reserves *theos* with the definite article for the Father, preserving some continuity with Jewish usage.

There is one further reference in this Gospel to Christ as *theos* (20:28), and it comes in the climactic confession, indeed the only fully adequate confession in the Evangelist's view, in this whole Gospel.[10] It must be kept in mind that Israel had previously expressed adoration to Yahweh as the "Lord our God" (Ps. 98:8 Septuagint; 99:8 in English trans.) and Rev. 4:11 indicates that the same sort of acclamation was used by Christians of the Father. There may also have been some special aptness in the phrase for John's audience, as when the Fourth Gospel was likely written the emperor was being extolled with the phrase "Deus et Dominus noster." As for the meaning of the phrase, it recognizes not only Christ's personal lordship over Thomas but also Christ's essential oneness with the Father, which then makes legitimate Thomas's worship of the risen One. Both *kyrios* and *theos* are titles here, not proper names, and the former probably implies but the latter explicitly affirms the deity of the risen Jesus.[11] Thus, what we have seen here is that this Gospel is framed by the confession that Jesus is deity, and all that comes in between is grounded in this confession.

Throughout the Fourth Gospel the question of Jesus' identity comes up in various forms—sometimes in the form of an acclamation, sometimes in the form of an assumption about where Jesus came from, sometimes in the form of a question, sometimes in the form of a statement. For instance, in John 1 we hear in v. 13 that Jesus, as Son of Man, is the only one who has both descended from heaven and ascended into it. We also hear in this chapter the acclamation of Jesus as the Lamb of God who takes away the world's sin (1:29), and in John 3:2 Nicodemus admits that Jesus is a teacher "come from God," but in this irony-laden Gospel he does not realize the full significance of what he says. Knowing where Jesus has come from and where he is going is the key to understanding who he is in this Gospel.

In John 3:14 is the first presentation of the theme that the Son must be lifted up on the cross in order for salvation to come. This is apparently the first stage of his ascent back to be with the Father in heaven (cf. 8:28), for the death on the cross is the moment at which Jesus is said to be glorified in this Gospel. This is his "hour" (cf. 13:31 and 17:1). What John 3:14 shows us is that the Fourth Evangelist's theology of the Son of Man is conditioned by the story of Wisdom, perhaps especially by *1 Enoch* 70:2 and 71:1, where Enoch ascends and is apparently identified as the Son of Man, and by *1 Enoch* 42, where Wisdom descends to earth and then returns to heaven rejected.[12] We see this influence again in John 6:62—"what if you were to see the Son of Man ascending?" But it is also his theology of Jesus as Son of God that is affected by sapiential ways of putting things, for it is as Son that the *logos* was sent into the world, as John 3:16–17 reveals.

If it is true that Jesus bestrides the Johannine stage as a God,[13] it is also true that the Fourth Evangelist goes out of his way to stress the true humanity of Jesus and his subordination to the Father, even to a degree not seen in the Synoptics.[14] For one thing, Jesus is called a man in this Gospel far more than in the Synoptics, and it is in this Gospel that it is stressed from the outset that he is the man born to die (see John 1:29 and contrast the earliest Gospel, where the passion theme really begins halfway through in Mark 8), a man who is said in John 20 to have nail-marked flesh. He is proclaimed in public at the climax of the trial in the form *ecce homo* (19:5). He is depicted, for instance in John 4, as one who experienced weariness, hunger, thirst. Yet on the other hand there is no Gethsemane agony or God-forsakenness on the cross in this Gospel. The most one gets is Jesus' remark in 16:6 that the disciples are sorrowful about his coming death; and by contrast Jesus repudiates the idea that he will ask to be saved from his "hour" (12:27). The cross scenes are suffused with glory, and even on the cross Jesus is still doing God's will and taking care of others.

In John 5:19 and many times thereafter, we hear things like "the Son can do nothing on his own, but only what he sees the Father doing." This in fact is part of a christological theme in the Fourth Gospel that is of importance. Using the Jewish language about agency,[15] this writer portrays Jesus as God's *šālîaḥ*, or agent and apostle on earth. He has been sent to earth for a specific purpose, namely, to complete the work the Father gave him (5:36–38; 6:29).[16] It is not just that the Son has come down from heaven, for that of course could be said of angels as well, but that he was sent down on a mission of redemption as the Father's divine emissary, fully endowed with the power and authority to carry out such a rescue operation. He has a special relationship with the Father, such that only he has seen the Father (6:46), and this equips him to reveal and speak for the Father (7:16–17).

If understanding Jesus in the Johannine way of thinking amounts to knowing where Jesus came from and is going, that is, knowing he is pursuing Wisdom's trajectory, then misunderstanding manifests itself in having a false conception of Jesus' origins or destiny. Thus, for example, in John 1:45–46 even disciples and potential disciples think they know who Jesus is by saying he comes from Nazareth and from the family of Joseph there, but they do not understand Jesus' ultimate origins. In John 7:25–27 the Jerusalemites say they know where Jesus comes from (i.e., Nazareth), but they do not know he came down from heaven. In John 7:41 it is asked "surely the Messiah doesn't come from Galilee, does he?" (cf. v. 52). In 8:41 it is implied that he was born out of wedlock (and thus his nature is dubious) while his opponents are true children of Abraham, to which Jesus rejoins that he preceded Abraham, which is far greater than descending from him. In 8:48 it is asked if Jesus is not from Samaria. In 18:5ff. the opponents stress that they are searching for Jesus from Nazareth. In each case the error comes from their not knowing his ultimate origins—that he is Son of Man, Logos, Son sent from God, God's Wisdom who descends and ascends. In John 7:35 the Jews misunderstand Jesus because they do not know where he is going. They ask if he may be heading for the Diaspora to teach the Greeks. Again in 8:21–22, when Jesus says he is going away, the Jews wrongly assume that this means he is going to kill himself. In 14:5 even the disciples misunderstand because they do not know where Jesus is going, and so can't follow him. Likewise, even after Easter in 20:16–17 Mary wrongly assumes that Jesus is back to stay and tries to renew merely earthly relationships with Jesus, calling him *rabbouni*. She does not understand that Jesus must ascend so she and other disciples can have a new form of relationship with Jesus. It is only when she understands the pilgrimage of Jesus as God's Wisdom that she is able to proclaim to the male disciples—"I have seen the (risen) Lord," the basic confession of the earliest Jewish Christians.[17] All of this should be more than enough to establish that John's Christology is sapientially shaped and that he thinks that to understand who Jesus truly is requires a knowledge of the path Wisdom, in the person of God's Son, took to and from earth. Notice how the Gospel proper ends, so far as Jesus' speaking is concerned, in John 20:29 with Jesus as Wisdom offering a Wisdom saying or beatitude to the disciples, just to reinforce the point that has been made all along about Jesus' character and nature.

Once one understands this key to the Son's true identity, then other puzzling aspects of Johannine Christology fall into place. For instance, the author's attempt to reveal the role the Son played begins with creation in John 1, but also Jesus assumes the roles often predicated of Wisdom in her relationship to Israel (see Wis. Sol. 10). For instance,

Jesus is the one who came into the world enlightening God's people all along, and so Moses and the prophets were inspired by him to write about him (John 1:45; 5:46). Of Abraham it is said he saw the Son's day (8:56). Isaiah even saw his divine glory (presumably in a vision; see Isaiah 6 and John 12:41). Not that anyone actually saw him before the incarnation, because like the Father he was purely divine and no one was able to see him (see 1:18; 6:46).[18] In other words, the Son existed before the incarnation and has had roles to play before that event as well. It is hard not to hear echoes of Wisdom of Solomon 10–11 here, where it is said that Wisdom aided Abraham (10:5), entered Moses allowing him to perform wonders and signs (10:16), gave him and others the gift of prophecy (11:1; cf. 7:27), and was present in the wilderness and sustained Israel with manna and water from the rock (16:26; 11:4; cf. John 4 and 6). The Johannine Jesus understands himself to be the one who has aided God's people to come through their trials in all previous generations.

There has been considerable debate about whether the use of *egō eimi* by Jesus in this Gospel is in some instances (e.g., 8:24, 28, 58; 13:19) a predication of the divine name to Jesus. This question is appropriately raised not least because we are told explicitly in John 17:6, 12, and 26 that Jesus has manifested the divine name and that it is a name the Father gave to the Son (v. 12). Furthermore, in the Hebrew of Isa. 51:12, and even more clearly in the Greek translation of this verse (which reads "I am 'I AM' who comforts you") "I am" is apparently taken to be the divine name. We may also point to the Greek translation of Isa. 52:6, which reads "My people shall know that 'I AM' is the one who speaks" (while the Hebrew simply says, "They shall know that it is I who speak"). We must conclude, then, that in all likelihood, in some cases the use of *egō eimi* by Jesus in the Fourth Gospel is a predication of the divine name to him.[19]

Further evidence that our author intends in various ways to say that Jesus is divine is found in John 5. Here Jesus heals a man on the sabbath and justifies this by saying that God continues to work (even on the sabbath) and so must he (v. 17). This passage draws on common Jewish beliefs that despite what Gen. 2:2–3 says, God could not have ceased all activities on the sabbath, because God had to maintain the creation in existence (cf. Philo, *Legum Allegoriae* 1.5). The point then of John 5:19–20 is to make clear that Jesus has God's full creative power and is undertaking the divine work which only God can or should do.[20] Philo puts it this way: "His creative power is called God [*theos*] because through it he placed and made the universe" (*De Vita Mosis* 2.99).

But not only did the Son preexist and so have intimate knowledge of what came before; he also has considerable foreknowledge of things (see, e.g., John 2:24; 11:4). He thus has a sovereignty in the face of adversity not emphasized in the Synoptics (see 8:59; 10:39; 18:36; 19:11, 30; 20:17). Unlike the Synoptic parables and Gospel material in general, there is little or no christological indirectness in this Gospel. Jesus' discourses directly reveal who he is and provoke immediate reactions of acceptance or rejection. There is a certain unearthly quality to the Johannine Jesus.

Another christological dimension of importance is of course the "I am" sayings with predicates that characterize Jesus variously as living bread, light of the world, the door, life, and the authentic vine (6:35, 51; 8:12; 10:7, 9, 11, 14; 14:6; 15:1, 5). All of these things were already said to characterize Wisdom in the earlier Wisdom literature. In Prov. 8:38 Wisdom says "he who finds me finds life" and in Prov. 3:18 Wisdom is said to be the tree of life. In Wisdom of Solomon Wisdom is said to be light, indeed a reflection or effulgence of eternal light. In Sir. 24:17ff. Wisdom is said to be a vine that buds and bears abundant fruit. In Prov. 9:5 Wisdom beckons, "Come eat of my bread." The point of these sayings in John, as in their analogies in the Wisdom corpus, is to make clear that whatever one truly longs for or needs can be found in Wisdom, who in the Fourth Gospel is identified with Jesus, the Son of God. Furthermore, the "I am" sayings are also linked to discourses that expand on the themes of these sayings, not unlike the Wisdom discourses in Proverbs, Wisdom of Solomon, and Sirach.

The "I am" discourses are of course about Jesus' true identity, and they are linked with his signs, which are in various ways different from the tales of mighty works in the Synoptics. The chief reason is that John has cast these miracle stories in the form that miracle tales appear in the Wisdom corpus. Like John, the author of the Wisdom of Solomon thinks of miracles as signs from God that point to something larger than themselves (Wis. Sol. 10:16). In Wis. Sol. 16:6 all the wonders performed by God in Egypt and in the wilderness are seen as and called "symbols or signs of salvation" for God's people. This same text helps explain John 3:14, which speaks of Moses lifting up the serpent in the wilderness, and it is likened to the act of salvation on the cross.

The connection becomes clear if one knows Wis. Sol. 16:6, where the lifting up of the serpent is seen as a "sign of salvation" signifying the means by which humans passed from death to life.

The use of this sort of Wisdom material is not surprising, because as in the Fourth Gospel the author of the Wisdom of Solomon believes in and articulates a theology of eternal life and also its negative counterpart. In both of these writers' views human beings were made not for death but for everlasting life (see Wis. Sol. 2:23–24; 3:1–2; 5:15). Furthermore, the discussion of the devil's role in the Fourth Gospel is close to what we find in the Wisdom of Solomon. Death entered the world through the devil's envy (Wis. Sol. 2:24); it did not come from God, which is similar to what Jesus says in John 8:44, where the devil is seen as the father of the wicked and a murderer from the outset.

The discussion about Jesus being the way—indeed, the only way to the Father in the Fourth Gospel—draws on what is said about Wisdom elsewhere. Thus, the coming of Wisdom to earth causes a division of human beings: some seek and find (Prov. 8:17; Sir. 6:27; Wis. Sol. 6:12) while others do not seek and regret it too late (Prov. 1:28). This same language is used in John of the effect of Jesus on human beings (7:34; 8:21; 13:33).

The Farewell Discourse especially is laden with language that encourages the identification of Jesus with Wisdom if one already knows the Wisdom material. Sirach 4:11–13 is especially helpful at this point: (1) Wisdom teaches her children (cf. John 14–16); (2) Wisdom gives help to those who seek her (John 14:16ff.); (3) whoever loves Wisdom, loves life (John 14:15); (4) those who seek Wisdom from early morning are filled with joy (John 15:11); (5) whoever holds fast to Wisdom inherits glory (John 17:22); (6) the Lord loves those who love Wisdom (John 17:26). Jesus' disciples are called in this discourse little children (13:33), just as disciples are said to be Wisdom's children in Prov. 8:32–33 and Sir. 4:11 and 6:18.

There is a great deal more that can be said along these lines when one begins to compare John's Gospel and especially the christological material with the Wisdom corpus. The above will suffice, however, to explain perhaps the major reason why John's Gospel is so different from the Synoptics—it is about Wisdom come in the flesh, and everything is spun out on the basis of the insight shared in the *logos* hymn in John 1. In fact not only this hymn but also the V-shaped plot of the career of the Son, the "I am" sayings, the conception of miracles, the use of Father language, and various other aspects of Christology are all indebted to Wisdom material, especially the late Wisdom material found in Sirach and the Wisdom of Solomon. This is not all one needs to say about Johannine Christology, but it is perhaps the most important thing one can say. Jesus is the very exegesis of the Father, because he is Wisdom come in the flesh, not merely one who proclaims what God is like.

Another window on Johannine Christology comes from examining the structure of the Fourth Gospel. On the simplest level we have a book with a prologue (1:1–18), an epilogue (chapter 21), and an account of the ministry in between in three major parts: (1) 1:19–12.50, the so-called Book of Signs; (2) 13:1–17:26, the farewell discourses; (3) 18:1–20:31, the passion and resurrection narratives. What this does not in any way convey is the manner in which we have a crescendo of miracles in this Gospel climaxing with the giving of sight to the blind in John 9 and the raising of a man four days dead in John 11, and also a crescendo of confessions that become more and more insightful and adequate until in chapter 20 Thomas's confession matches that of the prologue. Furthermore, the sign miracles are woven together with discourses, probably seven of each, indicating that in Jesus the perfect revelation or Wisdom of God has appeared on earth and that if one wants the benefits of life and light that God offers one must accept God's agent on earth—Jesus. The overall impression left by having this large quantity of extended discourse material unlike what we find in the Synoptics is that the presentation of Jesus is much more by word than by deed. Our author is far more interested than the Synoptic Gospels in raising and answering christological questions. This is shown in the way the material is arranged (a crescendo of confessions), the repeated discussions of Jesus' origins and destiny (which one can understand only with a knowledge of the prologue and Wisdom thinking), and the fact that the miracles are seen as signs pointing not so much to the presence of the kingdom but to the presence of the king.

In fact, the crescendo of the miraculous continues into the passion narrative such that the ultimate sign in this Gospel is Jesus' own death and resurrection, which the seventh sign, of Lazarus's raising, merely foreshadowed. By placing Lazarus's raising where he does in the Gospel, the author prepares to make a larger christological point in the passion material, namely, that the death and resurrection of Jesus are a sign and miracle of God, not a disaster. Like Lazarus's death, Jesus' own can be said to be for God's glory, and so the Son of God may be glorified through it (11:4). We may also contrast the emphasis in this

Gospel on the way the disciples grew in understanding and awareness of who Jesus was after Easter (see 2:22; 12:16), but unlike what we find in Luke's Gospel, nothing whatsoever suggests that this Gospel is a chronicle of Jesus' own growing awareness of who he is. Notice how the baptismal scene is basically omitted, or, better said, the elements of the scene that suggest Jesus learned something about his own identity and ministry are omitted. Instead, 1:29–34 suggests that John received the revelation and then testified about who Jesus was. Also omitted are the actual act of baptizing or anything else involved with that act which might suggest Jesus' subordination to John.

Another interesting window on the Christology of the Fourth Gospel comes from analyzing together the sometimes neglected Son of Man sayings in the Fourth Gospel.[21] These sayings in John, unlike what we find on the whole in the Synoptics, do not neatly fall into one of the three categories of ministry, suffering and death, or future coming sayings. One saying in John may refer to both suffering and future coming. This is not entirely surprising since for the Fourth Evangelist Jesus' death is already seen as a form of glorification and exaltation. In some ways, the Daniel 7 and Enoch material help us to understand some of the Johannine Son of Man sayings even more than most of the Synoptic ones. The concepts of representativeness, divine status and roles, glory yet in a context of suffering, and being in the presence of God, and perhaps corporateness, which are all present in the Son of Man material in Daniel and Enoch, are also found in the Johannine Son of Man sayings. We will look briefly at each of these sayings at this juncture. Before we do so it is apposite to bear in mind Schnackenburg's conclusion that these sayings show just how different the Fourth Gospel is from the Synoptics, for here the concentration is not on a future Son of Man coming on the clouds, but on his first coming to earth and what he accomplished from the time of the incarnation until the time he was lifted up on the cross. Vertical eschatology about the one who comes down and will be lifted up displaces an emphasis on horizontal eschatology.[22]

The first of these is John 1:51. This saying stresses that Jesus is like Bethel, the gate of God, the juncture between heaven and earth, God and humankind. In this context Jesus discovers and discusses the true Israelite, just as in a sense Jacob did after wrestling with the angel. The saying reflects the notion that Jesus is the locus or center of divine activity, even in a sense holy ground, which raises the question of whether this saying prepares for what we find in John 2, where Jesus is seen as the temple.

The second of these sayings is found in 3:13, and here again a true Israelite is found in the context—in this case Nicodemus. Here the Son of Man is himself an ascending and descending figure, though it appears from 3:14 that the ascending has to do with Jesus being lifted up on the cross. John 3:13 probably reflects the idea that the Son of Man has both preincarnate and postincarnate existence, being eternal. Yet he is also human because he came to earth in human form and died.

John 5:27 reflects the judgment theme found in the Synoptic future Son of Man sayings and in Daniel. Jesus judges because he is the Son of Man given this role in Daniel 7. This presumably means that Jesus will judge after he has lived and himself has been a defendant and a witness for others. He is able to do so because he knows in his own human nature and experience what humans are like, but he can defend precisely because he is the vindicated Son of Man.

In 6:27 and 53 the Son of Man is the provider of eternal life for God's people. It is as Son of Man that Jesus suffers and is able to provide flesh and blood (i.e., life) for the believer. Believers must be incorporated into him. This idea may go back to Daniel and imply the Son of Man's divinity since one can't be incorporated into an ordinary mortal.

In 6:62 ascending is mentioned again in association with the Son of Man phrase. This ascending is taken as evidence that Jesus is in fact the Son of Man and also evidence that he will be able to provide eternal life. His exaltation provides life for those who believe.

John 8:28 is a crucial saying, for it indicates that recognition of the Son of Man will only come when he is crucified. The point is that only then will Jesus be seen as the representative suffering figure of Daniel 7. In addition, knowing that Jesus is eternal ("I am") seems also to hinge on the lifting up of the Son of Man. The "I am" here is followed immediately by a statement about Jesus' utter dependency on the Father. It is then not an attempt to equate the Son of Man with the Father, but perhaps a way of indicating that, like the Father, the Son is eternal. It is interesting how, precisely because Jesus is a dependent obedient Son, he can also be called eternal, *theos*, Word, and the like. His correspondence with the Father's character and will are somehow related to or affected by his behavior. It is precisely as obedient Son that he manifests he is eternal Son. John 8:28 means that when Jesus has been obedient even unto death this will reveal that he is all he claimed to be, including being Son of Man.

John 9:35 is the only place in the Gospels where anyone is asked if he believes in the Son of Man. Only here could the phrase be seen as a confessional title, and here the phrase seems to be almost a circumlocution for "I." That is, Jesus is asking, "Do you believe in me?" There is certainly nothing like this in the Synoptics.

John 12:23 reflects typical Johannine language, though the idea here is not terribly different from the suffering Son of Man sayings in the Synoptics (cf. Mark 14:41). Again the debt to Daniel 7 seems likely. One must also consider John 12:34, where the phrase is found on the lips of the crowd, who fail to even understand who the Son of Man is. The connection of the Son of Man being lifted up, which entails suffering and yet glory, shows the correlation of this saying with others in John and also with the background in Daniel and Enoch.

John 13:31 is the tenth and last of these sayings, and once again passion and glory are associated, and the Son of Man's relationship to the Father is expressed. The Son of Man's glory also belongs to the Father.

Having briefly reviewed all these sayings, it is time to draw some conclusions about Johannine Christology. All these sayings appear in the first half of this Gospel, with the exception of the last one, and all are relatively uniform in their meaning or range of meaning. It seems clear that all are better understood when read in light of the background of Daniel 7 and the Enoch material. It is clear enough that our author wants to reveal the ascending descending divine one in these sayings—in other words, the one who fleshes out the roles predicated of Wisdom in Jewish Wisdom literature. The phrase is used to help focus on the idea that Jesus is the juncture of the divine and the human, heaven and earth, and so they focus not just on his roles but on his identity. Indeed at one point the question is even raised as to who this Son of Man is so he can be not merely identified but believed in. In these sayings are allusions to the full scope of Christ's work as it is envisioned by the Fourth Evangelist—he has a preincarnate existence; he becomes incarnate; he dies, is exalted, and will serve a judging function.

The Son of Man is thus a heavenly and earthly figure but also an eschatological figure who is human and dies, yet has divine authority. In these sayings John intends to present the full cosmic and historical scope of the work of Christ. There is exaltation even in death; there is present suffering but then vindication; there is salvation and yet also judgment; there is representativeness but also corporate personality. In short, the Son of Man sayings are another expression of the familiar Johannine high Christology. All such titles tend toward the revelation that the Son is in the Father and vice versa, which is to say they are preoccupied with making clear who Jesus is in relationship both to the Father and to human beings, especially his followers.

If we turn to the specific use of Son or Son of God language in the Fourth Gospel there is no question that this language is more prominent here than in the Synoptics. Already we find the term Son in the prologue, and it is present with some frequency in John 3, where it is made clear that the Son was sent by the Father (hence the Son preexisted, as the prologue stated), and sent for the purpose of saving the world. The Son is not only the one sent; he is also the sole descendant of the Father (see above on *monogenēs*), and the one in whose hands God has placed all things, like an heir to the Father's fortune.

The first major discussion of Jesus' sonship does not really transpire until John 5:19–20. This may be seen as something of a parable and could be called the parable of the apprentice. Jesus as Son does only what he sees the Father doing. He can do nothing on his own. He is a man under authority and under orders. Of course in relationship to all other human beings he is a man in authority and can give commandments or orders. The preexistence and divinity of the Son come out in these sonship sayings in a way that is seldom the case in the Synoptics, but other aspects of these sayings are not without parallel in the Synoptics.

In any detailed discussion of sonship language, besides the texts already mentioned one would also have to examine John 7:29; 8:28; 10:15, 37; 12:49; 13:3; 14:10; and 17:5, 25. Furthermore, since the Gospel begins in chapter 1 and ends in chapter 20 with sonship language (see especially the purpose statement in 20:31), there is something to be said for the conclusion that this is a key term or category for the Fourth Evangelist. The term "Son" or "Son of God" almost always comes up in contexts where the Father is also mentioned. In short, it is relational language. The term or phrase sometimes comes up in the same context as the phrase "Son of Man," but the terms do not seem to be interchangeable.

R. Bauckham sums up the evidence on Johannine sonship language in a helpful manner:

The Johannine idea of sonship may be regarded as a fuller exposition of what may be gathered of the filial consciousness of Jesus from the Synoptics, and it is important to stress its full content against the reduction of the meaning of sonship in developed Trinitarian theology. Sonship involves the unparalleled mutual intimacy of Father and Son. . . . The Son is the perfect reflection of the nature and character of the Father. . . . He represents the Father among men [*sic*] (Jn. 5.19 . . .). The Son is the Father's true Son only in his absolute renunciation of his own will and his whole-hearted identification of himself with his Father's will (Jn. 6.38). So far from heightening the Christology implicit in Jesus' use of Abba, the Fourth Gospel's tradition of his teaching stresses dependence and obedience of the Son to a remarkable degree. . . . This obedience of course is not the obedience of the slave but the obedience of the Son, who in love willingly identifies himself with the Father's purpose (Jn. 14.31). Neither in the Synoptics nor in John do we find that sonship is static being: sonship is a relationship to be fulfilled in mission, and as such both determines and is validated by Jesus' whole life and fate. The credibility of his claim to unique sonship cannot be separated from his path to the cross, nor from his resurrection as the Father's seal of approval on the accomplishment of the filial mission. This is why the glory of the Johannine Son is fully attained on the cross.[23]

We have seen in this survey the great importance to the Fourth Evangelist of three sorts of christological language: (1) the Wisdom language, which explains the most about this Gospel; (2) the Son of Man language, which helps bridge the human and divine sides of the Son; and (3) sonship language, which like the other two sorts of terminology can be used to express the full gamut of the career of the Incarnate One. There are of course other titles that are sometimes used, such as Shepherd, Lamb of God, Holy One of God (John 6:69), Teacher and Master (13:13–14), King of Israel (1:49), or in the passion account King of the Jews (chapters 18–19), but they play minor roles compared to these three categories we have discussed.[24] John of course uses the term "Christ" with some frequency and knows for instance that Christ is not just a name but is first a title (4:25–29), and one especially appropriate for a Jew to confess of Jesus (1:41; 7:26–31; 11:27). Indeed he thinks it is something Christians must believe and confess (20:31). But John wishes to go beyond more limited Jewish categories in order to say something about a universal savior, not unlike Luke did, and furthermore the verses where the term "Christ" appears do not really add much to what we have already noted from these other categories. Notably, Christ is almost never a term that Jesus uses to speak of himself in this Gospel (but cf. 17:3, where it is a name).

CHRIST COME IN THE FLESH: THE JOHANNINE EPISTLES

Whether one thinks the epistles predate or postdate the final form of the Fourth Gospel—and it is my view that the former is the case—it is clear enough that these epistles have a close connection with John's Gospel in the matter of Christology. This is not to say that these letters are loaded with christological material. For example, there is really nothing in 3 John of christological substance or significance at all, and so we will not discuss it.[25] 1 and 2 John, however, present us with some crucial data, and it has been said that the "nucleus of the teachings of 1 and 2 John is the view of Christ. No other NT writing stresses the importance of the humanity of Jesus for Christian faith as do these two documents."[26]

It also seems clear that these two documents have been formulated in the heat of a christological controversy over whether "Jesus Christ has come in the flesh" (2 John 7). They thus reflect what must have been one of the earliest christological controversies in church history.[27] It is not surprising, then, that our author is concerned about the "doctrine" (*didachē*) of Christ (2 John 9) and that these letters reflect in a fresh way that there is something called christological orthodoxy. Even in the first century, christological orthodoxy was forged or revealed in the fires of controversy. We will begin by examining 2 John and work our way back to 1 John.

At the outset of 2 John we find the characteristic emphasis on Jesus being the Father's Son. Verse 7 is the key confessional statement that we also find in 1 John. The author insists that Christians must acknowledge that "Jesus has come in the flesh." We will discuss this recurring phrase in some detail when we get to 1 John 4:2. Verses 9–10 express the typical Johannine exclusiveness—the only avenue to the Father is through the Son. Continuing in Jesus' teaching (or is it continuing in the doctrine about Jesus?) is the means by which one has God, both the Father and the Son. It is possible that Christ's divinity is implied by the parallel construction at the end of the clauses at v. 8a and 8b.

We turn now to 1 John and will concentrate our discussion on this important document. 1 John is probably not a letter but a homily that was circulated in the Johannine community (cf., e.g., Hebrews). It has often been noted that the beginning of 1 John is similar to John 1, but the differences are also telling. 1 John speaks of *what* was from the beginning, *what* we have heard (the *what* being identified at the end of v. 1 as "the word of life"). Furthermore, v. 2 also seems to indicate that the subject here is not a person but rather something—the eternal life that was with the Father or the word about it.[28] Yet it cannot be a mere oral message, for the author speaks of seeing it; and it cannot be a mere abstract concept, because he also speaks of touching it. Perhaps one may say there is some sort of interplay here between the Son as Word and what he brought to believers—the word and indeed the reality of eternal life. One may also ask what the phrase "from the beginning" means. Does it mean from the beginning of time, or does it refer to what has been heard from the beginning of Jesus' ministry? Perhaps the latter is more likely, not least because the author speaks of hearing, seeing, and touching this something. Yet we cannot be sure that the author means the Word of life has been *touched* or heard since the beginning. Supporting the conclusion that 1:1 is about something, a something that had a beginning in time, such as a message, is the closely parallel phrase in 3:11, where the subject is clearly "the message you have heard from the beginning" (again *ap' archēs* as in 1:1).

Verse 3 gives the first clear reference to Christ called "his Son Jesus Christ" and, as is typical in Johannine contexts, the reference is found in tandem with the mention of the Father. We see here already the characteristic ways Jesus will be referred to in this homily—as Jesus Christ (with Christ used as a name) and as God's Son. There are no references to Jesus as Son of Man in this document or in the Johannine epistles as a whole, which is perhaps something of a surprise with the emphasis on Christ having come in the flesh. The Son is Christ, and in our author's view to have fellowship with the Son is also to have fellowship with the Father.

1 John 1:7 brings into play the Elder's understanding of what Christ accomplished on the cross—"the blood of Jesus cleanses us from all sin." Though such a notion is perhaps implied in the Fourth Gospel, it is nowhere stated in this fashion, but then the Gospel is an example of narrative theology, not an assemblage of theological propositions. Both the Gospel and 1 John place plenty of emphasis on the importance of Jesus' death and its salvific benefits in general terms.[29]

In 1 John 2:1b Jesus is called "the Righteous One," a title we have already seen predicated of Jesus in Acts.[30] Not only did Jesus' death cleanse others from sin; he himself was without sin (cf. Hebrews). Also in this verse is a concept that comports with the forensic and trial language that occurs repeatedly in the Fourth Gospel—namely, that Jesus is the believer's Advocate. This presumably means that he is a witness or an intermediary for the defense of Christians in heaven. As an innocent or righteous one, he is qualified to represent human beings without bias. On top of this he is able to plead his own righteousness and his righteous deed on the cross in the believer's behalf (cf., e.g., Heb. 9:24; 1 Tim. 2:5).

The one who denies that Jesus is "the Christ" is said in 1 John 2:22 to be a liar. The use of the title rather than the name Christ here suggests the author's Jewish background and that he is familiar with how the term was used before it became a name. He goes on to say in the same verse that the denial that Jesus is the Christ is tantamount to denying both the Son and the Father. This is amplified and clarified in the following verse in the form: "No one who denies the Son has the Father; everyone who confesses the Son has the Father." It seems clear that these statements arise out of a context of controversy, where some, even some involved in the Christian community to whom the Elder is writing, were denying these crucial christological ideas. In other words, remaining in the Christian fellowship, which our author equates with remaining or participating in the Son and the Father (1:3),[31] requires that one believe certain things about Jesus. Spiritual incorporation is dependent on orthodoxy in some sense.

We are told in 3:8 why the Son was revealed—to destroy the works of the devil, which, in the Elder's view, are chiefly sin and death. The verb *ephanerōthē* implies the incarnation. The Son existed before he was revealed on earth. 1 John 3:16 states that believers know what love is by considering the cross. Love is defined by the christological paradigm—"he laid down his life for us, and we ought to lay down our lives for one another." Throughout this homily belief and obedience go together and nowhere is this more clear than in 3:23–24, where God's commandment (singular)[32] is that "we should believe in the name of his Son Jesus Christ and love one another" with the result that, according to v. 24 "all who obey his commandments abide in him."

Believing in the name of Jesus is a Jewish way of saying believing in the person and nature and character of Jesus. It is not as though the name is assumed to have some sort of magical quality; in Jewish thinking a name is not a mere label but normally connotes or conveys the nature of the one named. This formulation is quite striking if we compare it to texts like Mark 12:28–31 and par., where the two great Old Testament commandments (loving God and neighbor) are called a single commandment. Here we have a christianized version of this, where belief in Christ takes the place of loving God in the twofold single commandment. This is not a surprise, since for our author loving or believing in the Son also entails loving and believing in the Father. One may also wish to compare another and different christianized version of the *Shema* in 1 Cor. 8:6.[33]

The critical text of the letter thus far in christological matters is 1 John 4:2. The context has to do with the testing of the spirits—one can recognize a person who has the Spirit of God if their "spirit" recognizes that Jesus has come in the flesh. Every spirit that doesn't confess Jesus is not from God.[34] Now this confession does not mean simply that one recognizes that Jesus was human or a man but rather that he preexisted and took on human flesh, and thus is more than (though not less than) a human being. This is evident from what follows in 1 John 4:9, where we are told that God sent his Son. Someone must first exist before they can be sent. Our author is not talking about a mere concept in the mind of God that he then equates with or sees as embodied in a person named Jesus. Thus, the character of this crucial confession is really twofold: (1) Jesus was a real human being; (2) he was the divine Son of God, who came to earth and took on flesh. There is perhaps also a third implication, namely, that Christ is still in the condition of having flesh, though glorified flesh in heaven.[35] The concept of the incarnation is crucial to the Elder for several reasons, not the least of which is its present implications about Christ in heaven and about the life of the believer. In his view, Christ is still the God-man, albeit in a glorified state and place. He did not cease to be human or Jesus when he rose from the dead and ascended on high. In other words, in one sense the effect of the incarnation on God's Son is permanent, and the author can speak about the incarnation in the present tense even long after he believes it first came about. There is undoubtedly an anti-docetic thrust to some of the Elder's message, but there is also an anti-low Christology thrust as well. Our author wants to assert both the divinity and ongoing humanity of the Son.

1 John 4:14 again speaks about the Son who was sent from heaven by the Father, but here something new is added. He was sent as Savior of the world. This Hellenistic phrase, which would have seemed quite familiar to those who knew anything about the emperor cult in the first century may be an attempt by our author to better relate his essentially Jewish ideas to a largely Gentile audience in the Diaspora (in Ephesus perhaps). Verse 15 makes essentially the same sort of

remark we have already seen about acknowledging Jesus, only here instead of talking about acknowledging him as the Christ, the subject is acknowledging him as the Son of God. The former would have to do with his relationship to Israel, if the terms are being used specifically (i.e., he is the Jewish Messiah), the latter with Jesus' intimate relationship to the Father. Such a confession leads to mutual indwelling between the believer and God. Clearly the Elder thinks that one must believe something definite about Jesus to participate in Christian spiritual life.

1 John 5 begins again with a focus on confession. New birth hinges on belief in Jesus as the Christ. 1 John 5:6 is certainly one of the most debated verses in all of the Johannine corpus. Since at least the Middle Ages many have seen here a reference to Christ coming to the believer through the sacraments, baptism and the Lord's Supper. Bound up in this discussion is the relationship of this text to John 3:5–6. I have shown at length elsewhere that these texts must be interpreted in light of their Jewish background, not in light of later Christian thinking about the sacraments.[36] When this is done it will be seen that water is a frequent Jewish metaphor for various parts of the process of human conception and physical birth including (1) semen, which is called a drop of water and the wife a well where the water of life is to be placed; (2) the breaking of the waters as the process of birth begins in earnest; (3) the actual birth itself, with the fluids that come forth with the baby. John 3:5–6 provides us with a classic example of parallel structure—to be born out of water and of Spirit is explained in v. 6 to mean to experience physical birth and then spiritual birth ("flesh is born of flesh, and spirit is born of Spirit").

Likewise here in 1 John 5:6 the discussion is not about sacraments and their effects but about Christ, with water referring to his physical birth or incarnation and blood referring to his death. In our author's view the three that testify to the believer, telling the real truth about Jesus and who he is, are (1) the incarnation; (2) the atoning death of Christ; and (3) the Holy Spirit. The Elder in fact calls these three God's witness or testimony to who Jesus is. The coming of Christ to the believer spiritually could not have happened if Christ had not first taken on flesh; second, died on the cross; and third if the Spirit had not conveyed the benefits of the life and death of Jesus to that believer. Thus, the birth, the death, and the Spirit are the three great witnesses that testify Jesus is the Incarnate One and Redeeming One who is risen above and can send the Spirit.

The one who has the Son has eternal life, but the coming of God's Son not only conveys life to the believer but also light or understanding, as 1 John 5:20 makes evident. There has been some debate as to whether 1 John 5:20 provides us with another example where *theos* is predicated of Christ, but the Greek sentence structure and word order do not favor this conclusion. Verse 20 refers to "the one who is true" as someone distinct from the Son whom the Son has revealed to the believer, and furthermore the next major clause refers to "his Son Jesus Christ," again distinguishing the Son from the Father. With the twofold use of the phrase "him who is true" to refer to God the Father, it is only natural to take the final portion of the verse ("he is the true God and eternal life") to refer to the Father, not the Son. The believer is in both the Father and the Son, but the former is called "he who is true" not least because the elder has said in 1 John 5:9 that it is ultimately God who has testified to who Jesus is in a threefold manner.

It is clear enough that this homily is not a doctrinal tract or mere theological exercise. It is an attempt to combat christological problems which have caused soteriological misunderstanding and also practical problems of community division (see 1 John 1:18–19). Our author is polemical enough to call those whom he attacks antichrists because in his view they are guilty of aberrant, not merely inadequate, christological beliefs. He sees their presence in the community as a sign his churches are in the end-times (1 John 1:18). In response to the problems these now-departed persons have caused, our author stresses the incarnation and its implications and benefits. There is nothing here that does not comport with what we found in the Fourth Gospel, but there are nuances and expansions of the basic Johannine christological ideas here forged in the fires of controversy.

The Elder does not draw on the Johannine Son of Man material, nor on the whole does he reflect the deep indebtedness to the Wisdom corpus that we found in the Fourth Gospel, though his conception of the incarnation and of Christ as a corporate personality does seem to owe something to the Wisdom material. Our author is concerned with the affirmations about Christ as Son of God and as the Christ, and to a lesser extent as world Savior. Specifically he is worried about denials of the proposition that Jesus Christ has come in the flesh, denials that undercut not only the humanity of Christ but also his atoning work on the cross and present ongoing benefit to believers. In other words, the focus of this homily is more single-mindedly on the importance of the incarnation and its implications for the Christian's confession and faith. Doubtless we should not take these ad hoc documents as encompassing all of what the Elder thought about Christ. What we can, however, gather from these documents is that he had a very high Christology indeed, seeing Christ as both divine and human, and seeing the confession of that belief as essential to being a Christian. As we turn to the last of the Johannine documents in our next section, which seems to come from a hand different from that of the Elder, we must keep these fundamental Johannine ways of looking at and expressing things in mind.

THE LION AND THE LAMB:
THE CHRISTOLOGY OF THE APOCALYPSE

The book of Revelation is different enough in genre and Christology from the Gospel and Epistles of John that it could warrant a separate treatment, but it is similar enough to the other Johannine material to justify placing it in this chapter, especially because it likely is written by someone named John who was a part of that community, was influenced by the various ideas and themes we find in the Fourth Gospel and Epistles, and this has affected the way he articulates or communicates the various apocalyptic visions he had as a seer or prophet.

To say the book of Revelation is indebted to Jewish apocalyptic literature is to say too little. It is part of a corpus of such literature that shares many features of the genre including the recounting of heavenly visions and journeys, the use of hyperbolic and fantastic metaphors and multivalent symbols to speak about certain historical and eternal realities, the interest in how God will end human affairs and in matters of the general timing of such events, and a passion for justice for God's people, who are experiencing difficulties including persecution and in some cases even death. Apocalyptic literature is in general minority literature and speaks in a kind of symbolic and coded language about things that in many cases could not be aired in public. Often this literature is concerned with the question of theodicy, how God can be good and yet bad things happen to God's people.[37]

The book of Revelation was probably written during the last decade of the first century, and was certainly written to Christians in cities in western Asia Minor who were experiencing various difficulties. The lateness of the document does not prevent it from having a plethora of primitive and also some highly polished images of and ideas about

Christ. Since Revelation is a document meant to address Christians in physical and spiritual danger, we should not be surprised if it concentrates on images and ideas of Christ that would be helpful to address that situation. It is natural then for the author to stress the sovereignty of God, the power of Christ, Christ's judgment of the wicked for the saints, and the like.

Nor is it surprising that we do not really find a gentle Jesus meek and mild in this book but rather one who sits on the judgment seat with his Father, one who rides forth in judgment with a sword proceeding from his mouth, one who even when he can be seen as a lamb at the same time can also be seen as a lion. Here is a mighty and fearsome Christ indeed, with most of the emphasis on what Christ in heaven now is (an exalted Lord) or will be for believers when he returns. There is little attention then here to the ministry of Jesus or the merely human side of Jesus except by way of emphasizing his death and its benefits. There is some justification for Richard's conclusion that the author employs Christology to convey his apocalyptic message, but the reverse could also be argued.[38] Perhaps it is best to say that apocalyptic thinking has affected how this author expresses his Christology.

A quick survey of the various titles applied to Christ in Revelation reveals the following: Christ appears only seven times, Son of God once, Son of Man twice (but in each case as part of an analogy, not a title), Logos or Word once, but Lord twenty-three times (used also interchangeably of God and of Christ) and Lamb twenty-eight times. In this work none of the human titles of Jesus such as Teacher, Rabbi, Servant, Prophet, or human being are used. It is equally interesting that some of the more Hellenistic titles such as Savior or God are also notably absent. In other words, the terminology and titles of this book are very different from John's Gospel, where Son of God and Son of Man dominate the landscape and from the Epistles, where Christ and Son of God are prominent. The extreme Jewishness of this document and its different christological terms are enough to make one suspect it was not written by the same person who wrote either the Gospel or the Epistles or both, an opinion that is only reinforced when one notes the very different sort of Greek we have in this document compared to the rest of the Johannine corpus. This document has a very high Christology stressing Christ's heavenly exaltation and roles since and because of his death and resurrection.

The christological tone for the whole book is set in the very first chapter with the first christological vision of John of Patmos. The book begins with the assertion that this is "the revelation of Jesus Christ," and it is probably no accident that it is only in this chapter that we have the title Jesus Christ (three times). "The first Christian readers would need to be led from Jesus Christ to the Lamb, the name which dominates the second part of the book."[39] Jesus is the faithful witness, the firstborn from the dead, the ruler of the kings of the earth (1:5) and also the one who will come on the clouds in the future for judgment (1:7). Revelation 1:5 also mentions Jesus' redemptive death and blood.

It is also in this chapter that we have the first of only two references in this book to Jesus as one like a Son of Man; only here his garb makes clear his divinity. What is interesting about this is that the author begins here a trend that will continue throughout the work of applying Old Testament images and names formerly used of Yahweh but now applied to Christ or both the Father and Christ. Whereas it was the Ancient of Days in Daniel 7 that had such raiment, here it is Christ who is both divine and one like a Son of Man (1:13). It is not clear whether the person referred to as Alpha and Omega in Rev. 1:8 is God or Christ (see also Rev. 21:6), though it is probably God, but more clearly in 1:17–18 Christ is referred to as the First and Last (and in Rev. 22:13 he is the Alpha and Omega), the one who was dead but is now alive forever and has in his hands the keys of Death and Hades and also holds the churches in the palm of his hand, something a Christian under fire might find comforting. From this lofty christological height the book never descends.

It is worthwhile considering for a moment the significance of calling both God and Christ the Alpha and Omega. R. Bauckham is likely correct in suggesting that it conveys the idea that the person in question "precedes and originates all things, as their Creator, and he will bring all things to their eschatological fulfillment. The titles can not mean anything else when they are used of Christ in 22:13."[40] Furthermore, it needs to be stressed that when Jesus is called the First and the Last this seems to be grounded in Isa. 44:6 and 48:12, where it is a divine self-designation of Yahweh. Not only so, but it is used in a context where it aids in stressing the exclusive monotheistic proposition "besides me there is no God." Here in Revelation it probably does not mean anything very different from what Alpha and Omega mean.

This interpretation comports with Rev. 3:14, where Christ is called "the origin (*archē*) of God's creation," which likely does not mean that he is the first created being or the firstborn from the dead (for which other terminology is used), but rather is another way of saying about Christ what is said clearly in Rev. 22:13. In other words, Christ, as in the logos hymn in John 1, is seen as preceding all things and as in part the source or creator of all things, along with the Father. By saying that he is the Omega or the Last, we are probably meant to think of Christ's assumption of the role of the coming final judge on the eschatological Day of the Lord (see Revelation 19). It is Bauckham's conclusion about this First and Last/Alpha and Omega language that "as a way of stating unambiguously that Jesus belongs to the fullness of the eternal being of God, this surpasses anything in the [rest of the] New Testament."[41] It is not then surprising that in Revelation, perhaps more than in any other New Testament book, Jesus is the object of worship and adoration, which in this same book is said not to be appropriate for mere angelic supernatural beings (cf. 19:10; 22:8–9).

Because Jesus is included in John of Patmos's definition of God, he is seen as an appropriate object of worship. In Revelation 5 we are introduced to the image of Christ as the Lamb, which is to become the dominant image in the book thereafter. In Rev. 5:8 the Lamb, who has triumphed through his death and resurrection, is the focus of the circle of worship in heaven, which includes the worship of the living creatures and the elders, the representatives of all kinds of creatures both animal and human (cf. 5:6 and 7:17).[42] It is precisely as slain lamb that this Lamb conquers and then judges with righteous wrath (6:16). The worship of the Lamb is not somehow separate from or distinct from the worship of God but is seen as a part of it in 5:13. If a doxology is a clear indication of the object of worship, then the one offered to Christ alone in Rev. 1:5–6 surely indicates that he is being approached as deity. This doxology should be compared to two other such doxologies offered to Christ alone in 2 Tim. 4:8 and 2 Pet. 3:18, which suggest that the practices described in Revelation of worshiping Christ was not somehow an aberration but rather a widespread practice in a variety of Christian communities.[43]

It is perhaps right to note that John of Patmos does not, as is the case in the Fourth Gospel, really choose to use the concept of the Wisdom of God to include Christ in the Godhead. Indebtedness to Wisdom of Solomon does, however, seem to be apparent at one crucial point. In 19:11ff. the conquering warrior is called the Word of God. To this we must compare Wis. Sol. 18:16ff., where the Word or Wisdom leaps from heaven with a sharp sword.

John stresses that Christ shares the names, the throne, the work, and the worship of God.[44] While it is true to say that for Christians, because Christ functioned as God—namely, as creator, redeemer, present Lord, and coming future judge—he was thus worshiped, this is probably to say too little. At the end of the day, he believes that only God can perform what Christ performs, and thus there is at least an implicit assertion of Christ's divine nature in all this material. Consider what it means to say that the slaughtered lamb is seen on the throne and is worshiped for his overcoming through death and resurrection the powers of this world.

It must surely include the notion that God was in Christ reconciling the world to himself, but more to the point the way God rules the world is by and in the slaughtered and exalted Lamb. Christ's suffering and death are seen as the act of an eternal being thus having eternal efficacy and making evident how God has chosen to overcome evil and rule the world. Only God saves, and he has done this as the Lamb.

The one who is called ruler of God's creation in Rev. 3:14 is also in that same chapter called the one who holds the key of David (3:7), and thus is the Jewish Messiah. Just because John thinks Jesus is more than the Jewish Messiah does not mean he leaves behind this notion as unimportant. In Rev. 5:5 he is seen as Lion of the tribe of Judah and also the Root of David. The lamb image is of course also thoroughly Jewish, and a slaughtered lamb is the ultimate symbol of atonement for sins in a Jewish context. But John has transformed this image to speak not only of a lamb slain but of something else of which no early Jew who was not a Christian had spoken—a lamb once slain but now glorified and powerful. Here the story of Jesus has transformed this Jewish image into something unexpected, paradoxical, new. It is no surprise that the slain Lamb image arises repeatedly in a document written to Christians who are being persecuted. They too are lambs for the slaughter, but like Jesus they in the end will have victory over death and their human tormentors.

Another image transferred from God to Christ is the image of Jesus being the one who has the book of life and also the one who opens the scrolls that disclose God's future plan and will. Only he is said in Revelation 5 to be worthy enough to open not only the scroll but all the seals upon it. We see here the notion of Christ as the implementer of divine justice on earth.

The concept of redemptive judgment may seem foreign to us, but it is a prevalent concept in the Old Testament, especially Joshua and Judges. The idea in a nutshell is that God redeems his oppressed people by judging their enemies, hence the term redemptive judgment. Thus, our author is not saying anything novel by predicating both judgment and redemption of his deity; the only novelty is that Christ is said to be assuming these divine roles. He is both Savior of the saved and Judge of the wicked. The end result of the battle of good and evil will be and indeed in John's view already is that "the kingdom of the world has become the kingdom of our Lord and of his Christ, and he will reign forever and ever" (11:15). "Lord" here refers to God rather than Christ, and Christ is used in its titular and Jewish sense. Our author is not guilty of Christomonism, though he clearly includes Christ within his description of God alongside the Father. This way of putting things in 11:15 suggests that our author was in touch with the earliest Jewish Christian ways of confessing their monotheism, such as we have seen in 1 Cor. 8:6.[45]

Thus, the Lamb will triumph and one day invite his own to a wedding feast (19:9). He will also come as the pale rider, the grim reaper or executioner spoken of in Revelation 19. The Lamb is also the Lion. As Christ, he will reign for a thousand years with his martyrs (Rev. 20:4ff.), which may refer to his present reign in heaven with the martyrs already there, but in view of the discussion of resurrection in John 20, it probably refers to a future reign on earth at the close of the age. Christ is the one who began and will bring to a close God's plan for humanity.

At the end of Revelation we are told in Revelation 21 that Christ and the Lord God (here the Father) will be the temple and glory of God's people and they will dwell together forever—beyond disease, decay, death, sin, suffering sorrow, tears, or torment. For now, our author sees Christ as one who stands at the door of human hearts and knocks, but one day he shall burst on the human scene as a ravaging Lion destroying or at least judging the wicked and thereby rescuing the righteous. Thus believers are urged at the close of the book to urge him to come— the one who is Daystar dawning on history's horizon. Both horizontal and vertical eschatology fuse in the final vision of things such that heaven and earth in effect merge. The New Jerusalem descends from above, making a new earth to go along with a new heaven. The one who lies at the center of this vision, indeed the one who turns this vision into reality, is according to John none other than Jesus, who is at once Lamb, Lion, and Lord. We should have expected this Christo-centric and theocentric conclusion in view of the fact that we were told at the outset of the book that this is "the revelation of (and about) Jesus Christ."

It is well to ask at this point in what way or ways John of Patmos seems indebted to the Christology we find in the other Johannine documents. In some ways this is an easy question to answer. We may point to texts like Rev. 7:17, where we see Christ as Shepherd leading his people to springs of living water. This parallels what we find in John 10 (cf. John 21), where Christ claims to be the Good Shepherd. On the other hand, when we try to examine the way our author uses the term *logos* in the form "the Word of God" in Rev. 19:13 compared to what we find in John 1 the context is very different. Here the Word as in Wisdom of Solomon (cf. above) is involved in judgment, but in John 1 the image is used to speak of a role in creation and redemption. Or again we may ask about the similarities between the Lamb in John 1:29, 32 and in Revelation. It is immediately notable that a different Greek term for lamb is used in each (*amnos* in the Gospel, *arnion* in Revelation) and in the Gospel the Lamb is seen as purely redemptive, one who takes away sin, whereas in Revelation the Lamb's role involves both redemption and judgment. In John 10:7 Jesus is said to be the gate, while in Rev. 3:20 he stands outside it and knocks. In the Fourth Gospel, Son of Man is an important title with a cluster of key ideas surrounding it. In Revelation it is simply part of an allusion to the analogy found in Daniel 7.

The overall impression one gets is that John of Patmos knows Johannine Christology, but he is not interested in slavishly imitating it or simply passing it along. Rather he deliberately varies or modifies what he knows of Johannine Christology to suit the message he wants to convey. There is on the whole a much more varied scope of images and ideas that come into play in Revelation than in the other Johannine documents, but then the other documents are not apocalyptic literature and do not really use pictographic language.

All of the texts in the Johannine corpus share an emphasis on the importance of Jesus' death and an emphasis on both the true humanity and the divinity of Christ. It is repeatedly the Christ of glory, the exalted one, that appears in these documents, even in the account of the ministry in the Fourth Gospel. These documents have no problem with using the various names and titles of God for Jesus Christ, nor do they have any problem with offering worship to Christ as God. They all seem prepared to redefine Jewish monotheism to accommodate what they wish to say about Christ. Thus, we may say that certainly some of the highest Christology to be found in the New Testament can be found in these books. After these documents, the remainder of the canonical books will appear on the whole much less imaginative and challenging in their christological expressions as we shall now see.

NOTES

1. See the introduction to my commentary on the Fourth Gospel, *John's Wisdom* (Louisville: Westminster/J. Knox, 1995).

2. See the discussion of J. A. T. Robinson, "The Use of the Fourth Gospel for Christology Today," in *Christ and the Spirit in the New Testament*, ed. B. Lindars and S. S. Smalley (Cambridge: Cambridge University Press, 1973), pp. 61–78.

3. The chief difference from Matthew comes in the Johannine discourse material, where the focus is on Christology, while in Matthew the teaching focus tends to be on the coming of the kingdom and how disciples should respond to its arrival.

4. R. Schnackenburg, *Jesus in the Gospels: A Biblical Christology*, trans. O. C. Dean (Louisville: Westminster/J. Knox, 1995), p. 219.

5. See pp. 78ff. above.

6. See now the helpful discussion in Schnackenburg, *Jesus in the Gospels*, pp. 283–89, where he comes to much the same conclusion as this study about Jewish Wisdom thinking being the origins of most of the concepts here.

7. See, e.g., C. K. Barrett, *The Gospel according to St. John*, 2nd ed. (Philadelphia: Westminster, 1978), p. 156: "The absence of the article indicates the Word is God, but is not the only being of whom this is true."

8. See M. J. Harris, *Jesus as God: The New Testament Use of* Theos *in Reference to Jesus* (Grand Rapids: Baker, 1992), pp.74–84.

9. Notice also the careful distinction in 1 John 5:18 between the child and Son of God's relationship to God.

10. John 21 is an appendix to this Gospel added by the final editor or Fourth Evangelist.

11. See rightly Harris, *Jesus as God*, p. 129.

12. See pp. 17ff. above.

13. See E. Käsemann, *The Testament of Jesus* (Philadelphia: Fortress Press, 1968), pp. 8–9.

14. Schnackenburg notes that while the humanity of Jesus is clearly affirmed, his humaneness is not brought to the fore in the same way it is in Luke (*Jesus in the Gospels*, pp. 240ff.). For example, the terms mercy and pity do not really turn up in John in the way they do in the Synoptics.

15. See pp. 11ff. above. On the use of agency language in this Gospel, see E.

Richard, *Jesus: One and Many. The Christological Concept of New Testament Authors* (Wilmington, Del.: M. Glazier, 1988), pp. 208–9. He argues that high Christology in this Gospel develops because of and out of agency Christology. This is partially correct, but he fails to adequately consider the sapiential influence on this Gospel.

16. See Schnackenburg, *Jesus in the Gospels*, pp. 248–51.

17. See pp. 75ff. above.

18. Here I follow R. A. Culpepper, *Anatomy of the Fourth Gospel* (Philadelphia: Fortress Press, 1983), p. 106.

19. See the helpful discussion in Jerome Neyrey, *Christ is Community: The Christologies of the New Testament* (Wilmington, Del.: M. Glazier, 1985), pp. 160–61.

20. Ibid., pp. 162–63.

21. See S. S. Smalley, "The Johannine Son of Man Sayings," *New Testament Studies* 15 (1968–69), pp. 278–301.

22. Schnackenburg, *Jesus in the Gospels*, pp. 260–74. "The cross is the ladder on which Jesus climbs up to the glory of the Father" (p. 261).

23. R. Bauckham, "The Sonship of the Historical Jesus in Christology," *Scottish Journal of Theology* 31 (1978): 245–60, here pp. 259–60.

24. See Schnackenburg, *Jesus in the Gospels*, pp. 270–81. Jesus the eschatological prophet foretold by and like Moses could also be mentioned.

25. 3 John speaks about seeing God or being from him (v. 11), and there may be an allusion to Christ in the reference to traveling for the sake of the name (v. 7), but otherwise there is nothing of relevance in this document for our purposes.

26. R. Kysar, "John, Epistles of," in *The Anchor Bible Dictionary*, ed. David Noel Freedman (New York: Doubleday, 1992), 3:909.

27. Richard, *Jesus: One and Many*, pp. 224–25.

28. "The Eternal Life" could perhaps be a somewhat odd and oblique title for Jesus, but it is not clear that this is so here.

29. See the discussion in Neyrey, *Christ is Community*, pp. 190–91, about the stress in 1 John on the fact that flesh and earthly deeds matter in the eternal scheme of things.

30. See pp. 154 above.

31. The translation of *koinonia* in 1:3 as "fellowship" is probably not entirely apt. The term tends to have a more active sense of sharing something in common with someone or participating with someone in something. In short, fellowship would be the by-product of person's sharing the Father and Son in common, but our author is probably discussing the sort of spiritual union and active sharing involved in a living relationship with Father and Son, not just it effect on the relationship between believers, though that is mentioned first in v. 3 (there are two uses of *koinonia* in this verse).

32. The context indicates that the Father is meant; see vv. 20–22.

33. See pp. 116ff. above.

34. There may be some value in comparing 1 Cor. 12:3 at this point, where it is also affirmed that a true confession is possible only at the prompting of God's Spirit in one's life, and that by contrast a cursing of Christ proves that the Holy Spirit is not in a person's life.

35. P. Minear has attempted to argue that 1 John 4:2 is not about the incarnation but about Christ's spiritual entry into the believer's life. See his "The Idea of Incarnation in 1 John," *Interpretation* 24 (1970): 291–302. This mistakes the result or effect of the incarnation for the cause itself, and it is the latter with which our author is primarily concerned here.

36. See my "The Waters of Birth: John 3.5 and 1 John 5.6-8," *New Testament Studies* 35 (1989): 155–60.

37. A very useful survey of this kind of literature is J. J. Collins, *The Apocalyptic Imagination* (New York: Crossroad, 1984).

38. Richard, *Jesus: One and Many*, p. 425.

39. See D. Guthrie, "The Christology of Revelation," in *Jesus of Nazareth: Lord and Christ* (Grand Rapids: Eerdmans, 1994), pp. 397–409, here p. 398.

40. R. Bauckham, *The Theology of the Book of Revelation* (Cambridge: Cambridge University Press, 1993), p. 55. In the next few paragraphs I shall be echoing and amplifying some of Bauckham's arguments with which I am in agreement.

41. Ibid., p. 57.

42. Even as the Lamb, Christ is seen not as weak but rather as powerful and fully capable of overthrowing enemies, not unlike the lamb symbol in the *Testament of Joseph*. There is perhaps some indebtedness of John to the author of this work, for in *Test. Jos.* 19:8–9 we hear of the twofold Messiah who is presented as both Lion and Lamb.

43. Does it say anything to us that these three texts may all be addressed to Christians in Asia Minor in areas where emperor worship was prevalent?

44. Richard rightly stresses that the image of the throne occurs so frequently (the term is mentioned forty-six times) in order to stress God's or God in Christ's lordship over the entire historical process (*Jesus: One and Many*, p. 430). As he says, "The book is about power and the lack of power which the Christians of Asia Minor experienced during the reign of Domitian. . . ."

45. See pp. 108ff. above on this text.

8

The Suffering Servant and His Journey through the Heavens: The Christologies of the General Epistles

T HE SO-CALLED GENERAL EPISTLES are, for the most part, not really a homogeneous group of documents that could be said to belong together. Yet, apart from James and Hebrews, they do share certain things in common christologically and perhaps in terms of literary relationship as well. Clearly enough there is some sort of relationship between 1 and 2 Peter, which present us with the most christological substance among these letters, except for Hebrews. Equally clearly, there seems to be some sort of relationship between Jude and 2 Peter, as a close comparison between Jude 5–16 and 2 Peter 2 will show. Yet what then do we make of the fact that we find similar ideas about Christ in Jude 6; 2 Pet. 2:4–6; *and* also 1 Pet. 3:18–20? Hebrews, on the other hand, does not seem to have any literary links with these other documents but does share a Jewish Christian way of viewing matters. There is then some justification for treating three of these documents together in this study, and Hebrews is included at this point because of its traditional inclusion in the so-called General Epistles.

JAMES: SUBMERGED CHRISTOLOGY[1]

James can be dealt with rather rapidly; indeed, we could have and perhaps should have included it much earlier in our study in the discussion of early Jewish Christian Christology. It may well be one of the earliest of our New Testament documents, and it certainly reflects deep indebtedness to Jewish sapiential literature, which was one of the hallmarks of earliest Jewish Christian thinking about Christ and other subjects.[2]

There is in fact very little overt Christology in this tract or homily, which led some Christians in previous generations to see this document as little more than a Jewish ethical tract or, as Martin Luther described it, "a right strawy epistle," and so dispensable. Apart from the mention of Jesus' name along with two titles in the form "the Lord Jesus Christ" in 1:1 and 2:1 (with the latter text perhaps referring to the exalted Christ now in heaven, in view of the term "glorious"), and a possible reference to Jesus as Lord in 3:9 as the object of confession,[3] a reference to the second coming of the Lord in 5:7–8, and finally a reference to anointing people in the name of the Lord (5:14), there would appear to be no Christology to discuss. Yet this conclusion is a bit premature, because in fact there is an implied Christology in the ethical substance in this letter.

It has been increasingly recognized by scholars that there are detailed parallels between the ethical teaching in Jas. 1:2–5:12 and the Sermon on the Mount, as the following chart will show:

James	1:2	=	Matt. 5:11–12/Luke 6:22–23
	1:4	=	Matt. 5:48
	1:5	=	Matt. 7:7
	1:17	=	Matt. 7:11
	1:22	=	Matt. 7:24/Luke 6:46–47
	1:23	=	Matt. 7:26/Luke 6:49
	2:5	=	Matt. 5:3, 5/Luke 6:20
	2:10	=	Matt. 5:18–19 (cf. Luke 3:9)
	2:11	=	Matt. 5:21–22
	2:13	=	Matt. 5:7/Luke 6:36
	3:12	=	Matt. 7:16–18/Luke 6:43–44
	3:18	=	Matt. 5:9
	4:2–3	=	Matt. 7:7–8
	4:4	=	Matt. 6:24/Luke 16:13
	4:8	=	Matt. 5:8
	4:9	=	Matt. 5:4/Luke 6:25
	4:11	=	Matt. 7:1–2/Luke 6:37–38
	5:2–3	=	Matt. 6:19–21/Luke 12:33
	5:6	=	Matt. 7:1/Luke 6:37
	5:10	=	Matt. 5:11–12/Luke 6:23
	5:12	=	Matt. 5:34–37[4]

In all probability our author knew some form of the Matthean version of the Q material, perhaps even at a preliterary stage of this material's existence. The careful comparison of these parallels shows that James is no mere Jewish tract to which a few christological phrases have been added. Rather, the author has carefully woven into his own argument sayings material from the Jesus tradition, making the material his own rather than directly quoting the tradition. The Jesus tradition is viewed in James as a further development of the Jewish sapiential tradition. The implied Christology in this material is considerable. The author assumes that Jesus was the great master teacher, whose teaching can be used and reused to address new situations, perhaps especially situations involving the dilemmas that some of the earliest Jewish Christians faced. The authority of the tradition is not argued for; it is assumed. Moreover, it seems to be that the audience is familiar with the source of much of this teaching, for there are no phrases such as "as Jesus said." Yet this Jesus material is seen as having the same authority as the Old Testament, which is occasionally cited (2:8–11; 2:23). Both are to be heard and heeded. The phrase "the Wisdom which is from above" is a key one (3:17), especially when compared to texts like Jas. 1:17, which says every good gift comes down from above, from the Father of lights (cf. 1:5). The implication would seem to be that since Jesus' teaching is so often drawn on in this document, it is an example of that wisdom which comes down from above. In other words, Jesus was a revealer and conveyor of divine wisdom. Are we meant to see Jesus himself as the paradigmatic gift that came down from above, from the Father? The author does not say so, but the above evidence should cause us to look again more carefully at the overt christological references in this document.

What we learn from a closer scrutiny of Jas. 1:1; 2:1; 3:9; and 5:7–8 is considerable. First, we learn that our Jewish Christian author already treats Christ as a name of Jesus, not unlike what we find in the Pauline epistles.[5] Second, the term "Lord" seems to be used in this homily interchangeably for both Christ and God. Third, our author has an eschatological view of Christ's roles; he looks for Christ's return, as 5:7–8 probably shows. The question about 3:9 of course is whether "Lord and Father" are viewed as two persons or as one. The single article before "Lord" might favor the view that only the Father is meant, but on the other hand we do not find this double phrase elsewhere in the New Testament applied to God. More to the point, Jas. 1:1 shows that our author couples God and Jesus together as objects of faith and those that he serves. In any case, Jas. 1:1 and 2:1 seem to reflect Christian faith in and confession of the risen Lord (hence the term "glorious" in 2:1). Finally, if our author knows the tradition that Jesus was a healer, then it is quite believable that 5:14 is about anointing sick people in the name of the great healer. Here there may be a relationship to the healing narratives we find in Acts, where Jesus' name is invoked for healing (see Acts 3:6; 9:34; 16:18; 19:13). There is, then, a basic Christology underlying and occasionally surfacing in the homily of James, to which too little attention has usually been paid.

JUDE: JESUS, MASTER AND LORD

Jude is an even more promising source of material, even though it too is basically a Jewish Christian ethical tract or homily. The document is theocentric rather than Christocentric when it refers to divine activity (see vv. 5–15).[6] In the first verse of Jude Christ is used as a name for Jesus, not a title. In this document there is a certain dual emphasis on the Father and on Jesus, something we have seen in James. Believers are said to belong to Christ and are either kept safe for or by him (v. 1) (if it is "for," then the Father is doing the keeping). In v. 4 Jesus is called "our only Master and Lord, Jesus Christ," though this may be another example of an expression involving two persons, in which case we should translate it "our only Master and our Lord Jesus Christ." It appears from v. 9 that our author has no problem with calling the Father Lord as well, and so we see the application of certain titles to God and to Jesus as well.

In v. 14 we have to deal with the ambiguity caused by the dual use of terms. Is this a reference to Christ's future parousia with ten thousand angels or to a past judgment on sinners by Yahweh? It is probably the former for two reasons: (1) This document is a word of warning about intruders presently troubling the audience (v. 4), and it is said they were long ago destined for condemnation. (2) The judgment spoken of in v. 14 seems to be the final one when the Lord will "execute judgment on all. . . ." Our author then shares the early Christian faith that Christ will return to judge the world and redeem the saints, something even the very earliest Jewish Christians who prayed in Aramaic sought.[7] Verse 14 is in fact a quotation from *1 Enoch*, except that Jude has inserted the word *kyrios* to indicate that he is referring to Christ. Verse 17 uses the same formula we saw in James, "the Lord Jesus

Christ," and he is called "our." Christ's mercy is mentioned in v. 21 as something to be waited for, and this refers to mercy on judgment day. This verse makes more certain that v. 14 is about Christ rather than God.

In the doxology in v. 25 we find a remark of real christological substance—"to the only God our Savior be glory, majesty, power, and authority, through Jesus Christ our Lord, before all ages now and forever more." The first half of the doxology is drawn from traditional Jewish ascriptions calling the Father the savior of God's people. This doxology is surely a sign that we are dealing with very primitive Jewish Christian material here, perhaps one of the very earliest documents in the canon. Note, however, that God is said to be the believer's savior through Jesus Christ. What are we to make of the end of this doxology? Does it refer to the eternality and/or preexistence of Christ as well as of God? Since Christ is the nearest antecedent, it would seem likely that at least the preexistence of Christ is referred to in v. 25c and his everlastingness (existing from now on forever), if not also his eternality.

The Christology of Jude that we have thus far examined can be summed up easily. The author sees Christ as Lord over believers and the one who will come to judge the world with his angels (cf. the similar primitive formula in 2 Thess. 2:7 [cf. 1 Thess. 4:16]). As the Lord's possession, the believer is being kept safe for him until Christ's return. The author is happy to place Christ together with the Father in doxological remarks, indicating that he includes Christ in his devotion to and worship of God, and presumably prays to both Christ and the Father.

It is now time for us to consider perhaps the most intriguing christological motif found not only in Jude but in both Petrine letters:

Jude 6	*2 Peter 2:4*	*1 Peter 3:19–20*
and the angels who didn't keep their own position, but left their proper dwelling, he has kept in eternal chains in deepest darkness for the judgment of the Great Day	For if God did not spare the angels when they sinned, but cast them into Tartaros and committed them to chains of deepest darkness to be kept until the the judgment	[Christ] went and made a proclamation to the spirits in prison, who in former times did not obey when God waited patiently in the days of Noah.

Obviously, the first two of these texts are more similar to each other than the third is to either one. R. Bauckham has shown at considerable length that there is very likely a literary link between Jude and 2 Peter, as this and other material from the same parts of these documents show.[8] The first two of these texts are not obviously of christological import, though if the reference to Christ as Lord in Jude 4 prepares for v. 5, where the Lord is the one who saved the people from Egypt and then kept the angels in chains, then we have a comment on Christ's preexistence and roles in Israel's history, drawing on Wisdom ideas not unlike what we find in 1 Cor. 10:4 (cf. Wis. Sol. 11:4) . The author of 2 Peter, however, would clearly seem to see God and not Christ as the one who chained the disobedient angels.

In all these texts the reference is to the story in Gen. 6:1–4, where God was so outraged by what the angels (sons of God) did with the daughters of humanity that God brought a flood upon the earth. This Genesis context is more obvious in the use of this material in 1 Peter 3, and it is in 1 Peter 3 that we find something of clear christological importance. Here Christ (v. 18 makes clear that this is who it is) goes and preaches to these angels in prison. Though the 1 Peter 3 text has been the basis of the creedal statement "he descended into hell" and also the basis of various "second chance" theologies, it is doubtful that this text has anything at all to do with such notions. Indeed, nothing is said about Christ's "descent" anywhere. We are simply told that after Christ died and was "made alive in the Spirit" he went and preached or made a proclamation to these spirits or angels. There may be a trace of this whole theological development in the hymn fragment in 1 Tim. 3:16, where we hear that Christ was "vindicated in spirit," which remark is immediately followed by "seen by angels." Commentators have always thought this remark was out of place. If it referred to Christ's entry into heaven, it would be better placed just before or after the last line of the hymn, which reads "taken up in glory." This reference to being seen by angels, however, may not be out of place at all if it is about Christ's visit to Tartaros. It is also not impossible that Eph. 4:8 is of relevance here as well, for there it is said of Christ quoting Ps. 68:18 with alterations "When he ascended on high, he led (or made) captivity itself captive."

To understand this material a certain knowledge of Jewish angelogy and demonology is necessary. The powers and principalities and indeed Satan himself were believed to inhabit the realm between heaven and earth. This is one reason why the planets were sometimes assumed to be heavenly beings or angels ("the heavenly host") and is also why Satan is called in the New Testament "the Ruler of the Power of the Air" (Eph. 2:2). It would appear, then, that 1 Peter 3, far from being about a descent to humans, is about Christ's ascent to the angels on his way to heaven at which point he proclaimed his victory over such powers and thereby made their captivity all the more permanent and their doom sure. This material, then, would provide us with another strand of evidence of the development of cosmic Christology or Christus Victor (over the powers), and it would show that this is not simply a Pauline development. We must now turn to some of the other relevant material in the Petrine corpus.

1 Peter: Jesus the Shepherd

This letter is more theocentric than Christocentric, and it reflects primitive Jewish Christian thinking about Christ at various points (see, e.g., 4:19, where it is God rather than Christ who is called the Creator). It may in fact, like Jude, be one of the earlier non-Pauline letters in the New Testament. Several general features deserve note: (1) an emphasis on proof from prophecy that Jesus is the Christ—or, perhaps better said, a stress on Christ being the fulfillment of prophecy, as we saw in Acts;[9] (2) the idea of Christ as the Suffering Servant perhaps receives its largest attention among New Testament books in this document; (3) the Pauline phrase "in Christ" occurs in 3:16; 5:10; and 5:14 but only as a sort of cliché, not in its pregnant sense of spiritual union with or incorporation into Christ; (3) Jesus is called Jesus Christ some eight times and simply Christ twelve additional times in this letter; (4) various other titles occur once or twice, such as "Lord Jesus Christ" (once), Lord (twice as a form of address), Shepherd (once), and Overseer or Guardian (*episkopos*) (once); (5) Christians are called upon to reverence Christ as Lord; (6) the term Lord is used of both God and Christ such that in some texts it is not clear which one is meant (cf. 1:25; 2:3; 3:12).

The letter begins with an address that has at least an implicit trinitarian ring mentioning Father, Spirit, and Christ with distinctive roles for each in the economy of salvation. As in the Pauline corpus, we see the raw stuff of trinitarian thinking but not any developed reflection on the subject. Jesus is called "our Lord" and the risen One in 1:3, and in v. 7 we are reminded about the future "revealing of Jesus," which is this author's way of referring to the second coming. This same language comes up again in 1:13 and should be compared to what is said about the revealing of salvation and glory at the eschaton (1:5; 4:13; 5:4). This is apocalyptic language, though not in a particularly apocalyptic book, and refers not only to the idea that Christ is now hidden, being invisible since entering heaven, but that one day believers will again see him (1:8; 4:13b). In the meantime, Christ and the believers' inheritance is reserved in heaven (1:4).

Only once does our author speak of the first coming of Christ as an appearance (1:20—only 2 Thess. 1:7 elsewhere in the New Testament also uses this language of revelation, *apokalypsis*, of Christ's second coming), which may mean that our author subscribes to the notion of Christ's pre-existence. Strictly speaking, however, all that 1:20 really says is that God foreknew Christ before the creation of the world. An indirect but perhaps clearer piece of evidence that the author believes in Christ's preexistence comes in 1 Pet. 1:11, where we have the interesting phrase "the Spirit of Christ," which might refer to Christ's preexistence; but some think it refers to the Holy Spirit sent to believers by Christ.[10] We see in this document a certain subordination of the Spirit to Christ just as there is a subordination of Christ to the Father so far as function and activity are concerned.

1 Peter is a document written to Christians under pressure, and in some cases probably already suffering, and it is therefore not surprising that two of the major images of Christ are (1) Christ as God's sacrificial lamb, and (2) Christ as God's suffering servant. Our author is also more interested than some in the ethical implications of such a Christology, for he will urge the *imitatio Christi* upon them. Christology is used for parenetic purposes.[11] Christians too must be prepared to suffer and die and be taken up into heaven as Christ was.[12] In 1:19 we hear about the precious blood of Jesus, who was a lamb without blemish, the one chosen before all worlds began but revealed in this last age. The Greek actually reads here "precious blood *as* of a lamb," so we are dealing with an analogy rather than a direct identification of Christ as the Lamb of God, as we saw in the Johannine literature. Isaiah 53 may lie in the background at this juncture (see Isa. 53:7), but in any case the point will be made that Christ truly suffered as a human being and so provides an example of how disciples should react to or endure suffering. 1 Peter 1:2 mentioned the "sprinkling with the blood of Christ" (cf. Exod. 24:3–8). Jesus is seen by our author not merely as a passive victim or bearer of sin but an active carrier of sin as 2:24 makes evident: "He himself carried our sins in his body to the

cross, so that we, having parted with those sins might live for what is right. By his wounding you have been healed."

Our author subscribes to the notion that Christ's death was a penal substitutionary atonement (Christ suffered for you [2:21]). Of course Christ himself is seen not as a sinner (2:22) but as the one who carries sins to the cross for others and does away with them and their consequences for believers (4:1, cf. 2:24; 3:18). His perspective in these matters seems close to what we find in Hebrews (though without the high priestly Christology) and to a lesser degree what we find in the Pauline corpus.

If the death of Jesus is a crucial christological moment for our author, so is the resurrection of Jesus. For instance, it is by raising Jesus from the dead that God gave Christians both new birth and a living hope (1:3). It is also through the resurrection of Jesus that "baptism saves" (3:21). Christ's resurrection has the function of making it so that the believer's faith and hope will be in God (1:21).

> If the cross is the basis of Christian ethics [for our author], the resurrection is the basis of Christian experience.... It is quite apparent that Peter's interpretation of the death and resurrection of Jesus Christ in relation to Christian experience is neither a perfect carbon copy nor a pale shadow of Paul's interpretation of these saving events. It is a theology of Christian salvation in its own right, worthy of attention alongside of the other major witnesses within the NT canon to the meaning and significance of Christ's saving work.[13]

1 Peter 2 provides us with an interesting and distinctive christological concept—Christ as a Living Stone. The terminology suggests that Christ is the living founder or, better said, foundation of the church. Christ is unique in that he is the living stone, with disciples being copies of the original. The word "stone" here in Greek refers to a stone tooled by an artisan, not a rough, uncut stone. It could refer to a precious stone, but more likely here refers to a building stone. This living stone was rejected by human beings but selected by God. Again, Isaiah 53 may lie in the background, and it may also be significant that it is Peter who is portrayed as using Ps. 118:22 of Christ in Acts 4:11 (cf. Eph. 2:20).

1 Peter 2 provides us with several different christological expressions or images besides those just mentioned. For example, in 2:25 Christ is called both Shepherd and *Episkopos,* or Overseer. This implies Christ's present role as one who watches over and out for his flock. This in turn implies his present rule, power, and active concern

for and involvement with God's people in history. It is possible also that "Lord" in 1 Pet. 2:13 refers to Christ (based perhaps on Christ's teaching about "render unto Caesar . . .").[14]

In 1 Pet. 3:15 believers are told to acknowledge Christ as the holy Lord, perhaps a variant on the most primitive confession of the earliest Christians.[15] In any case, 3:18 seems to preserve a primitive Christian confessional formula. Christ's death is once for all, and so he is both righteous and the representative of all. He was killed in the body but made alive by the Spirit (or does this elliptical Greek phrase mean made alive in the spiritual realm?). The point of christological import of what we find in 1 Pet. 3:18–22 is that Christ is Lord even over the spirit realm, and is judge over all. This point is made quite explicitly in 3:22—Jesus has gone to heaven, and all angels and powers are now in submission to him.

It is quite certain, given the numerous references to Christ's bodily suffering in this epistle, that we do not have a docetic Christ in 1 Peter. 1 Peter 4:1 is further evidence for this conclusion. There is a certain stress on Christ as the mediator or vehicle through whom one approaches the Father and through whom the Father approaches humankind, in particular believers (cf. 4:11 and 2:5). In 4:13 there is a reference, which almost sounds Pauline, to believers sharing in Christ's sufferings. This is perhaps not an example of Christ mysticism but *imitatio Christi*, where the believer endures the same sort of sufferings as Christ because she or he bears the name of Christ (4:14). In 1 Pet. 5:4 Jesus is once again called the Shepherd, and this time the reference is to the second coming, at which time Christ will dispense crowns of glory to his long-suffering followers. In 5:10 we seem to have a clear Paulinism—believers share in God's eternal glory "in Christ."

It is a mistake to miss the narratological underpinning of the Christology of this letter. In particular, as Richard has pointed out, there are hymn or creedal fragments throughout this letter (see 1:20; 2:21–24; 3:18–22), which makes clear that the author knows of the V pattern manifested in early christological hymns, which charts the course of Christ's career in three stages: preexistence, earthly existence, return to heavenly existence.[16] Though various scholars have tried to argue that 1 Pet. 1:20 does not suggest the personal preexistence of Christ, these arguments are quite unconvincing for several reasons:[17] (1) The author is drawing on a hymnic pattern widely represented in early Christian sources, and clearly enough in various of these V-pattern hymns Christ's preexistence is discussed (e.g., in Col. 1:15ff.; John 1;

and, I would argue, in Philippians 2 as well). (2) As the context (cf. v. 19) and grammar make clear 1 Pet. 1:20 is talking not merely about a pre-existent or foreknown plan or purpose but a preexistent person, someone who can be revealed or manifested at the end of the ages. (3) The attempt to draw an analogy with Rom. 16:25–27 must be said to fail. There clearly Paul is talking about some*thing*, the revelation of a long-hidden mystery, hidden in the prophetic writings. Here the person of Christ is the subject. In short, the author of 1 Peter believes not just in a preexistent plan of God but also in a preexistent Christ who is at the heart of that salvation plan and who returned to glory from whence he came. There was no evolution from preexistent plan to preexistent person in early Christian Christology. Both were affirmed from an early date.

There is much fresh material in this letter from a christological point of view. The images of Christ as Suffering Servant, as Shepherd and Guardian, or as Living Stone are presented with some finesse and care. There is a clear focus on what is true about Christ from his death until his second coming. In other words, there is really no significant reflection here on Christ's earthly ministry prior to his death. Our author is comfortable calling Christ Lord, especially the believer's Lord, and he also in 1 Peter 3 shows a development of the idea of Christ's lordship over the principalities and powers. Christ's death is seen as a unique atoning sacrifice, but it is also true that our author thinks believers must be prepared to follow Christ on the way of the cross and beyond into heaven. Christ then is seen as something of a pioneer or trailblazer in this regard, not unlike what we find in Hebrews.[18] Christology in this epistle is a subject broached not for abstract contemplation but rather for pastoral application and encouragement for Christians under duress and suffering. Though the letter is very theocentric in orientation in the traditional Jewish sense of the term, we do see the beginnings of a trinitarian way of thinking in 1:2. We will bear these things in mind when we scrutinize 2 Peter and see if the Christology of what is probably the latest document to make it into the canon sounds like what we have heard here.

2 PETER: JESUS "GOD AND SAVIOR"

From the very beginning of 2 Peter there is a notable difference from 1 Peter in the way this author refers to Christ. Although we find the usual name Jesus Christ in 1:1, we also find another phrase, which may use *theos* of Christ. On the one hand it could be argued that 2 Pet. 1:1 has a parallel in v. 2, "the knowledge of God and Jesus our Lord," where God and Jesus the Lord are distinguished. Thus, various commentators have argued for such a distinction at the end of v. 1 as well. This conclusion is probably wrong for several reasons: (1) Everywhere else in 2 Peter the term "Savior" refers to Christ (see 1:11; 2:20; 3:2; 3:18). (2) The phrase "God and Savior" was in fact a stereotyped formula in both the Old Testament and in the Greco-Roman world. It is found on coins and inscriptions and was used in each case to refer to one person, not two.[19] Especially close to our phrase in 2 Pet. 1:1 is Isa. 45:21, which refers to Yahweh as "a righteous God and Savior." (3) The word "Savior" here lacks the definite article, and usually this means that the two coordinated nouns are being used of one and the same person. (4) The doxology in 2 Pet. 3:18 suggests a person prepared not only to worship but to give the praise only God should have to Christ. We thus conclude that *theos* here does refer to Christ. Since there is a definite article before *theos*, the titular rather than the generic aspect of the matter is being emphasized in regard to Christ. This verse appears to reflect an author willing to go further than the author of 1 Peter in the sort of language he would predicate of Christ.

The second thing to stress about 2 Pet. 1:1 is that the use of "Savior" also sets this document off from the terminology we found in 1 Peter. *Sōtēr* is on the whole a Hellenistic, not a Jewish, term. It is found only sixteen times in the whole of the New Testament, five of which are in 2 Peter and four in the Pastoral Epistles. This probably tells us something about the provenance of this document and its author.

In 1:8, 14, and 16 the by now familiar formula "Lord Jesus Christ" occurs, which we also noted in James. 2 Peter 1:11 tells us that Jesus is both Lord and Savior, and he is said to have an eternal kingdom, which believers enter only on the last day.

Though the case for 2 Peter having the same author as 1 Peter is weak on the grounds of style and vocabulary (2 Peter is Asiatic Greek) as well as at the level of thought, there is one section of 2 Peter that seems very Petrine indeed in vocabulary and style and in other respects as well—2 Pet. 1:16–2:3a, the Petrine testimony to the transfiguration experience.[20] On this occasion, it will be remembered, Jesus was called God's Son by the divine voice.[21] We are told that Christ received honor and glory from God the Father and that the voice said:

"This is my Son, my Beloved with whom I am well pleased." This account is actually closer to what we are told the voice said to or about Jesus at the baptism, but for our purposes what is interesting is that v. 16 suggests that the author sees the transfiguration as a preview of Christ's future coming in power. This is one of the rare occasions in the epistles where an episode from the life of Jesus that occurred prior to his death is recounted and its christological importance commented on. That the final editor of 2 Peter is concerned about the second coming is shown clearly from 2 Pet. 3:10, and so it is unlikely that 2:16 is about Christ's first coming in power, though this is not impossible, coming as it does from the pen of someone who began his letter by stating Christ was *theos*.

In 2 Pet. 2:20 we are told that the key to escaping corruption is knowing "our Lord and Savior Jesus Christ." This is certainly one of the most expansive christological formulas in the New Testament, involving as it does three titles and one personal name, though Christ is used in effect as a second name here. This same formula is used again at 3:18, where we are told of Christ's grace. The implication is that he dispenses grace, as only God can do. The letter ends with the ascription of glory to Christ now and forever.

One final matter is worth commenting on. If we compare 2 Pet. 3:10 and 3:12 we find the phrase "day of the Lord" followed by "day of God." The question is whether both Lord and God in these texts refer to Christ or the Father. In view of 3:8 it is perhaps likely that "Lord" does not refer to Christ in these texts, in which case we find that the author of 2 Peter, like so many other New Testament writers, uses the term "Lord" interchangeably for the Father and the Son. If 3:12 does not refer to Christ, then, bearing 2 Pet. 1:1 in mind, we also find the phenomenon that "God" is used of two different persons in this letter as well. Thus, we have found in this letter more evidence of high Christology, though not a great deal of creativity in its expression. The same cannot be said for the last New Testament document we must examine—Hebrews.

HEBREWS: THE HEAVENLY HIGH PRIEST

The Christology one finds in the sermon we call Hebrews is a perfect example of the fact that the dominant terminology used is not necessarily always the most distinctive terminology used. Without question, the major christological category or terminology in Hebrews, and the term used to cover the scope of Christ's work, is "Son." In this regard the usage is very similar to what we found in the Pauline epistles, where Son could be used to describe the preincarnate, earthly, and postincarnate stages of Christ's career.[22] But in Hebrews there is something quite distinctive—the notion that Christ is the believer's high priest, the heavenly high priest still at work for the believer in the ultimate Holy of Holies—heaven. There is also a third major motif in Hebrews. Though this author nowhere calls Christ God's Wisdom, he repeatedly clothes Christ in the garb, with the attributes, and in some cases with the tasks of Wisdom. These three christological ideas are not developed discretely in separate portions of the document but rather are neatly woven together in an impressive tapestry. It must be stressed that this document is a sermon or homily in excellent rhetorical form; it is not a theological treatise where the author intends to speculate on merely arcane or abstract notions. As W. L. Lane has rightly said about its witness to Christ: "The key to that witness is the recognition that christology in Hebrews is pastoral response to crisis."[23] Like Paul, our author writes as a pastor, and also like Paul he grounds his ethical exhortations in a high Christology at point after point—though it is doubtful our author *is* Paul.

That high Christology is evident immediately in the sermon's exordium in 1:1–4, which, as we have already said, is probably taken from an early Christian hymn.[24] Here Christ is affirmed to be the eternal Son of God. Throughout this document there is a sustained christological focus, as our author wants to stress the superiority of Christ over angels and all other lesser beings that might garner human attention and worship. But his interest is not just to speak of a hierarchy of being; he wants also to speak of a consummation of a plan for human history, and so he also uses the terminology and ideas that suggest that Christ eclipses all that has come before him, that the revelation in the Son is full-fledged and completely fulfilling of God's plans and purposes, while that revelation which came before was partial and piecemeal.

More than many other New Testament documents, Hebrews seems to be built around at least five biblical texts, or in one case a combination of texts: (1) 1:3–2:4 is based on a catena of texts, in particular, 2 Samuel 7, the Psalms, and Deuteronomy 32; (2) 2:5–18 is based on Ps. 8:4–6; (3) 3:1–4:13 is based on Ps. 95:7–11; (4) 4:14–7:28 is based on Ps. 110:4; and (5) 8:1–10:39 is based on Jer. 31:31–34. Hebrews 11–13 is largely a parenetic section grounded in the previous christological and exegetical discussion.[25] What this demonstrates is that our author is more concerned than some to explain how the Christ-event is grounded in the Hebrew Scriptures, probably because his audience was made up largely of Jewish Christians for whom this was a crucial issue. It is also possible to divide the document up thematically as follows: (1) 1:1–4:13 proclaims Jesus as the Son of God who is superior to angels; (2) 4:10–10:31 focuses on Jesus as high priest; (3) Christ as perfector of faith is stressed from 10:32 on in order to appeal to the audience to persevere.[26] On this showing, it is the christological perspective which gives the document its structural unity.

In the first two chapters our author indicates both the full divinity and humanity in a variety of ways. But, roughly speaking, the first chapter deals with Jesus as the eternal Son of God, and the second chapter deals with him as a human being. In 1:2 Jesus is said to be the heir of all things and also the agent through whom God made the universe. The author uses the language of Wisdom to describe Christ's work, but he is not dealing merely with a preexisting idea or a personification of Wisdom; he is talking about a preincarnate person— indeed, an eternal one.[27] In v. 3 we are told that the Son manifests God's glory, bearing the very stamp or exact representation of his nature, something said of Wisdom in Wis. Sol. 7:21–27. At the end of v. 3 we are told of Jesus' exaltation to the right hand. The main stress is on what Christ in heaven is now for the believer; in fact this is a constant theme in this homily, though our author is also interested in the role of Jesus in history as well.

The first major section of the homily, which continues up to 2:4, endeavors to show the vast superiority of Jesus to angels, the other heavenly beings who have previously been messengers for God and mediators of a covenant with God's people. Jesus, by contrast, is not merely a messenger or a mediator; he was also involved in creating and now in sustaining all things by his powerful word. Jesus is seen as uniquely God's Son in a way that could not be said of either angels or human beings. It may be that our author is putting things as he does because there were those in early Judaism who were given to angel veneration.

In 1:8 is the important citation of Ps. 45:6–7, which appears rather clearly to call a duality of persons God. In all likelihood the traditional rendering of Ps. 45:7a, "Your throne, O God, is for ever and ever," is the correct one. It would appear that Heb. 1:8 provides us with the first of three places where the Father addresses the Son—in vv. 8, 10, and 13. In other words, the Son's role as the agent of creation and as God's co-regent that is spoken of in what follows is seen as flowing out of his essential divinity. This is not a surprising conclusion after we have heard in v. 3 that a person called the Son is the effulgence of God's glory and the visible and exact representation of God's being. Just as we will be told that the Son is set apart from sinful humans in that he was holy and without fault (7:26), so here we are told that he is set apart from the angels in that he is appropriately called *theos*.[28] In v. 10, Ps. 102:26–28 addresses Jesus as Lord, which is a natural corollary to the address of him as God.[29]

In v. 13 our author goes on to celebrate the exaltation of the Son to God's right hand, drawing on Ps. 110:1. This is by no means unique, but what is unique is that our author goes on to use Ps. 110:4, "You are a priest forever just like Melchizedek." As Lane says:

> No other Christian writer of this period draws attention to this passage, but in Hebrews there are more references to Ps. 110.4 than to any other biblical text. In addition to three quotations of the passage (5.6; 7.17,21), there are eight allusions to it in chap. 5, 6 and 7 and each of the allusions is distinctive in form and function. The primary reason for the emphasis on Ps. 110.4 in Hebrews is that it supplied a scriptural basis for the writer's priestly christology.[30]

The point of mentioning this here is that in the first chapter our author has already established the divine credentials of the Son, which helps to prepare for the claim that he has a forever priesthood. The main emphasis in the crucial first chapter is to show that Jesus is Son, Creator, Lord, even God, and this makes possible the discussion in what follows of Christ as a unique sort of priest.

In Hebrews 2 we learn of Jesus as son of humanity. Our author uses Psalm 8 to bring out this theme and interprets that Psalm christologically, such that Jesus is the Son of Man who has been crowned with glory and honor and given dominion over the works of God's hand. Jesus was made a little lower than the angels for a little while during his time on earth and even went so far as to die, but now he is crowned with glory. It is characteristic of this homily that it moves from Jesus' death to his exaltation without discussing the resurrection.[31] Jesus' crowning happened because he suffered death—it was in a sense his reward for perfect obedience to God. The importance of certain key psalms, especially Psalms 8 and 110, to our author's christological reflections should not be underestimated, but it also becomes clear that our author knows the substance of some earlier christological hymns, and apparently also the Pauline handling of a hymn such as we find in Philippians 2.

In Hebrews 2:10, Christ is called the *archegos* of their salvation (i.e., believer's salvation), who was made perfect through sufferings. The key Greek term, which recurs at 12:2, means something like pioneer or trailblazer, someone who does something first. In this case our author is suggesting that Jesus blazed a trail into heaven through many sufferings and so paved the way for believers to follow him. The question is, In what sense was he made perfect through sufferings? Probably a knowledge of Platonism is necessary to understanding the author's logic here. In our author's view heaven is the perfect realm; earth is the realm of incompleteness, transience, imperfection. By suffering Christ is translated into the realm of perfection and eternality. Thus, the point is that Christ's tasks were not complete, and so his work was not perfected until he reached heaven. The author is not commenting on the moral imperfection of Christ while on earth, as 4:15 (cf. 7:26) makes clear.

Hebrews 2:14 indicates that Jesus had real flesh and blood and that his death destroys the power of the one who had previously held sway over humans by death—namely, the devil. This motif is somewhat reminiscent of what we find in Pauline texts such as Col. 2:15 and Eph. 4:7, where the powers and principalities are said to be disarmed by Christ's death. Our author wishes to stress that Jesus was made like humankind in every regard, except that he was sinless, so that he could be the believer's brother and faithful helper, but most of all so that he could be the believers' faithful and holy high priest, making atonement for sins, with himself as the sacrifice.

Christ is seen as both priest and sacrifice, as both atoner and atonement. His humanity is such that he could and did suffer temptation, and so he is able to help others who suffer temptation. Obviously, the author is attempting to walk a fine line here. To be tempted is not the same as sinning, but to be tempted does imply a struggle and suffering. It implies the real possibility that one might be led to do what he ought not to do. There is no hint that this author thinks Jesus' temptations were somehow unreal or that Jesus was merely play-acting but not really tempted.

The very reason our author sees Christ's life and death as meritorious (and rewarded) and his obedience as salutary and to be imitated is that Christ could have acted otherwise. That Jesus was sorely tried, tested, or tempted implies that he actually considered the possibility of doing something other than God's will, especially in regard to going the route of the cross. Hebrews 5:7–10 may recount Jesus' agony in the Garden of Gethsemane or the way he responded to his trials in life in general. In either case, in the end he always submitted to God's will, and his prayers were heard because of his reverent submission to God, even though the God who was able to rescue him from death did not do so.

In Heb. 3:1 Jesus is called both the apostle and high priest of the Christian confession—in other words, both God's sent one, who represented God on earth and also the believer's representative in the heavenly sanctuary. The author pictures heaven as a great sanctuary and Jesus as the believer's priest there offering himself as sacrifice to the Father for humanity's sake, and offering up prayers for believers in God's very presence. What is interesting about all this is that our author sees Christ as continuing to fulfill the human tasks of the priest even after his death. It is not just as divine but also as human that he acts in heaven. For Jesus to be the believer's priest he had to be fully human, and to be the believer's sacrifice he had to be truly alive in the flesh and so capable of being killed.

Jesus is seen as greater than Moses in all these matters. Moses was a servant in God's house, while Jesus is a Son over God's house (i.e., God's people). Salvation amounts to sharing in Christ (3:14), and so here we see the notion already present in the Pauline corpus of incorporation into Christ as a divine being.[32] Jesus has gone up into heaven as the believer's great high priest, but also as the Son of God (4:14). The real thrust of 4:15 seems to be that Jesus suffered the gamut of the sorts of trials and temptations humans suffer, and yet did not sin. The pastoral thrust of these christological observations is clear. The point is that Christ understands and feels the tempted believer's difficulties and dilemmas and can relate to the situation.

In Hebrews 5 we hear that the Son is a priest forever just like, or after the order of, Melchizedek. Why this order? The author seems to have had two reasons: (1) Jesus could not be a priest after the order of Aaron or Levi (or Zadok), for Jesus was of the line of Judah; (2) the author wishes to speak of a permanent or forever priesthood. The author goes on to say that Jesus prayed for believers on earth and continues to do so in heaven. He offered himself as sacrifice on earth and continues to present this or offer this to God in heaven. In addition, he learned obedience from what he suffered, obedience to God's will.

The author returns to the Melchizedek argument at this juncture. He points out that this Melchizedek was without father or mother, without beginning or end of days, being a priest forever. This is a typical example of the early Jewish exegesis of the silences of the Old Testament, silences that are assumed to be pregnant. Because Melchizedek's origins and descendants are nowhere mentioned, because his birth and death are nowhere recorded in the text, this allows for the conclusion that he was a priest forever. Of course, our author's real interest is in saying these sorts of things about Christ, not about Melchizedek.

Jesus may be seen as the ante-type of Melchizedek, with the latter only as the type. In typology the two figures are carefully compared but not identified, and here we see again the emphasis on Christ's superiority to all others he might be compared to—angels, Moses, Melchizedek. In any event, Lane is surely right to stress that "the use that is made of Melchizedek in 7.1–10 is thoroughly christological. He has no independent significance; he is introduced only for the sake of clarifying the character of the Son. His function is prophetic. He is illustrative of those prophecies of the OT that pointed to the insufficiency of the old order and to the superiority and sufficiency of the new."[33]

Jesus lives forever and so has a forever priesthood. Jesus inaugurates a covenant that is permanent, not partial or temporary. Jesus has a greater nature and name than any angel. In short, Jesus is just what the believer needs—a priest and sacrifice who is truly holy, blameless, set apart from sinners, exalted above the heavens where nothing can prevent his fulfilling and completing his role for the believer (6:26ff.). In the author's view, he always lives to intercede for the believer.

The portrait of Christ oscillates back and forth between the images of Son and priest, and one aspect of the former is the suggestion that Jesus is a kingly figure who sits down at the right hand of the Father (8:1ff.). This in turn is followed by a resurgence of the priestly images such that in Heb. 9:11ff. we hear of the efficacy of Christ's blood. His blood, offered in the heavenly sanctuary, obtains eternal redemption, and its effect is to cleanse human consciences. Jesus is both mediator of the covenant and the ransom price paid to reconcile the two parties. Christ's sacrifice is once for all time, for all people, for all sins; it does not need to be repeated. Thus, the one-time act of dying on the cross was sufficient, and the presentation of it to the Father effective for all the rest of human history.

As has been noted by more than one scholar, our author is drawing an analogy between Christ's sacrifice and the sacrifice offered in the Temple in Jerusalem on Yom Kippur, the Day of Atonement by the high priest. This sacrifice not only deals with the sins of the past, but is seen as a covenant-inaugurating act (cf. 9:15–22), fulfilling the promises given through Jeremiah of a new covenant (Heb. 8:7–13; 10:16–17). It is precisely because this sacrifice inaugurates a new covenant that it has direct implications for believers, not the least of which is that believers are called upon to follow Christ's example of self-sacrifice through their own obedience unto death (12:1–3).[34]

Hebrews 12:1–2 must be read in light of the hall-of-faith passage in Hebrews 11. Christ is being portrayed as the ultimate example of faith and the crucial verse is to be translated, "looking to Jesus the pioneer and perfecter of faith." The word "our," usually added before faith even though the Greek text does not support such an addition (no doubt it is done on the basis of the assumed analogy with the earlier reference to the *archegos*), misses the point. Our author is writing pastorally and suggesting that Christ, by being obedient even unto death, set the ultimate and only complete example of faithfulness. He not only sets the example; he makes truly Christian faith possible by dying and ascending to the right hand to aid believers thereafter. There may also be the suggestion that the perfect manifestation of faithfulness for the believer as well is that one suffers for and dies in one's faith. Christ endured the cross for the joy set before him, and his followers can likewise endure suffering because they have "the assurance of things hoped for" (11:1).

In Heb. 13:8, Jesus is contrasted with all human leaders and priests as mediators. They all died, and their deaths ended their service to other human beings. By contrast, Jesus' service and tasks go on—he is the same yesterday, today, and forever. Jesus then is finally seen as the permanent great shepherd of the sheep—always looking after and interceding for believers. Believers can count on the heavenly high priest never to change or change his mind about his followers.

Here then in this homily we have seen a very well balanced presentation of Jesus as both fully human and divine, as one who exercises his character and roles both on earth and in heaven. In the author's mind, Christ is both the believer's heavenly high priest and the preincarnate Son of God, who in fact can be called God by the Father. He is also the one who died on the cross, and because of all this is greater than and superior to angels, prophets, priests (including Melchizedek), and even Moses. There is none to compare to the one who is both Son of God and Son of Humankind. The narrative logic of our author's presentation is evident. He must speak of the entire pilgrimage and ministry of the eternal Son, including his preincarnate, incarnate, and postincarnate roles.[35] In this regard his approach is like that in Paul's letters, and before that in the christological hymns. Underlying all of this is the hermeneutical move of assigning the status and roles of Wisdom to God's Son. This is a common thread running from Jesus through the earliest Jewish Christians who compiled Q, through Paul, to the author of Hebrews. It is one of the things that binds New Testament Christology together.

Perhaps more than any other New Testament writer, the author of Hebrews shows how the divinity and humanity of Christ are interconnected and interdependent:

> By insisting that Jesus is the preexistent Son and the exalted High Priest, the author sets the stage for the description of Jesus' soteriological role, since he is both an earthly and heavenly being who connects the heavenly and earthly realms. Employing traditional apocalyptic categories and applying current Platonic ideal categories, the author sees Jesus as the only real link between the world of shadows or copies (9:1–10) and the heavenly reality (8.5). His earthly existence (his sacrifice) established an eternal bond between earth and heaven and provided an entrance for all who would draw near.[36]

This brings us to the end of our survey of the christological material found in these General Epistles. We have found none of these epistles barren land for such discussions. Even James proves to have more christological substance, albeit largely by implication, than is usually thought. It is clear enough that James, Jude, and 1 Peter were written by Jewish Christians who do not yet show the boldness of the author of 2 Peter in calling Christ God. Nevertheless, there are various other ways that worship and lordship and various divine attributes and functions are ascribed to Christ in these documents. 1 Peter has a powerful focus on Christ's death and his role as exemplar even while being the unique Suffering Servant. There is a wide variety of christological formulae in these documents, but there is a notable tendency to pile up titles such as Lord Jesus Christ, or even Lord and Savior Jesus Christ. We discovered an interesting connection between Jude and 1 and 2 Peter in regard to the story of Christ's witness to the angels or spirits in prison, apparently on the way to heaven. This is an interesting development and shows not only the expansion of the implications of cosmic Christology but also the tendency to think in narratological fashion about Christ, even when thinking about the sequel to his death.

We did not find any Son of Man material in these books, nor any significant reflection on the incarnation, except perhaps in 1 Peter, where we hear about Christ's appearing. By and large these documents, like the other New Testament epistles, concentrate on what is true of Christ from his death onwards, and especially on his present roles in heaven. We did, however, notice the interesting exception to this rule in 2 Peter, where there is a reflection on the significance of the transfiguration as a sort of preview of the second coming. By far the most interesting of all these documents for our purposes is Hebrews, especially because of its high priestly Christology. All of these documents continue to reflect the early Christian hope in the return of Christ. The Christologies of the New Testament are many and varied, and we have seen just in these five documents a small testimony to this variety and thus to the fertility of christological thought in the canonical period. In our next chapter we must consider the question of whether in the end any evolutionary or devolutionary or developmental schemes really tell the tale or help us analyze this remarkable diversity in the New Testament. We must also sum up our christological conclusions about the canonical period. Afterwards we will consider the budding Christologies of the period between the writing of the New Testament books and the great ecumenical councils.

NOTES

1. A phrase coined by E. Richard, *Jesus: One and Many. The Christological Concept of New Testament Authors* (Wilmington, Del.: M. Glazier, 1988), p. 380.

2. See my discussion of this document in *Jesus the Sage: The Pilgrimage of Wisdom* (Minneapolis: Fortress Press, 1994), pp. 236–47.

3. There is doubt about this because in 5:4 "Lord" seems to refer to God.

4. I have drawn this list chiefly from the helpful study by P. J. Hartin, *James and the Q Sayings of Jesus* (Sheffield: Sheffield Academic Press, 1991), pp. 144–45, though I have made some changes.

5. That our author knows something about Pauline ideas, if not also one or more letters of Paul, is shown by Jas. 2:18–26. I would suggest that our author in fact is dealing with the misunderstanding of certain key Pauline ideas.

6. Richard, *Jesus: One and Many*, p. 389.

7. On *marana tha*, see the discussion on pp. 74–75 above.

8. See R. J. Bauckham, *Jude and 2 Peter* (Waco, Tex.: Word, 1983).

9. There are in fact a number of notable similarities between 1 Peter and Acts in the way christological matters are handled. In both documents the real focus is on Christ's death and resurrection and his going to heaven and the benefit to believers of these three events.

10. P. J. Achtemeier points to 1:11 as referring to the idea of Christ inspiring and being present with the prophets, and supports this by showing how the notion was common shortly after this period ("Suffering Servant and Suffering Christ in 1 Peter," in *The Future of Christology: Essays in Honor of Leander E. Keck* [Minneapolis: Fortress Press, 1993], pp. 176–88, here pp. 186–87) (cf. Ignatius, *Letter to the Magnesians* 8.2; *Barnabas* 5.6; *Hermas Similitudes* 9.12.1–2; Justin Martyr, *Apology* I.31–33; 62.3–4; Irenaeus, *Adversus Haeresis* 4.20.4; *2 Clement* 17.4).

11. See the discussion by E. Richard, "The Functional Christology of First Peter," in *Perspectives on First Peter*, ed. C. H. Talbert (Macon, Ga.: Mercer University Press, 1986), pp. 121–39. Richard, however, tends to underestimate the at least implicit ontology of some of the christological remarks in 1 Peter.

12. See Richard, *Jesus: One and Many*, p. 386.

13. J. R. Michaels, *1 Peter* (Waco, Tex.: Word, 1988), p. lxxii.

14. On the meaning of Christ's teaching on the secular authorities, see pp. 36–38 above.

15. On which see pp. 75ff. above.

16. See the discussion of the hymnic material on pp. 79ff. above, and Richard's discussion in "Functional Christology," pp. 127–33.

17. See Richard, "Functional Christology," pp. 128–31. He quotes and is following J. D. G. Dunn, *Christology in the Making* (Philadelphia: Westminster, 1980), p. 238.

18. See pp. 213ff. above.

19. See the discussion in M. J. Harris, *Jesus as God: The New Testament Use of Theos in Reference to Jesus* (Grand Rapids: Baker, 1992), pp. 230–38.

20. I have argued this case at some length in "A Petrine Source in 2 Peter," in *Society of Biblical Literature 1985 Seminar Papers*, ed. K. H. Richards (Atlanta: Scholars Press, 1985), pp. 187–92.

21. See the discussion of this story on pp. 47ff. above.

22. The connections with the Pauline epistles have often been noted. In fact the Western church accepted this document into the canon on the understanding that it was part of the Pauline corpus. See Richard, *Jesus: One and Many*, p. 365.

23. W. L. Lane, *Hebrews 1–8* (Waco, Tex.:Word, 1991), p. cxxxviii.

24. See pp. 84–86 above.

25. See R. N. Longenecker, "The Melchizedek Argument of Hebrews," in *Unity and Diversity in New Testament Theology*, ed. R. Guelich (Grand Rapids: Eerdmans, 1978), pp. 161–85.

26. Richard, *Jesus: One and Many*, pp. 366–69.

27. Here and elsewhere the efforts of Dunn to suggest that only the idea of Christ or Christ's role preexists are unconvincing (*Christology in the Making*). Only persons act in the way our author says the Son acted before and during the creation of the world.

28. It is not impossible that in v. 9 we have a second reference to the Son as God. Probably "your God" refers to the Father and should not be seen as a vocative—translated "O God" as in v. 8.

29. See the discussion in R. E. Brown, *An Introduction to New Testament Christology* (New York: Paulist Press, 1994), pp. 185–87.

30. Lane, *Hebrews 1–8*, pp. cxlii-cxliii.

31. This might be a clue to the earliness of this document, since we also find this phenomenon in the christological hymns, but on the other hand this document seems to reflect a knowledge of various Pauline epistles, or at least of their substance.

32. See pp. 107ff. above.

33. See Lane, *Hebrews 1–8*, p. cxlii.

34. So H. W. Attridge, "Hebrews, Epistle to the," in *The Anchor Bible Dictionary*, ed. David Noel Freedman (New York: Doubleday, 1992), 3:97–105, 102–3; see also his commentary on Hebrews (*The Epistle to the Hebrews*, ed. Helmut Koester [Philadelphia: Fortress, 1989]).

35. See Lane, *Hebrews 1–8*, p. cxxxix: "the writer sees the eternal Son, the incarnate Son, the exalted Son."

36. Richard, *Jesus: One and Many*, p. 374.

9

Summing Up and Moving On

CHRISTOLOGY AND METHODOLOGY IN REVIEW: THE NEW TESTAMENT FACES OF THE CHRIST

W E HAVE NOW COMPLETED our exegetical and theological review of the Christologies of the New Testament and are in a position to draw some conclusions. The first of these may be surprising to some, but it will be self-evident for those who have followed the argument of this study carefully. This conclusion is that there is a great deal of very high Christology, including the predication of *theos* of Christ in various strands of tradition in the New Testament. We find this high Christology at least as early as the christological hymn material which goes back to the earliest Jewish Christians; we find it in the Pauline corpus, in Hebrews, in the Johannine corpus, and also in 2 Peter. In terms of chronology, then, we find it early, middle, and late in the first century. The ascription of not only divine functions and attributes but also divine names and titles, including calling Christ "God," is not a development that can be said to have arisen only in the last decade of the first century, though it does appear that the further one gets into the first century the more frequent these kinds of statements are.

This first conclusion leads to another, namely, that any evolutionary view of the development of Christology—for example, from low to high Christology— is unsatisfactory and probably historically inaccurate. On the one hand we have some very high christological material in some of the earliest strands of material; indeed, some high christological notions are at least implied already in the material that arguably goes back to Jesus himself. On the other hand, we have some later documents that appear on the whole to reflect lower Christology. Any adequate discussion of the growth and development of New Testament Christologies will have to reckon with the probability that some Christians understood what they took to be the fuller implications of the Christ-event sooner than others, and so the expression of a high Christology took place sooner in some settings than in others. We have evidence, for example, from the Corinthian correspondence, or from the Johannine letters, that higher christological notions did not catch on as quickly in some places as they did in others, or at least they received significant challenge even within the Christian communities themselves. If we must generalize, it appears that those documents that arose out of a pre-70 c.e. Jerusalem or Palestinian context, such as is arguably the case with James and Jude, tended to have less explicitly high christological expressions, *although* even in these communities prayers like *marana tha,* and some of the earliest christological hymn and creedal material already expressed a high Christology at least in devotional and worship practices.

It cannot be said with certainty that high Christology is simply a product of what happened when the Jesus movement reached the Diaspora and absorbed even more hellenized ways of thinking. There is in fact very little evidence of purely hellenized presentations of Christ in any of the evidence we have discussed in this study, apart perhaps from the use of a title such as Savior. This is hardly surprising, for all the authors of the New Testament, with the possible exception of Luke, were Jews, well grounded in Jewish ways of thinking about theological matters, although they were also at least partially hellenized Jews. Even in the case of Luke, it is entirely possible in view of his knowledge of the Old Testament that he had been a God-fearer before he became a Christian. The Christologies of the New Testament, including most of the higher christological material, are by and large plants growing out of the fertile soil of early Judaism. Even the First and Fourth Gospels, which reflect a good deal of high Christology, had roots in Palestinian soil even if, as is probable, they were written elsewhere.[1] New Testament Christology as a whole represents a radicalizing of various Jewish notions.

One of the more remarkable facts about the early church is how long it took for it to process and fully come to grips with some of the seminal and creative christological ideas and expressions we find in the

New Testament. There is nothing to compare with the Pauline and Johannine material until well after the first century. Not even Origen or Tertullian approach the level of christological profundity we find in the canon.

Our next conclusion will be controversial in some quarters and completely taken for granted in others. It is that there are various Christologies in the New Testament, and they do not all blend or dovetail nicely together. Nor can one set up a history-of-ideas schema and argue that Son of Man Christology led to Son of God Christology, which in turn led to God Christology. This is not to say that I think we have dueling Christologies in the New Testament, or Christologies that assert flatly contradictory things about Christ, only that we have considerable diversity that needs to be recognized and appreciated. Even when we are dealing with a title like Son of Man, the meaning of the phrase has different nuances in different passages and books. For instance, in the Fourth Gospel, the Son of Man material reflects not only the Daniel background but also Wisdom thinking about the descending and ascending Wisdom of God. This latter is something we do not really find in the Synoptics.

Perhaps the model of the sun with various beams radiating out from it is more apt than the linear development model. Some of the beams are closer together and more similar in intensity than others. There is, for example, a similarity between the incarnation theology found in John and the preexistence discussions in Paul, but one can't simply amalgamate the two.[2] All these christological expressions were later deemed by the church to be true light, but not all are on the same wavelength nor do they all illuminate the same subjects. The Christ-event produced a great deal of light and not a little heat in the lives of many of Jesus' early followers, and the Christologies of the New Testament reflect the impact of this event on different lives and different ways of thinking. There was of course also the passing down of traditions and cross-fertilization along the way, especially the later one gets in time from the Christ-event. The New Testament writers were not all operating independently of each other or independent of shared christological traditions. Notice, for example, the Pauline "in Christ" formulae in 1 Peter, or the Pauline influences in Hebrews.

Another important conclusion is that it appears that some christological forms proved more serviceable than others when Gentiles began to become the majority in various congregations. It would appear, for instance, that Son of Man Christology fell more and more into disuse the more the Gospel moved into the non-Jewish portions of the Greco-Roman world. Some of the Jewish titles such as Christ seem to have quickly become mere ciphers or names for Jesus. Sometimes a group of appellations were strung together, such as the Lord Jesus Christ, but we do not find simply two titles juxtaposed such as "the Lord Christ" in writers like Paul who understood what Christ originally meant. Others titles such as Servant or Prophet seem to have existed on the margin, while terms such as Christ and Lord and the phrase Son of God seem to have been the most widely used terms and titles.

Some Christologies, such as the *logos* Christology, were destined to be used in various ways after the New Testament era, as we shall see in the last section of this chapter. Others, such as Jesus as the Living Stone, seem not to have left much of an enduring impact. This does not mean that the ideas or metaphors were less interesting or important but only that as time went on Christians tended to express their faith in more conventional ways than in the New Testament era. There are other titles, such as Savior, that seem to have first come to prominence when Christians began to approach Gentiles in earnest with the Gospel, and they have been with us ever since that time.

Where did all of this vast array of christological thinking come from? Ultimately, we have argued, it in many cases goes back to Jesus himself, or to the earliest Jewish Christian followers of Jesus. A good deal of the earliest Jewish Christian christological material seems to have arisen in the context of worship—when Jesus began to be confessed, prayed to, sung about, and even addressed as Lord or God in doxologies and other liturgical formulae. I am suggesting, then, that high Christology arose in part out of thinking through the implications of Jesus' own self-presentation in words and deeds and relationships and in part out of the experience of Jesus as the risen Lord, not primarily as a result of ideas from other religious contexts being imported into the christological discussion. Borrowing there was of terms such as Savior, but the ideas were taken up and transformed and made serviceable for the praise of Jesus Christ. These were but building blocks or tools used to express a faith in Christ already known and experienced; they were added to the Jesus tradition, which was already being passed along.[3] Implicit in the worship of a historical figure of the recent past named Jesus of Nazareth by Jewish Christians who were still monotheists was that Jesus had to be in some sense divine. To no other person but God would a true Jew offer prayers and worship or call the divine name.[4]

There were of course, as we shall see, Christologies that developed after New Testament times that cannot be said to be legitimate developments of notions already found in the New Testament. One such Christology, which goes back at least to Clement of Alexandria and Tertullian, involved the idea that Christ was the angel of the Lord in the Old Testament. This angel of the Lord is identified as Gabriel in the birth narratives in the New Testament and the book of Hebrews is very specific about Christ being of a higher order than that of angels (cf. also Col. 2:18). The book of Revelation in addition condemns angel worship. Perhaps some New Testament writers already knew that the incarnation had to be understood to have transpired at a particular point in time at the inception of Jesus' life, and not before.

Two final questions need to be broached before we consider what we have learned about methodological matters by undertaking this study: Does the New Testament call Jesus God? Does the New Testament formulate a doctrine of the Trinity? It seems to me beyond reasonable doubt that we have several texts from different sources that affirm that it was appropriate to call Jesus God. A minimal list would include Rom. 9:5; Titus 2:1; Heb. 1:8; John 1:1; 20:28; and 2 Pet. 1:1. In addition, the idea but not the exact term seems clearly present in various other texts, such as the Christ hymns in Philippians 2 and Colossians 1.[5] This practice was continued with vigor early in the second century in a variety of contexts, which provides further evidence that it did not spring up after New Testament times in some particular place (cf. Ignatius, *Letter to the Ephesians* 1.1; 15.3; etc; *Didache* 10.6 [this may be a first-century text]; and of course there is the famous reference in Pliny from about 115 C.E. speaking of Christians singing a hymn to Christ as to a God [*Letter* 10.96]). In short, there is evidence in the New Testament and in the literature from shortly thereafter of what might be called binitarian thinking.

This thinking led in at least some quarters in the New Testament era to a reconceiving of what the term *theos* actually meant. It was no longer understood to refer simply to Yahweh or the Father.

The reconfiguration of the *Shema* in 1 Cor. 8:6 reveals that this process was set in motion already within two decades or less of Jesus' death. Christology in this period is rightly seen as an aspect of theology, so long as it is understood that christological thinking was leading to a reconceiving of what *theos* did and had always meant. Christians continued to affirm that God is one, but they had notions different from those of non-Christian Jews about who God was. In other words, it was true but not adequate to speak of God being in Christ, unless one was also prepared to speak of God as Christ. It was not adequate to speak of Christ embodying or manifesting the divine presence unless one was also prepared to speak of Christ being the divine presence on earth in the flesh.

Whether one thinks of the christological hymns or Pauline theology, or even the Petrine notion of Christ inspiring the Old Testament prophets, it seems clear enough that in various quarters Christians were already prepared in the early and middle decades of the first century to speak about the personal preexistence of Christ, not merely the embodiment in Christ of qualities or character traits or powers that preexisted in Yahweh. This is especially evident in the christological hymns that speak of Christ playing a personal and active role in the creating of the universe.[6]

What about the Trinity? First, it must be admitted that while we find the stuff or raw data out of which a doctrine of the Trinity can be composed, we do not find in the New Testament an attempt to clearly articulate or explain such a doctrine, much less argue for it. The trinitarian formulae that we have in the New Testament come in baptismal formulae (e.g., Matt. 28:19) or prayerlike salutations and benedictions (2 Thess. 2:13f.; 2 Cor. 13:14; 1 Pet. 1:1f.; Jude 20f.) or confessional formulae (Eph. 4:4–6, cf. 2:13). In none of these places are we told clearly how the Spirit relates to Father and Son, nor are we able to find simple remarks like "the Spirit is God," nor is there any clear evidence that the Spirit was prayed to in New Testament times. Nonetheless, the Spirit is said to be "of God" or "of/from Christ," and there are various places, such as in the Fourth Gospel, where we see the same sort of subordination of (and dependence on) the Spirit to Christ as we saw for the relationship of Christ to God the Father. Equally clearly, in various places the Spirit functions as and for God and/or Christ and is not merely treated as a power or force. For example, in Luke 1 the Spirit is a personal presence that overshadows Mary.

There is of course a proper distinction between calling God spirit (in reference to the divine substance or nature) and talking about the Holy Spirit sent by Christ to believers. Especially in the Fourth Gospel and in the Pauline letters the Spirit is seen as a personal representative or agent (called another Paraclete or Advocate in the Fourth Gospel) and in a sense a substitute for Christ while he is absent from earth. It is also true that it is assumed that the Spirit can be omnipresent—with all believers everywhere at once. This is an attribute of God. There is thus a good case to be made for the divinity of the Spirit as something early Christians believed in, though they seem to have spoken of this matter far less than about the nature and titles of Christ. This in turn means there is at least the raw data for trinitarian thinking in the New Testament and some movement to articulate what that means in some of the formulae of worship. It is at the same time important to stress that the New Testament writers see themselves as monotheists from first to last, not as tri-theists. They were all, with one possible exception, Jews. The New Testament does not tell us how there can be one in three or three in one, or the details of the interrelationship, though there are some statements about the Son being in the Father, and the Spirit coming from Christ to believers. The intricacies of the Trinity were left for subsequent generations to ponder and hammer out.

METHODOLOGY AND MEANING

Perhaps the first thing to be said on this score is that the very variety of Christologies in the New Testament discourages evolutionary or history-of-ideas kinds of thinking about this subject. It is wrong to come to the text with an assumption that these Christologies are all examples of the imposition of christological garb on a nonmessianic Jesus. We have seen at the beginning of this study that there is a considerable case to be made that Jesus is the ultimate source of a great deal of New Testament Christology, both in his person and in his work, both in his relationships and in his words. This means that there is a case to be made that the Christologies of the New Testament are not fairly characterized as examples of piety outrunning the historical evidence.[7]

A second methodological point is that one must do one's best to examine all the New Testament evidence if one is going to talk about the Christologies of the New Testament. Furthermore, one must commit oneself to doing careful contextual exegesis. Phrases and titles must not simply be snipped out of their contexts. This study is based on that sort of painstaking exegesis, though it was quite impossible to display it all in so short a compass as this book affords. In other words, the focus must lie on what is in the text, not primarily on what may

lie behind or beyond the text. We must not begin with certain theological agendas and then do the exegesis, or at least we must be aware
of our theological biases as we come to the text and make allowances
for them. While there are some hints of development or "unfolding"
here and there, the New Testament is not unilinear but rather involves
a variety of valid trajectories moving out from the source.

In particular, whether one likes low or high christological ideas, it is
not in order to assume that we must start with the one and move to
the other. The evidence is complex, and often the same document
emphasizes both the humanity and the divinity of Christ. This is so
even of some of the earliest New Testament material, which should
warn us about using texts to fight theological battles, especially if we
are at odds with the conclusions of the New Testament writers themselves. Respect for the givenness of the text, however much one may
dislike its content, is crucial to any historical or theological enterprise
if it is to have integrity.

A further methodological point is that, though scholars like to think
in discrete categories (e.g., suffering Son of Man sayings in one category, future coming Son of Man sayings in another), a good deal of our
material overlaps. Not only do different sorts of Son of Man sayings
bleed over into each other's territory, but we see Son of Man and Son
of God material overlapping, or Son of God and Wisdom material, or
Lord and Savior material and so on. The New Testament reflects synthetic thinking about the Christ and we must take this into account.
Martin Hengel puts it this way: "The development of Christology was
from the beginning interested in synthesis: otherwise it was impossible to give satisfactory expression to the eschatological uniqueness of
God's communication of himself in the man Jesus."[8]

Part of what it means to recognize the synthetic thinking of the
New Testament writers involves seeing that Christology in the New
Testament is so bound up with soteriology that it is quite impossible
and wrong methodologically to consider the person of Christ apart
from his works. Often the christological and soteriological statements
come together and arise out of each other. For example, it was believed
that Christ could not have been Savior and Lord had he not died and
risen again from the dead. His mission both expressed and determined
his identity for believers. Romans 1:3–4 says quite clearly that he was
only appointed Son of God in power as a result of and since the resurrection. Before that he was Son of God in weakness.

It is also crucial to bear in mind the distinctiveness of early christological thinking and not just its indebtedness to early Judaism and other sources of ideas. There was no other religious community of that era that proclaimed or worshiped a crucified Son of God, much less told the story of a preexistent Son who came to earth, was crucified, raised, exalted to God's right hand, and was expected to return. This was a very strange story indeed. Pagans did not talk about the death of a god in human form, and the evidence still suggests that Jews did not talk about a crucified Messiah. Hengel is right that in most ways this strange story put a damper on mythologizing because it was believed that Jesus was a nonpareil. The insistence that a Jewish manual worker from Galilee was God's unique Son seems to have resulted on the whole in the avoidance of various sorts of possible pagan embellishments of the story. What narratological developments we do find come out of early Jewish literature, such as the Wisdom literature, not by and large out of Greek or Roman mythology.

It was precisely because it was believed that Christ was unique and his claims on his followers exclusive that the New Testament writers sought to apply as many grand titles and ideas to Christ as they could. He was seen as creator, redeemer, sustainer all wrapped into one. Most of the various titles and functions of the Jewish God were predicated of him. All of the Old Testament institutions were thought to be completed or summed up in him. All Old Testament prophecy was thought to point forward to him, for he was seen as the climactic revelation of God and the hermeneutical key to all that have been revealed before his time.

He was seen as the real preexistent Wisdom of God (not Torah), the greatest revealer, eclipsing Moses, a forever priest, eclipsing the levitical and all other merely human priesthoods, the perfect once for all sacrifice making all other sacrifices unnecessary, the Jewish Messiah but also the Savior of the world, the only begotten Son of God, unlike all the other sons and daughters of God. Indeed, it was believed by various New Testament writers that only God's names including the term God and Lord were big enough to express adequately the reality and meaning of the Christ. It was believed that Christ was larger than any one idea or image or title could encapsulate, and therefore a multiplicity of images and ideas was required.

This continued to be the case in the postcanonical period. Precisely because the New Testament was not canonized for a long time after the New Testament era, christological development continued in various forms. It is important to see how this process led to the key ecu-

menical and christological councils, at which point the issues of orthodoxy and canon became clearer if not entirely fixed.

CHRISTOLOGY AND CANON:
THE ORGANIZING OF ORTHODOXY

When we get beyond the first century C.E., we discover that the christological landscape remains varied and interesting. We also discover
that christological speculation tended to run in certain directions and
to favor certain concepts (e.g., *logos* Christology), whereas other concepts such as the Son of Man tends to drop almost completely out of
view. In addition, new ideas arose, and there was amplification of some
New Testament concepts that had been only minor notions or barely
hinted at or mentioned in passing in the New Testament.

We shall see also that many of the major controversies within the
church of the second and third centuries involved Christology. There
was the attempt to define the relationship of Christ's divine nature to
the Godhead, and also the relationship of the Holy Spirit to the Godhead. Probably the major subject of the council of Nicaea in 325 C.E.
was Jesus' relationship to the Deity, while the western church at the
council of Chalcedon in 450–451 sought to define without error the
relationship of Christ's humanity to his divinity.[9] Of course none of
the formulations of these councils was immune to error, but they were
seen as definitely better than the alternatives. While both Nicaea and
Chalcedon were in-house discussions of important matters, when the
smoke cleared some parties found themselves outside the house. It
will be noted that especially at Chalcedon the christological defini-
tions tended to proceed by negatives, in other words ruling out of
bounds certain notions without trying to describe exhaustively what
was the case about Christ. This was an exercise in boundary definition,
which thereby makes clear what is not orthodox thought. None of the
major viewpoints was denying the divinity or humanity of Christ at
Chalcedon, but there were significant differences of opinion about
how the two were related.

No doubt it will come as something of a surprise to some that there
was a relatively lively debate among the ante-Nicene fathers about the
deity or preexistence of Christ. As we have seen, these ideas are in evidence in the New Testament, but they are found infrequently, whereas
they seem to have been taken as a matter of course in the second and

third centuries in many Christian quarters.[10] For instance, we find the idea of the preexistence of Christ in Clement of Rome, and Ignatius of Antioch does not hesitate to call Jesus "our God" on various occasions.

As S. Duffy has pointed out, Ignatius seems to have been the first to take some of the Pauline ideas about Christ found in the christological hymns and other material in his letters and combine them with Johannine ideas.[11] He speaks repeatedly about "Jesus Christ my God." He also affirms the personal preexistence of Jesus (see, e.g., *Letter to the Magnesians* 6.1; 7.2). Ignatius begins to speculate about the paradoxical nature of the incarnation. Jesus is both flesh and spirit, both born and yet not born, God in the flesh, yet as flesh subject to death (see *Letter to the Smyrnaeans* 1.2; *Letter to Polycarp* 3.2; and especially *Letter to the Ephesians* 7.2). Ignatius is in fact perfectly comfortable with saying "Our God Jesus Christ was carried in the womb by Mary" (*Ephesians* 7.18). Yet Ignatius can also speak of Jesus becoming God's Son at his conception in Mary's womb, though he also affirms Christ's preexistence.[12] Ignatius of course lived in a primarily pagan environment where there was affirmation of many gods, so this may have been one reason he felt comfortable in speaking as he does about Christ as "my God," but Ignatius was no polytheist.

Apart from the Shepherd of Hermas, there is relatively little evidence of adoptionist Christology in the usual sense of the term between the late first and early third centuries. There are, however, other strange formulations in Hermas's writings. For instance, it is in Hermas that we hear that the Son of God was Michael the archangel before the incarnation. This attempt to rank the Son among the created beings was ultimately to meet with condemnation.

It is clear enough that calling Jesus God led to a variety of speculations about how one could say such a thing and remain a monotheist. One solution came to be called monarchianism—the idea that God was a monad or numerically only one, so that the Father and the Son were one and the same being and person. This led to the untenable conclusion that there was no God in heaven while the Son was on earth and also that the Father must have died on the cross with or, better said, *as* the Son (this view was called Patripassianism). Sabellius, for instance, wanted to call the one Christian God the *huiopater*—the SonFather. This idea was eventually abandoned for a variety of reasons, one of which was that the Greek notion of the impassibility of God (God's inability to suffer) was adopted by Christian thinkers and was understood to rule out God suffering on the cross.

There was also floating around in the second century the idea that Jesus and the Spirit were one and the same so that it was Jesus as Spirit that overshadowed Mary descending into her womb and taking on flesh. This has sometimes been called a Spirit or pneumatic Christology. There were many developments of this kind as Christians tried to work out the implications of calling God, Christ, and the Spirit God or Lord.

One of the most important second-century figures was Justin Martyr, who spent his time trying to harmonize the Greek and Stoic idea of the *logos spermatikos* with the Johannine idea of the *logos*. The Stoics were basically pantheists who believed that the principle of rationality and moral order (the germinal *logos*) pervaded the universe. Justin used this idea to argue that before Christ came to earth there were seeds of the *logos* in humanity, so they were able to come up with a fragmentary knowledge of the truth. Apparently then, for Justin the *logos* was defined impersonally before the incarnation as the Father's rational thought or intelligence, which became personal only when the *logos* took on human flesh.[13] This denied to Christ any personal preexistence. This attempt to harmonize New Testament thought with Greek philosophical notions, or at least to use the latter to express the former, was not an unusual practice in this period when christological experimentation was common, without a canon to act as a norm.[14] Justin, despite such speculations, helped the church along in that he does deal with a divine triad, talking about the divinity of Father and Son and Spirit, though as was common in this period Spirit seems to have been called or treated as some*thing* rather than some*one*. On the other hand, Justin also introduced the Greek philosophical notion of God's impassible nature into the discussion about the incarnation, which caused no end of difficulties when not only the incarnation but also Christ's death was discussed in the next two centuries.

Without doubt, the theologian who summed up the thought of the second-century church and dominated the intellectual landscape prior to Origen was Irenaeus. He too held that the *logos* was God's immanent rationality used in creation, and that in fact the Word coexisted with the Father from all eternity. Irenaeus gave a fuller role to the Spirit and its divine status than others had before, and no doubt this helped foster further trinitarian reflection. It is interesting that Irenaeus identified not Christ but the Spirit as the preexistent Wisdom figure. Thus apparently the Spirit was also coeternal and preexistent.

Though Irenaeus is closer to trinitarian thinking than anyone before Tertullian, he still did not talk about three coequal persons in a Trinity, but rather a Father with his rationality or wisdom. This was not accidental, however, because Christianity had had to struggle on two fronts—against pagan polytheism and against charges of polytheism from Jews, both of which caused Irenaeus to insist on the belief that God is One. While it can be said that at points Irenaeus learned from and echoed Justin Martyr, he repudiated the latter's subordinationist tendencies, and affirmed the true divinity of Christ.[15]

After Irenaeus, the next crucial figure is Tertullian (160–220 C.E.). Tertullian is the first to actually use the word "Trinity," and perhaps one of the first to insist on the personal preexistence of the Son, though he also argued that the Son was begotten for the work of creation. Tertullian also called the Word or Son before the incarnation a *persona* (person). He also says that the three are manifestations of the One divine power. They may be distinguished but not divided. Father, Son, and Spirit are one in substance; in fact he concluded that Father and Son are one identical substance extended. He adds, however, that the Father is the whole substance, and the Son is a part of the whole. In other words, God is the name of the substance, the divinity. At some points he was also willing to say, since the Godhead is one, that the Father and the Son are one identical being. In other words, Monarchianism or traces of it were found even in those who were later deemed orthodox on the Trinity. It was apparently not until near the end of Tertullian's life as the second century closed and the third dawned that what was later seen as the standard pattern of trinitarian thinking began to emerge. Nevertheless, Tertullian helped to shape the conciliar discussion that was to follow not only on the interrelationships within the Trinity but also on the two natures but single personhood of Christ (see *Against Praxeas*).[16]

About 250 C.E. Novatian picked up where Tertullian left off and went further not only saying that the Son was a second preexistent person but insisting that the generation of the Son is not tied to creation but is totally pretemporal. Since the Father is always the Father, there must have also always been a Son, a view Tertullian appears not to have affirmed. Still we must bear in mind that we do not yet have the three-in-one formula, because Novatian still argues that the Father connotes the unique Godhead.

Origen (roughly 185–254 C.E.) is next and one of the most influential figures in this whole discussion. His views were both brilliant and eclectic. He argued that God is a monad (one, not three), but that God always needed to have objects to exercise his goodness and power. So God brought into existence a world of spiritual beings or souls coeternal with him. This idea came to him from Middle Platonism, which spoke of the eternality of the world or matter. But to mediate between God and the world, the Son was generated before time and the world. The Son is therefore called by Origen a second God and is said to have existed before all time. Origen is willing to state that there are three persons in God, and each of the three *hypostases* is distinct. Father, Son, and Spirit are one in essence but different in subsistence. Sometimes when Origen talks about oneness, it appears that he means the three persons of God are united in a moral union. They are said to be one in unanimity, harmony, and identity of will. The Father is the fullness of deity, from which the Son and Spirit derive their deity, though these latter two are eternally and really distinct.

There were, however, problems perceived with Origen's use of Middle Platonic notions to help flesh out the understanding of God and the world. Origen himself seems to have seen some of the difficulties because in his later writings, which reflect his late discovery of the letters of Ignatius, he begins to speak of the passibility of God, God's ability to suffer and feel emotions comparable to human emotions.[17]

For one thing, if one maintains the eternality of the world this would seem to impugn God's absolute sovereignty and transcendence over the world, not to mention raising serious questions about what Genesis 1 might mean by talking about creation out of nothing. Sometimes too Origen slipped into a sort of subordinationism whereby he argued that the Son should not be prayed to, because he was an emanation from the Father or even a creature—the first in a chain of emanations (another Platonic idea). This notion was to be expanded on by the Gnostics in the second and third centuries, who seem to have independently drawn on Platonic (and Zoroastrian?) ideas. What is at issue here is whether the divine Son stands fundamentally on the side of the Godhead or on the side of the creature. In the west it was only haltingly that the idea of God as a monad gave way to the view of three persons, so powerful were the belief in and the stress on divine unity.

Much, perhaps most, of the christological debate in the West which led up to Nicaea centered on the question of what John meant when he said the Word became flesh. Hippolytus, the student of Irenaeus, had argued that in fact the preexistent Son put flesh on as one puts on a garment. Tertullian, however, articulated what was to become the standard notion of the two natures of Christ (calling them two *substantiae*, two substances). The Son, being a divine spirit, is said by Tertullian to have descended into the Virgin and to have had a real human birth, really assuming human flesh. Foreshadowing issues that were not to be settled until 451 at Chalcedon (if they can be said to be fully settled even then), Tertullian argued that Jesus' human nature was complete, including a real human soul. This view was later to be disputed by some who wanted to argue that the divine *logos* took the place of the human soul so the *logos* dwelt in a human body. This view, however, was seen to deny Christ's true humanity, and also that he had two complete natures.

Clearly there was a lot of ferment on these issues between 300 and 450. Some still seemed to argue (as Justin Martyr had earlier) that the divine in Christ should be called spirit, and was sometimes confused with the Holy Spirit. This spirit Christology, however, was largely displaced by the idea that *logos* was the term for the divine in Christ. Both Ignatius and Irenaeus simply called the *logos* the Son. *Logos* and Son of God became the dominant titles in the second and third centuries and were used to explain all the main passages in the Gospels and Epistles that were already gathered and being treated as at least sacred tradition.

Matters seem to have been brought to a head by Arius, who argued that (1) the *logos* was a created being; (2) that God was impassible but the *logos* was mutable; (3) that Jesus was then not fully human, being subject to change. The real issue here was whether God's nature could incorporate change (i.e., take on a body). If this was not so, then apparently Jesus as the *logos* could not be called God, strictly speaking. For Arius, only God was God; the divinity was a monad, not a triad.

To respond to Arianism, the church turned to the word *homoousios*, and to the phrase "begotten, not made." This in part amounted to saying that Christ came from the *ousia,* or essence or very being, of the Father. The point at issue was whether or not the preexistent *logos* was of the same stuff or nature as the Father. If the answer was yes, then he had to be placed on the divine side of the dividing line between God and humans, not on the other side and not merely in between. This point was crucial not only for Christology but also for soteriology because if only God could save human beings, then Jesus must be in some sense God, or sharing in the same divine nature. But some then asked, If we affirm that Christ is of the same nature as God, does this mean sharing the same *kind* of nature (or made of the same substance) or sharing the same identical substance (numerical identification)?

This discussion led some in the early fourth century to argue for a compromise term, *homoiousios* (of like substance). At Nicaea this compromise term was rejected in favor of *homo-ousios*, meaning that the Son was to be seen as of the same identical substance as the Father, not just a similar or same kind of substance. This in turn preserved a union between the Father and Son, avoided tri-theism, and still allowed for a distinction between Father and Son as different persons. Father and Son were distinguishable but not separable. The logic behind the decision at Nicaea appears to have been that since the divine nature is immaterial and indivisible, any being sharing in the Godhead must share the very same divine substance as the Father. Thus, in the end the unity of the Godhead and the deity of Christ were affirmed at Nicaea in 325 C.E.

This is not to say that there were not residual concerns. Some saw *homo-ousios* as a convenient translation of Tertullian's earlier phrase *unius substantiae*. But some worried that this negated the threeness, the three *hypostases* of the deity. The problem boiled down to the fact that *hypostases* was a proper Greek translation for the Latin term *substantiae*. When some Greek-speaking Christians heard the arguments for *unius substantiae*, they assumed that this meant one *hypostasis*, which was not Tertullian's or Nicaea's view. These problems were argued about during the entire period between 325 and 450, and the dogma of the Trinity was not hammered out before that latter date. Until then there was still much debate and discussion.

One of the more overlooked aspects of the discussion was what one should say about the Spirit. It does not appear that there was any substantial Christian document written about the deity of the Spirit before the second half of the fourth century—in others words, not until well after Nicaea. Nicaea had primarily been about the relationship of the Father and the Son. As late as 380, Gregory of Nazianzus summed up the problem as follows: "of the wise among ourselves, some have conceived of him [i.e., the Holy Spirit] as an activity, some as a creature, some as God; and some have been uncertain what to call him." Clearly pneumatology was trailing along behind Christology at this stage of church history.

One of the key figures who helped to lead to the resolution of various important matters was Athanasius. He made a start toward sorting out several of these issues by pointing out the following: (1) The Spirit was called the Spirit of the Lord; hence it was of God. (2) To blaspheme against the Holy Spirit meant to blaspheme against God. (3) The Holy Spirit was God because it did what only God could do—sanctify or make holy human beings. Athanasius pointed to the baptismal formula in Matthew 28 and stressed that the church only baptized people into God. This was very helpful, but what was still needed was clarity by means of one agreed-upon term for the oneness of God and another for the threeness of God. In general it would be accepted that in Greek the formula would speak of one *ousia* and three *hypostases,* and in Latin one *substantia* with three *personae*. It would appear that it was not until the time of Augustine that the church became really comfortable with talking about three persons in the Godhead. Athanasius, however, stressed that whatever is said of the Father, in the matter of divinity, may also be predicated of the Son, except that the Son is not and should not be called the Father.[18] Furthermore, he stressed that since only God could provide salvation or redeem humanity, Jesus must have been truly God.

What sort of dilemmas led to the Council of Chalcedon in 451? First, there was the growing influence, especially in the Eastern portion of the church, of Greek philosophical ideas on theological thinking about God. If God was absolutely impassible and unchangeable, then God could not suffer. What then did one do with the New Testament, which presented the church with phrases such as "they crucified the Lord of glory"? How could God as Lord be said to die on the cross? If it was not God, who died on the cross? How can Christ's death be said to have infinite or universal effect? Or again, the Fourth Gospel says the Word became flesh. Did this mean a divine being took on a human nature or that the Word turned into flesh, leaving divinity behind? Or was one to think of some sort of amalgam of divine and human natures in Jesus, so that his flesh had become divinized? Another question being broached was whether it was possible to conclude that some remarks in the Gospels and epistles applied only to Jesus' human nature and others only to his divine nature? Thus, for instance, it was asked, When a text says Jesus died and one concludes that this applied only to his human nature, where did his divine nature go? Why did Christ cry out "My God my God why have you forsaken me?"

Some pointed out that the Gospel traditions and the epistles simply referred to Jesus as a person, with all the various remarks predicated of him as a person. In other words, these sacred traditions didn't make the sort of nice distinctions that were later seen as important. Wouldn't it be better to say that all these statements are predicated of Jesus the God-man as a whole person, for in all such remarks the whole person of Jesus is always the subject or object of the discussion? It is the person who wills and acts and is the object of actions, not just his nature. Unless one separates the two natures and so comes up with two Sons (one the human Jesus, the other the divine Son), you must say what happened to one nature also happened to or at least affected and was evident to the other. These were the kinds of discussions and conundrums that the church pondered and which prompted the Council of Chalcedon.

Athanasius proved helpful in this discussion as well. He argued for the helpful notion of the *communicatio idiomatum*, or the communication of properties, such that predicates that might technically be said only of the divine nature of Christ could also be said of the human one as well, so closely were the natures united. Yet there were those who, like Apollinarius, wanted to maintain that there was but one nature in Christ, both divine and human. He maintained that only so could Christ be one person. How could one talk about Jesus growing in wisdom and stature, if he was omniscient as the Incarnate One? How could he be like other human beings in all essential respects if he did not experience human limitations of time, space, and knowledge?

How could he undergo temptation and it be a real temptation if it was impossible for him to sin (his divine nature making it impossible)? How could he be fully human if he didn't really have a human spirit or soul? The problem then could be summed up as follows: The divine and human had to be united in Christ closely enough to effect divine salvation for humans, but the union must not mean the obliteration of his true humanity (so that his human life was but a charade and he did not really undergo temptation or weakness or anxiety or fear and so on). Nor could the union be such that it meant that the divine suffered, something strictly speaking impossible if one meant feeling bodily pain, since God is spirit.[19]

The way the Council of Chalcedon dealt with these knotty problems was severalfold. First, it was said that one must not talk about Jesus' natures without setting up a timetable. Are we talking about the Incarnate One during his earthly ministry, or the preexistent Word before the incarnation, or the God-Man after the resurrection and ascension, now in heaven with a glorified body? The narratological

Christology found in the hymns in the New Testament would seem to have encouraged this sort of approach. Different remarks were seen to apply to the whole person at different stages of his career. The fathers at Chalcedon were careful not to go the "kenotic" route in interpreting Philippians 2, careful to say that this text did not mean Christ gave up his divinity in order to become human. Rather, it was viewed as the bending down of divine compassion, renouncing divine privilege or status but not divinity. One and the same Christ was the subject of all christological predicates. The final decision at Chalcedon was a compromise and combination of several previous statements by various people such as Athanasius. The final statement was not intended to answer all the questions but was to ensure that the church believed in one Christ but with two united but distinct natures. It will be worthwhile to quote the key portion of the council's decision at this point:

> Following therefore the holy fathers, we confess one and the same Lord Jesus Christ, and we all teach harmoniously [that he is] the same perfect in Godhead, the same perfect in humanity, truly God and truly human, the same of a reasonable soul and body; *homo-ousios* with the Father in godhead, and the same *homo-ousios* with us in humanity, like us in all things except sin; begotten before ages of the Father in Godhead; the same in the last days for us and for our salvation [born] of Mary the virgin *Theotokos*,[20] in humanity one and the same Christ, Son, Lord, unique; acknowledged in two natures without confusion, without change, without division, without separation, the difference of the natures being by no means taken away because of the union, but rather the distinctive character of each nature being preserved, and [each] combining in one person and *hypostasis*—not divided or separated into two persons, but one and the same Son and only-begotten God, *Logos*, Lord Jesus Christ; as the prophets of old and the Lord Jesus Christ himself taught us about him, and the Symbol[21] of the Fathers has handed down to us.

We have provided only the flavor of the christological discussion and debate between 100 and 450 C.E. Much more could in fact be said, for instance, about the Council of Constantinople (381 C.E.), which came between Nicaea and Chalcedon. At this time the views of Apollonarius were condemned, safeguarding Christ's humanity.[22] Our focus has been on chronicling how the discussions about the Trinity, and especially Christ's role in the Trinity, progressed and developed. A good deal of the discussion went beyond what is said in the New Testament, and in some cases it could be said to go against what was said in the New Testament. For instance, the Greek notions of the impassibility and unchangeableness of God cause severe problems for the doctrine of the incarnation, for surely Christ's taking on a human nature constitutes a change in condition. Was one to pattern the way one read the sacred traditions by the council decisions, or the other way around? It is not an accident that during this same period, 100 to 451, the church was also sorting out its doctrine of the canon. A chart will help us see the situation:

Development of Christology and Canon

Development of Canon	Development of Christology
(27 books in NT agreed upon)	
	325 Council of Nicaea
	Rejects Arianism
	Promulgates Nicene Creed
	Asserts *homo-ousios* doctrine
367 Athanasius (in the East)	
	381 Council of Constantinople
382 Synod in Rome	Rejects Apollinarianism
Pope Damascus [Jerome]	Safeguards Christ's humanity
393 Synod in N. Africa	451 Council of Chalcedon
403 Pope Innocent I [West]	Two natures doctrine

What this chart indicates is that there was a rather widespread agreement on what constituted the New Testament canon before the christological issues were all ironed out. Doubtless this helped the christological process in 451 C.E. such that the council had an agreed-upon sacred tradition as a basis for the christological discussions.

In this section the discussion has centered not so much on the sort of christological issues that we have dealt with throughout this book—the meaning of titles and terms in their various forms and the exegesis of key texts in the New Testament sources. Instead, larger and sometimes philosophical issues that were not broached in the New Testament period dominated the discussion. The issue of the two natures of Christ or the interrelationships within the Trinity are not really discussed in the New Testament, though the raw data for such discussions were certainly present, even to the point of Christ being called God in various sources. The humanity of Christ is not so much discussed as assumed and displayed in the New Testament. Strangely enough, there seems to be more material on or interest in the relationship between Christ and the Spirit in the New Testament (especially in the Johannine and Pauline literature) than there is in the subsequent discussions about the Trinity, at least up until the fourth century.

Another interesting difference between what we find in the New Testament and especially what we find at Chalcedon is that in the end the latter relied on the *via negativa,* the path of negations, to better define the relationship between Christ's two natures. The New Testament, by contrast, concentrates on saying positive things about what is true about Christ as a person, without making nice distinctions as to whether the remarks are mainly about his humanity or his divinity. More could be said along these lines, but we have said enough to indicate the character of what was happening after the New Testament era in matters of Christology. Certain image and ideas from the New Testament documents became dominant, and certain things mentioned in passing in the New Testament were later seen as crucial (e.g., the meaning of the phrase "they crucified the Lord of glory").

The agendas of the New Testament writers were not always, some would say not often, the agendas of the later formulators of the creeds. Nevertheless, it cannot be said that these councils said anything that really *contradicted* what the New Testament sources said or suggested, except perhaps in the matter of the impassibility of God. By and large these councils were simply extrapolating what was implied in various New Testament texts, or putting together ideas that were found separately in different New Testament texts. In other words, the fathers were undertaking the task of systematic theologians more than that of exegetes.

In this study we have attempted to do the descriptive task, exposing the reader to the Christologies of the New Testament era and to a lesser extent of the period 100–451 C.E. We have not undertaken much of the synthetic task because that must be based on the descriptive task. In other words, that sort of discussion will have to be reserved for another time and another place. Here we have attempted to expose the reader to the many faces of Jesus as viewed and portrayed by the earliest Christians. F. Buechner has summed things up well in saying:

> Whoever he was or was not, whoever he thought he was, whoever he has become in the memories of [people] since and will go on becoming for as long as [we] remember him—exalted, sentimentalized, debunked, made and remade to the measure of each generation's desire, dread, indifference—he was a man once, whoever else he may have been. And he had a man's face. . . . *Ecce homo* Pilate said—Behold the man—and yet whatever our religion or lack of it, we tend to shrink from beholding him. The risk with Jesus is too great; the risk that his face would be too much for

us if not enough, either a face like any other face to see, pass by, forget, or a face so unlike any other that we would have no choice but to remember it always and follow or flee it to the end of our days and beyond.

So once again, for the last time or the first time, we face that face . . . take it or leave it, if nothing else it is at least a face we would know anywhere—a face that belongs to us somehow, our age our culture; a face we somehow belong to. Like the faces of people we love, it has become so familiar that unless we take pains we hardly see it at all. Take pains. . . . He had a face . . . [that was] not a front for him to live his life behind but a frontier, the outermost visible edge of his life itself in all its richness and multiplicity. . . . The *faces* of Jesus then—all the ways he had of being and of being seen. The writers of the New Testament give no description of any of them because it was his life alive inside of them that was the news they hawked rather than the color of his eyes. . . . See it for what it is and see it whole, see it too for what it is just possible it will become: the face of Jesus as the face of our own secret and innermost destiny: The face of Jesus as our face.[23]

If this book has helped the reader see and understand afresh some of the various faces of Jesus in the New Testament and beyond the New Testament, I am content. In the end, one is always in more danger of saying too little about Jesus than in saying enough or too much. The faces of Jesus are many, as are his interpreters, and having withstood the onslaught of two thousand years of scrutiny without exhausting the subject, there is always room for one more look at the subject. The reader must judge whether this survey has proved helpful or not.

NOTES

1. Here I think M. Hengel, in his seminal study *The Son of God* (Philadelphia: Fortress Press, 1976), has the focus right when he says that the most plausible sources for the christological ideas and images we find in the New Testament are (1) the Old Testament and early Jewish literature; (2) hellenized Judaism as it existed in Palestine; (3) Diaspora Judaism; (4) last and least, purely Hellenistic notions.

2. Another good example would be comparing the idea of the incarnation with the virginal conception. The latter tries to explain how and also who was the initiator of Jesus' human life, whereas the incarnational idea deals with the taking on of flesh by a preexistent being. The latter does not address how this event of incarnation transpired. The two ideas are not incompatible, but they are different. Real incarnational thinking leads to conclusions that will startle some. For instance, Jesus the human being from Nazareth properly speaking

did not exist prior to his conception in Mary. To put it a different way, Jesus as God-man had a human beginning in space and time. Christian faith is in a real historical person. At the same time various New Testament writers assert that the divine Son did exist before the incarnation; indeed, the christological hymns say he existed before the creation of the universe. It is not surprising that some such formulation as Nicaea or Chalcedon and the two natures doctrine arose to account for how these sorts of christological insights fit together.

3. See R. T. France, "The Worship of Jesus," in *Christ the Lord: Studies in Christology presented to Donald Guthrie,* ed. H. H. Rowdon (Downers Grove, Ill.: Inter-Varsity, 1982), pp. 17–37.

4. On how angel worship was handled in Revelation, see pp. 192ff. above.

5. In addition to the detailed study of M. J. Harris (*Jesus as God: The New Testament Use of* Theos *in Reference to Jesus* [Grand Rapids: Baker, 1992]) compare and contrast A. W. Wainwright, "The Confession 'Jesus is God' in the NT," *Scottish Journal of Theology* 10 (1957): 274–97; and V. Taylor, "Does the New Testament call Jesus God?" in his *New Testament Essays* (London: Epworth, 1970), pp. 83–89.

6. Here I must disagree with J. D. G. Dunn's assessment of the situation in "Christology as an Aspect of Theology," in *The Future of Christology: Essays in Honor of Leander E. Keck,* ed. A. J. Malherbe and W. A. Meeks (Minneapolis: Fortress Press, 1993), pp. 202–12, especially when he wishes to deny the conclusion that Christ was conceived of as personally preexistent well before the end of the first century C.E.

7. The issue of truth claims is another matter. For instance, it could be argued that Jesus did see himself as the Messiah and the like, and that the New Testament writers did develop such ideas from a historical basis, but that Jesus was wrong about himself and so were his followers. In view of the New Testament evidence, this argument seems more plausible than the one that simply says Jesus was a humble teacher or prophet about whom later devotees said far too much.

8. Hengel, *Son of God,* p. 75.

9. The eastern church never really accepted the results of Chalcedon.

10. No doubt trinitarian discussion was sparked at least in part by the continuing and amplification of the tendency to call Jesus God.

11. S. Duffy, "The Early Church Fathers and the Great Councils: The Emergence of Classical Christianity," in E. Richard, *Jesus: One and Many. The Christological Concept of New Testament Authors* (Wilmington, Del.: M. Glazier, 1988), pp. 435–86.

12. In other words, Ignatius thinks of Christ as preexistent, just not a preexistent Son, an odd conclusion in view of the early christological conclusion.

13. Some moderns have in fact argued in a fashion similar to Justin that this is what we find in the New Testament apart from John 1, not personal preexistence but something less than that. See J. D. G. Dunn *Christology in the Making* (Philadelphia: Westminster, 1980), passim.

14. See Duffy, "Early Christian Fathers," pp. 441–43.

15. Ibid., p. 444.

16. Tertullian, however, spoke of one *persona* with two *substantiae*, namely, flesh and spirit. See Duffy, "Early Christian Fathers," pp. 447–48.

17. See Duffy, "Early Christian Fathers," pp. 451–52.

18. See the discussion in ibid., pp. 457–59.

19. See the helpful discussion of all these matters in J. Pelikan, *The Christian Tradition, Volume 1* (Chicago: University of Chicago Press, 1971), pp. 172–77; and also J. N. D. Kelly, *Early Christian Doctrines* (New York: Harper & Row, 1958), pp. 56–60, 83–162.

20. This controversial Greek term means "God-bearer."

21. This term was the way the Apostle's Creed was referred to at this time.

22. On Apollinarius, see Duffy, "Early Christian Fathers," pp. 462–64.

23. F. Buechner, *The Life of Jesus* (New York: Harper & Row, 1989), pp. 9–14, excerpts.

Bibliography

This bibliography is not intended to be exhaustive, but rather to provide guidance for those who wish to pursue the subject of this book further. It is limited to works available in English.

There are several introductory surveys of the Christologies of the New Testament that are readily accessible. I would especially commend the following:

Brown, R. E. *An Introduction to New Testament Christology.* New York: Paulist Press, 1994.

Cullmann, O. *The Christology of the New Testament.* London: SCM, 1959.

Dunn, J. D. G. *Christology in the Making.* Philadelphia: Westminster, 1980.

Fuller, R. H. *The Foundations of New Testament Christology.* New York: Scribner, 1965.

Hahn, F. *The Titles of Jesus in Christology.* London: Lutterworth, 1969.

Marshall, I. H. *The Origins of New Testament Christology.* Downers Grove, Ill.: Inter-Varsity, 1994.

Moule, C. F. D. *The Origin of Christology.* Cambridge: Cambridge University Press, 1977.

Neyrey, J. H. *Christ is Community: The Christologies of the New Testament.* Wilmington, Del.: M. Glazier, 1985.

Richard, E. *Jesus: One and Many. The Christological Concept of New Testament Authors.* Wilmington, Del.: M. Glazier, 1988.

Of volumes of collected essays on our subject the following are some of the more helpful:

Charlesworth, J. H., ed. *The Messiah.* Minneapolis: Fortress Press, 1992.

Fuller, R. H. *Christ and Christianity: Studies in the Formation of Christology.* Valley Forge, Penn.: Trinity Press, 1994.

Green, J. B., and M. Turner, eds. *Jesus of Nazareth Lord and Christ: Essays on the Historical Jesus and New Testament Christology.* Grand Rapids: Eerdmans, 1994.

Hurst, L. D., and N. T. Wright, eds. *The Glory of Christ in the New Testament: Studies in Christology in Memory of George Bradford Caird.* Oxford: Oxford University Press, 1987.

Lindars, B., and S. S. Smalley, eds. *Christ and the Spirit in the New Testament.* Cambridge: Cambridge University Press, 1973.

Malherbe, A. J., and W. A. Meeks, eds. *The Future of Christology: Essays in Honor of Leander E. Keck.* Minneapolis: Fortress Press, 1993.

Rowdon, H. H., ed. *Christ the Lord: Studies in Christology presented to Donald Guthrie.* Downers Grove, Ill.: Inter-Varsity, 1982.

Introduction and Chapter One

Charlesworth, J. H. "From Messianology to Christology: Problems and Prospects." In *The Messiah*, edited by J. H. Charlesworth, pp. 3–35. Minneapolis: Fortress Press, 1992.

Collins, J. J. *The Scepter and the Star: The Messiahs of the Dead Sea Scrolls and Other Ancient Literature.* New York: Doubleday, 1995.

———. "The Son of God Text from Qumran." In *From Jesus to John*, edited by M. De Boer, pp. 65–82. Sheffield: JSOT Press, 1993.

de Jonge, M. "The Use of the Word 'Anointed' in the Time of Jesus." *Novum Testament* 8 (1966): 132–48.

———. "The Earliest Christian Use of *Christos:* Some Suggestions." *New Testament Studies* 32 (1986): 321–43.

Fuller, R. H., and P. Perkins. *Who is this Christ?* Philadelphia: Fortress Press, 1983.

Hooker, M. D. "Christology and Methodology." *New Testament Studies* 17 (1970–71): 480–87.

Keck, L. "Toward the Renewal of New Testament Christology." *New Testament Studies* 32 (1986): 362–77.

Neusner J., W. S. Green, and E. Frerichs, eds. *Judaisms and their Messiahs at the turn of the Era.* Cambridge: Cambridge University Press, 1987.

Nickelsburg, G. W. E., and J. J. Collins. *Ideal Figures in Ancient Judaism: Profiles and Paradigms.* Chico, Calif.: Scholars Press, 1980.

Schiffman, L. H. "Messianic Figures and Ideas in the Qumran Scrolls." In *The Messiah*, edited by J. H. Charlesworth, pp. 116–29. Minneapolis: Fortress Press, 1992.

Talmon, S. "The Concept of *Masiah* and Messianism in Early Judaism." In *The Messiah*, edited by J. H. Charlesworth, pp. 79–115. Minneapolis: Fortress Press, 1992.

Witherington, B. *Jesus the Sage: The Pilgrimage of Wisdom*. Minneapolis: Fortress Press, 1994.

Chapter Two

Barr, J. "Abba and the Familiarity of Jesus' Speech." *Theology* 91 (1988): 173–79.

———. "Abba Isn't Daddy." *Journal of Theological Studies* 39 (1988): 28–47.

Borg, M. *Conflict and Holiness and Politics in the Teaching of Jesus*. New York: Edwin Mellen Press, 1984.

———. *Jesus: A New Vision*. San Francisco: HarperSanFrancisco, 1987.

———. *Meeting Jesus again for the First Time*. San Francisco: HarperSanFrancisco, 1994.

Collins, J. J. "The Son of Man in First Century Judaism." *New Testament Studies* 38 (1992): 448–66.

Caird, G. B. *Jesus and the Jewish Nation*. London: Athlone Press, 1965.

Crossan, J. D. *The Historical Jesus: The Life of a Mediterranean Jewish Peasant*. San Francisco: HarperSanFrancisco, 1991.

Dahl, N. "Messianic Ideas and the Crucifixion of Jesus." In *The Messiah*, edited by J. H. Charlesworth, pp. 382–403. Minneapolis: Fortress Press, 1992.

Dunn, J. D. G. "Messianic Ideas and their Influence on the Jesus of History." In *The Messiah*, edited by J. H. Charlesworth, pp. 365–81. Minneapolis: Fortress Press, 1992.

Hengel, M. *The Charismatic Leader and His Followers*. New York: Crossroad, 1981.

———. "Christological Titles in Early Christianity." In *The Messiah*, edited by J. H. Charlesworth, pp. 425–43. Minneapolis: Fortress Press, 1992.

———. *Studies in Early Christology*. Edinburgh: T & T Clark, 1995.

Horsley, R. *Jesus and the Spiral of Violence*. San Francisco: HarperSanFrancisco, 1987.

Lapide, P., and U. Luz. *Jesus in Two Perspectives: A Jewish Christian Dialog*. Minneapolis: Augsburg, 1985.

Lindars, B. "Enoch and Christology." *Expository Times* 92 (1980-81): 295–99.

Meier, John P. *A Marginal Jew: Rethinking the Historical Jesus.* 2 vols. New York: Doubleday, 1991–94.

Neusner, J. *Judaism in the Beginning of Christianity.* Philadelphia: Fortress Press, 1984.

Sanders, E. P. *The Historical Figure of Jesus.* London: Penguin, 1993.

——. *Jesus and Judaism.* Philadelphia: Fortress Press, 1985.

Theissen, G. *The Miracle Stories of the Early Christian Tradition.* Philadelphia: Fortress Press, 1983.

Wink. W. *John the Baptist in the Gospel Tradition.* Cambridge: Cambridge University Press, 1968.

Witherington, B. *The Christology of Jesus.* Philadelphia: Fortress Press, 1990.

——. *The Jesus Quest: The Third Search for the Jew of Nazareth.* Downers Grove, Ill.: Inter-Varsity, 1995.

Wright, N.T. *Jesus and the Victory of God.* Minneapolis: Fortress Press, 1996.

Chapter Three

Black, M. "The Christological Use of the Old Testament in the New Testament." *New Testament Studies* 18 (1971–72): 1–14.

Dodd, C. H. *The Apostolic Preaching and its Developments.* London: Hodder & Stoughton, 1936.

Evans, C. A., and J. A. Sanders. *Luke and Scripture.* Minneapolis: Fortress Press, 1993.

Freed, E. D. "Theological Prelude and the Prologue of John's Gospel." *Scottish Journal of Theology* 32 (1979): 257–69.

Gundry, R. H. "The Form of the Hymn in 1 Tim. 3.16." In *Apostolic History and the Gospel*, edited by W. W. Gasque and R. P. Martin, 203–22. Grand Rapids: Eerdmans, 1970.

Hamerton-Kelly, R. G. *Pre-existence, Wisdom, and the Son of Man.* Cambridge: Cambridge University Press, 1973.

Harris, M. J. *Jesus as God: The New Testament Use of* Theos *in Reference to Jesus.* Grand Rapids: Baker, 1992.

Hurtado, L. *One God, One Lord.* Philadelphia: Fortress Press, 1988.

Longenecker, R. N. *The Christology of Early Jewish Christianity.* Reprint, Grand Rapids: Baker, 1981.

Meier, J. P. "Structure and Theology in Heb. 1.1–4." *Biblica* 66 (1985): 168–89.

Sanders, J. *The New Testament Christological Hymns.* Cambridge: Cambridge University Press, 1971.

Stanton, G. N. "On the Christology of Q." In *Christ and the Spirit in the New Testament,* edited by B. Lindars and S. S. Smalley, pp. 27–42. Cambridge: Cambridge University Press, 1973.

Suggs, M. J. *Wisdom, Christology, and Law.* Cambridge, Mass.: Harvard University Press, 1970.

Wright, N. T. *The Climax of the Covenant.* Edinburgh: T & T Clark, 1991.

Chapter Four

Bassler, J. M., ed. *Pauline Theology, Volume 1, Thessalonians, Philippians, Galatians, Philemon.* Minneapolis: Fortress Press, 1991.

Hay, D. M., ed. *Pauline Theology, Volume 2, 1 & 2 Corinthians.* Minneapolis: Fortress Press, 1993.

Kim, S. *The Origin of Paul's Gospel.* Grand Rapids: Eerdmans, 1982.

Kremer, W. *Christ, Lord, Son of God.* London: SCM Press, 1966.

Metzger, B. M. "The Punctuation of Romans 9.5." In *Christ and the Spirit in the New Testament,* edited by B. Lindars and S. S. Smalley, pp. 95–112. Cambridge: Cambridge University Press, 1973.

Stanton, G. N. "Incarnational Christology in the New Testament." In *Incarnation and Myth: The Debate Continued,* edited by M. D. Goulder, pp. 151–73. Grand Rapids: Eerdmans, 1979.

Thrall, M. E. "The Origin of Pauline Christology." In *Apostolic History and the Gospel,* edited by W. W. Gasque and R. P. Martin, pp. 304–16. Grand Rapids: Eerdmans, 1970.

Witherington, B. "Christology." In *The Dictionary of Paul and his Letters,* edited by G. F. Hawthorne, R. P. Martin, and D. G. Reid, pp. 100–115. Downers Grove, Ill.: Inter-Varsity, 1993.

———. *Paul's Narrative Thought World.* Louisville: Westminster/J. Knox, 1994.

Chapter Five

Brown, R. E. *The Virginal Conception and Bodily Resurrection.* New York: Paulist, 1973.

Burridge, R. A. *What are the Gospels?* Cambridge: Cambridge University Press, 1992.

Carson, D. A. "Christological Ambiguities in Matthew." In *Christ the Lord: Studies in Christology presented to Donald Guthrie,* edited by H. H. Rowdon, pp. 97–114. Downers Grove, Ill.: Inter-Varsity, 1982.

Kingsbury, J. D. *The Christology of Mark.* Philadelphia: Fortress Press, 1984.

————. *Matthew: Structure, Christology, Kingdom.* Philadelphia: Fortress Press, 1975.

Machen, J. G. *The Virgin Birth of Christ.* Grand Rapids: Baker, 1930.

Schnackenburg, R. *Jesus in the Gospels: A Biblical Christology.* Translated by O. C. Dean. Louisville: Westminster/J. Knox, 1995.

Styler, G. M. "Stages in Christology." *New Testament Studies* 10 (1963–64): 398–409.

Tannehill, R. C. "The Gospel of Mark as Narrative Christology." *Semeia* 16 (1979): 57–93.

Tuckett, C., ed. *The Messianic Secret.* Philadelphia: Fortress Press, 1983.

Chapter Six

Moessner, D. P. "The 'script' of the Scriptures in Acts." In *History, Literature, and Society and the Book of Acts*, edited by B. Witherington, pp. 218–50. Cambridge: Cambridge University Press, 1996.

Moule, C. F. D. "The Christology of Acts." In *Studies in Luke-Acts*, edited by L. E. Keck and J. L. Martyn, pp. 159–85. London: SPCK, 1968.

Schweizer, E. "The Concept of the Davidic 'Son of God' in Acts and its Old Testament Background." In *Studies in Luke-Acts*, edited by L. E. Keck and J. L. Martyn, pp. 186–93. London: SPCK, 1968.

Smalley, S. S. "The Christology of Acts." *Expository Times* 93 (1961–62): 358–62.

————. "The Christology of Acts Again." In *Christ and the Spirit in the New Testament*, edited by B. Lindars and S. S. Smalley, pp. 79–84. Cambridge: Cambridge University Press, 1973.

Chapter Seven

Bauckham, R. "The Sonship of the Historical Jesus in Christology." *Scottish Journal of Theology* 31 (1978): 245–60.

————. *The Theology of the Book of Revelation.* Cambridge: Cambridge University Press, 1993.

Brown, R. E. "The Theology of the Incarnation in John." In *New Testament Essays*, pp. 96–101. New York: Paulist, 1982.

Collins, J. J. *The Apocalyptic Imagination.* New York: Crossroad, 1984.

Culpepper, R. A. *Anatomy of the Fourth Gospel.* Philadelphia: Fortress Press, 1983.

Edwards, R. A. "Christological Perspectives in the Book of Revelation." In *Christological Perspectives*, pp. 139–54.

Fortna, R. T. "Christology in the Fourth Gospel." *New Testament Studies* 21 (1974–75): 489–504.

Guthrie, D. "The Christology of Revelation." In *Jesus of Nazareth Lord and Christ: Essays on the Historical Jesus and New Testament Christology*, edited by J. B. Green and M. Turner, pp. 397–409. Grand Rapids: Eerdmans, 1994.

Käsemann, E. *The Testament of Jesus*. Philadelphia: Fortress Press, 1968.

Minear, P. "The Idea of Incarnation in 1 John." *Interpretation* 24 (1970): 291–302.

Robinson, J. A. T. "The Use of the Fourth Gospel for Christology Today." In *Christ and the Spirit in the New Testament*, edited by B. Lindars and S. S. Smalley, pp. 61–78. Cambridge: Cambridge University Press, 1973.

Smalley, S. S. "The Johannine Son of Man Sayings." *New Testament Studies* 15 (1968–69): 278–301.

Witherington, B. *John's Wisdom*. Louisville: Westminster/J. Knox, 1995.

———. "The Waters of Birth: John 3.5 and 1 John 5.6-8." *New Testament Studies* 35 (1989): 155–60.

Chapter Eight

Black, M. "The Maranatha Invocation and Jude 14,15." In *Christ and the Spirit in the New Testament*, edited by B. Lindars and S. S. Smalley, pp. 189–98. Cambridge: Cambridge University Press, 1973.

Campbell, J. C. "In a Son: The Doctrine of the Incarnation in Hebrews." *Interpretation* 10 (1956): 24–38.

Giles, P. "The Son of Man . . . in Hebrews." *Expository Times* 86 (1974–75): 328–32.

Glasson, T. F. "Plurality of Divine Persons and the Quotations in Heb. 1.6ff." *New Testament Studies* 12 (1965–66): 270–72.

Hartin, P. J. *James and the Q Sayings of Jesus*. Sheffield: Sheffield Academic Press, 1991.

Longenecker, R. N. "The Melchizedek Argument of Hebrews." In *Unity and Diversity in New Testament Theology*, edited by R. Guelich, pp. 161–85. Grand Rapids: Eerdmans, 1978.

Richard, E. H. "The Functional Christology of First Peter." In *Perspectives on First Peter*, edited by C. H. Talbert, pp. 121–39. Macon, Ga.: Mercer University Press, 1986: 121–39.

Thompson, J. W. "The Structure and Purpose of Heb. 1.5-13." *Catholic Biblical Quarterly* 38 (1976): 352–63.

Williamson, R. "Hebrews 4.25 and the Sinlessness of Jesus." *Expository Times* 86 (1974–75): 4–8.

———. "The Background of the Epistle to the Hebrews." *Expository Times* 87 (1975–76): 232–37.

———. "Philo and New Testament Christology." *Expository Times* 90 (1978–79): 361–65.

Witherington, B. "A Petrine Source in 2 Peter." In *Society of Biblical Literature 1985 Seminar Papers,* edited by K. H. Richards, pp. 187–92. Atlanta: Scholars Press, 1985.

Chapter Nine

Caird, G. B. "The Development of the Doctrine of Christ in the New Testament." In *Christ for Us Today,* edited by N. Pittenger, pp. 66–80. London: SPCK, 1968.

Childs, B. *The New Testament as Canon.* Philadelphia: Fortress, 1984.

France, R. T. "The Worship of Jesus." In *Christ the Lord: Studies in Christology presented to Donald Guthrie,* edited by H. H. Rowdon, pp. 17–37. Downers Grove, Ill.: Inter-Varsity, 1982.

Hengel, M. *The Son of God.* Philadelphia: Fortress Press, 1976.

Kelly, J. N. D. *Early Christian Doctrines.* New York: Harper & Row, 1958.

Lane, A. N. S. "Christology beyond Chalcedon." In *Christ the Lord: Studies in Christology presented to Donald Guthrie,* edited by H. H. Rowdon, pp. 257–81. Downers Grove, Ill.: Inter-Varsity, 1982.

Moule, C. F. D. "The New Testament and the Doctrine of the Trinity." *Expository Times* 88 (1976–77): 16–19.

Osborne, G. "Christology and New Testament Hermeneutics." *Semeia* 30 (1984): 49–62.

Pelikan, J. *The Christian Tradition, Volume 1.* Chicago: University of Chicago Press, 1971.

Taylor, V. "Does the New Testament call Jesus God?" In *New Testament Essays,* pp. 83–89. London: Epworth, 1970.

Wainwright, A. W. "The Confession 'Jesus is God' in the New Testament." *Scottish Journal of Theology* 10 (1957): 274–97.

Index of Ancient Sources

Index of Modern Authors